To Renée

PREFACE

*T*HE BIOGRAPHY of Molière will receive but scant attention in these pages.[1] All we need know for our purposes is that the author of *Le Misanthrope* belonged to the generation of La Fontaine and Pascal, that from early manhood he lived by and for the theater, that he wrote, directed and performed comedies for the entertainment of a traditionally Catholic society from which he was officially and canonically alienated. Had he wished, he might have led the useful life of an interior decorator with literary tastes. He chose instead a somewhat riskier profession, one that gave him an exhilarating but precarious vantage ground from which to survey the world below or above him. Not only did he achieve material success, but he gained free access, as entertainer, to the highest social circles; quite understandably, the moral viewpoint expressed in his plays tends to be aristocratic, as M. Paul Bénichou has so convincingly shown in his *Morales du grand siècle*. Indeed, Molière almost invariably mirrors the attitudes and prejudices of the court, and espouses its contempt for middle-class values. At the same time, he uses this assumed eminence, and his illusory immunity as a sort of king's jester, in order to challenge all types of conformity. Consciously or unconsciously, he transforms entertainment (*divertissement*) into a form of subversion if not of liberation. For this reason, one cannot really compare Molière's stormy career to that of a Sacha Guitry who, as actor, director, and playwright hardly threatened the status quo, and who was no more alienated from his contemporaries than any other wealthy merchant or manufacturer of *l'article de Paris*.[2]

[1] Gustave Michaud has dealt most adequately with all aspects of Molière's biography in his trilogy: *Jeunesse de Molière, Les Débuts de Molière à Paris,* and *Les Luttes de Molière* (Paris: Hachette, 1923, 1924, 1925).
[2] For studies of Molière as a man of the theater, see René Bray, *Molière, homme de théâtre* (Paris: Mercure de France, 1954), and W. G. Moore, *Molière:*

The unique moral situation of Molière underlies the esthetic and dramatic discoveries that mark even the slightest of his farces. He chose the theater, and the chief purpose of the present study will be to assess his achievement as a creator of dramatic and poetic forms. The inner coherence that characterizes the tragedies of Racine is not absent from the comedies of Molière.[3] Each of his plays has its own peculiar unity, its own dramatic as well as metaphorical structure. And it is precisely by their moral vision, and by their inner coherence that his comedies differ from the vast majority of contemporary productions. Such talented writers as Thomas Corneille, Quinault, and Scarron constructed and versified their comedies with as much skill as any playwright before or since. If we take the well-made play as sole criterion, *Don Bertrand de Cigarral, La Mère coquette, Don Japhet d'Arménie* can rival such recognized masterpieces as *Le Misanthrope, L'Avare* and *Tartuffe.* However, Molière's witty contemporaries were quite content to put into cleverly contrived situations strikingly insignificant characters, who existed only to produce mirth. These works, which undoubtedly could hold the stage today, amuse an audience without really involving or compromising it. They do not contain a challenge—the kind of challenge that characterizes the majority of Molière's comedies and that is present in such remarkable plays as Jean de Rotrou's *Sosies,* which we intend to discuss in connection with *Amphitryon* and Pierre Corneille's *Menteur.*

As Charles Péguy has shown, Dorante is an heroic liar who, in another situation, would easily accomplish the sort of exploit he so readily invents.[4] Like Matamore, like Rodrigue, like Cléopâtre, he arouses the astonished admiration of the audience. Dorante, who previously had led the uneventful life of a law student in the sleepy town of Poitiers, has decided, with his father's consent, to join the turbulent ranks of the *noblesse*

A New Criticism (London: Oxford, 1949). Professor Moore by no means neglects the more literary aspects of Molière's art, and his highly suggestive book must indeed serve as a prolegomenon to all future interpretations of our author as a creative writer.
[3] Cf. my *Essai d'exégèse racinienne* (Paris: Nizet, 1956).
[4] Cf. *Note conjointe* (Paris: N.R.F., 1935), pp. 170 ff.

d'épée. Actually, he has just discovered his true vocation. His first fibs—those he tells Clarice—enable him to manufacture a suitable past, quite in keeping with his present ambitions and, one might even say, with his authentic being, that of a swash-buckling, spendthrift hero. In fact, he would appear to be quite untrue to himself if he told without embellishment the story of his humdrum existence. Now, in many of Corneille's serious dramas, the protagonist's inner being transcends external reality, which must passively take on any shape or color he chooses to give it. Dorante, unfortunately, happens to live in the France of Richelieu and not in some imaginary Aragon or literary Rome. Therefore, in order to realize his true potentialities, he must invent, in the manner of an artist, suitably spectacular events. He boldly and unhesitatingly creates his own exploits instead of letting the situation do it for him. Corneille stresses throughout the ironical discrepancy between that heroic and ideal realm, where he usually situates his plays, and the inconsequential or trivial world of the present. Rodrigue had swiftly shaped his own future while remaining faithful to all the values of the past and the present. Our impatient liar, on the contrary, is constrained to create an enviable and fascinating past in order to make up in one day for all the years he had lost in belying his own nature.

The play itself takes the form of a duel between haphazard encounters—the term *hasard* and similar expressions recur quite frequently—and the hero's breath-taking improvisations. Corneille might have entitled his comedy *Les Menteurs,* for nearly every character concerned does his or her best to show a false front to a confused but credulous world. They monotonously create illusions while remaining themselves in a state of insecurity, for they rarely succeed in fathoming the real intentions of others. This situation prevails particularly in the relationships between the sexes. The young men and women in the play manage to set up a fairly inviting façade, which, unlike Dorante's projected image, hides their genuine personality. Alcippe and Clarice have known one another for two years and consider themselves engaged. Nonetheless, Clarice has little faith in Alcippe's

promises. Because all she really wants in life is a suitable husband, she would not hesitate to replace her would-be fiancé
with any likely candidate who happened to ask for her hand.

Corneille repeatedly dwells on the mercenary attitudes and
general falsity that prevail in the modern world. Cliton,
Dorante's valet, claims that "Paris est un grand lieu plein de
marchands mêlés: / L'effet n'y répond pas toujours à l'apparence." This discrepancy between appearance and reality causes
a lack of stability in the realm of human values: "Comme on s'y
connaît mal, chacun s'y fait de mise, / Et vaut communément
autant comme il se prise" (I, 1). Thus Paris has become, in
certain respects, a market place and vanity fair peopled by
morally self-made men and women. Dorante's servant cannot
identify two pretty girls who are about to enter the scene, for
he deals in cheaper goods: "Non: cette marchandise est de trop
bon aloi" (I, 1). As for Clarice, she regards prospective husbands as a type of merchandise whose true value she does her
best to assess: "Le dedans paraît mal en ces miroirs flatteurs; /
Les visages souvent sont de doux imposteurs / ... Et que de beaux
semblants cachent des âmes basses!" She concludes: "Et pour
moi, puisqu'il faut qu'elle [la chaîne] me donne un maître, /
Avant que l'acceper je voudrais le connaître, / Mais connaître
dans l'âme." In short, the business-like Clarice fully realizes the
difficulties involved in getting her money's worth or at least her
dowry's worth in the marriage market. So far her efforts have
unearthed no better bargain than poor Alcippe: "Car Alcippe,
après tout, vaut toujours mieux que rien" (II, 2).

Dorante, in order to prove to Lucrèce that he really knows
her identity, describes her father in the following terms: "Il est
homme de robe adroit et retenu; / Dix mille écus de rente en
font le revenu" (III, 5). In such a world, commercial and financial values must strike people as more reliable than all other
human qualities combined. As a result, a true lover must show
his worth by the munificence of his gifts. Lucrèce reaches a
favorable estimate of Dorante's affection merely by adding up
the handsome tips he has so far given her servant. By thus regarding lucre as the sole criterion in all social relationships,

Corneille has wittily satirized the Paris of his time. Against this background of materialism and disguise, Dorante's venerable father, Géronte, stands out in bold if somewhat ludicrous relief: disinterestedness and truthfulness have long since ceased to be fashionable.

Paris, no less than its inhabitants, creates illusions and falsehoods:

> Paris semble à mes yeux un pays de romans.
> J'y croyais ce matin voir une île enchantée:
> Je la laissai déserte, et la trouve habitée:
> Quelque Amphion nouveau, sans l'aide des maçons,
> En superbes palais a changé ses buissons.

In other words, a mythological character, dear to the writers of court ballets, must have been at work in the city. And Géronte proceeds to develop his son's simile:

> Paris voit tous les jours de ces métamorphoses:
> Dans tout le Pré-aux-Clercs tu verras mêmes choses;
> Et l'univers entier ne peut rien voir d'égal
> Aux superbes dehors du Palais-Cardinal.
> Toute une ville entière, avec pompe bâtie,
> Semble d'un vieux fossé par miracle sortie,
> Et nous fait présumer, à ses superbes toits,
> Que tous ses habitants sont des dieux ou des rois (II, 5).

Thus nothing is as it seems, nothing tells the truth; but some beings and some objects manage to create falsehoods that have more artistic value than others. Dorante replaces by his vivid lies the conforming illusions of his contemporaries. His superiority arises from the fact that he knows how to build on the spur of the moment a far more attractive front than his rivals. And he resembles, in some respects, the dramatist himself. Corneille, like Dorante, had abandoned his law books in order to create heroic worlds where anything might happen and where dreams could have more substance and more stubbornness than facts.

Like Pierre Corneille, Molière, in the majority of his plays, will concern himself with the question of values; and he will frequently use terms borrowed from the world of commerce and finance as symbols of human relations. Indeed, we might apply La Rochefoucauld's well-known maxim: "La souveraine habileté consiste à bien connaître le prix des choses" not only to *Le Menteur* but to almost every character in Molière's works. This does not mean that Corneille's comic masterpiece must stand as a model for the plays of his younger rival. On the contrary. Whereas values or value judgments in Corneille's *Menteur* lack stability to such an extent that the first youth who chances along can bring about a state of confusion and very nearly turn his little world upside down, in Molière's comedies these values have become static, not to say inveterate. As such, they give rise to automatisms, to stereotyped reactions which must be swept aside. Although Corneille succeeded in devaluating contemporary social behavior, his satirical quips attack a relatively healthy and flourishing state of corruption, where the individual, for reasons of self-interest, tries to outsmart his rivals. Molière will launch most of his attacks not on dishonest or morally indifferent self-betterment, but on all forms of systematic behavior or ready-made attitudes. Far from exhalting the imagination, he will attempt to destroy all types of illusion or delusion, or rather of self-delusion. In fact, he will accept only one aspect of the imagination—the aspect that consists in creating new dramatic forms and new kinds of entertainment.[5]

In discussing the plays of Molière, I have usually followed the chronological order, for obvious reasons. All the major comedies are included in this study as well as most of the minor works. I have left out, however, two early farces: *Le Médecin volant* and *La Jalousie du barbouillé,* dramatic sketches of considerable merit, but which do not lend themselves to stylistic analysis. In fact, the text of these farces may not even be by Molière. Nor have I included his two polemical comedies, *La Critique de l'Ecole des femmes* and *L'Impromptu de Versailles,* adequately discussed by other critics, particularly by Dr. Robert

[5] The title of the present study is purposely ambiguous, for while Molière's comedies may have intellectual aspects, as do most seventeenth-century works of any importance, his general attitude appears to be anti-intellectual. Indeed, only an intellectual could possibly have launched so thorough and devastating an attack on the various abuses of systematic thought.

Nelson in his recent *The Play within the Play*. Moreover, I have left aside such *divertissements* as *Les Amants magnifiques* since they are much more spectacular than literary. Finally, I have neglected that patchwork masterpiece, *Psyché,* as well as *La Comtesse d'Escarbagnas,* which does not contain anything that cannot be found in other plays of the master.

Parts of this study have already been published. A section of chapter 5, "The Incompatible Lovers," appeared in *MLQ,* under the title of "The Comedy of Incompatibility in *Don Garcie de Navarre*" (Sept., 1960). Most of chapter 8, "A Burlesque Tragedy," appeared in *RSH*, under the title *"L'Ecole des femmes,* tragédie burlesque?" (Janviers-Mars, 1960). Chapter 13, "The Self-Deceivers," is included in the Morris Bishop homage volume. Chapter 17, "The Inhumanity of Harpagon," was published in *PMLA* under the title "Theme and Structure in *L'Avare,"* (March, 1960).

J. D. H.

CONTENTS

I   *Scappino*
                                      & Mascarille

𝓜 O L I È R E, an active admirer of the *com-
media* dell'arte, chose for his first important venture as a playwright to adapt into French verse Beltrame's *L'Inavvertito*. Beltrame's hero, the servant Scappino, appears to make up the plot
as he goes along, in typical commedia style; and on the spur
of the moment, he can invent any number of new tricks.
Scappino derives from the slaves of Greek and Roman comedy
who invariably used their manifold talents to serve youth and
further the course of nature. But these slaves of old functioned
as instruments of fate and, more often than not, turned out to
be gods in disguise. Not so Beltrame's Scappino who, even when
he proclaims himself a staunch ally of nature, tends to oppose
fate rather than impersonate it. Thus, if we must identify him
with a superior force, it had better be with the fertile imagination of the dramatist himself! His master Fulvio, however, unwittingly becomes the instrument of an impish destiny which
gleefully destroys Scappino's best laid plans. In short, we see
in Scappino a modern individualist and a strong believer in
efficiency, who militates against a mysterious, irrational, and
capricious force through the diligent use of purely human cleverness. His battle against Fulvio's demon, or against destiny itself,
ends, like Jacob's struggle with the angel, in an honorable draw,
for at the last moment fate decides to set everything right.

Scappino changes his name to Mascarille (little or half mask)
in *L'Étourdi* and becomes, if possible, more active, more in-
genious than in the Italian version. He completely dominates
the play, and René Bray has shown that he appears in more
scenes and speaks more lines than any other character in Molière's theater.[1] The French dramatist may have discovered in

[1] René Bray, *Molière, homme de théâtre* (Paris: Mercure de France, 1954,
pp. 195–196).

I

L'Inavvertito not only a promising plot and a part that happened
to suit his own histrionic talents, but also a literary device that
was to serve him well in the majority of his comedies: parody.
L'Inavvertito contains a satire of *marinismo*. Paradoxically,
Beltrame chose as exponent of preposterous conceits the swashbuckling Capitano Bellorofonte Martelione. True, the Capitano,
who brags of his military prowess even more often than he
eulogizes the beautiful Celia, does not play a very important
part. Nonetheless, this slight satirical element may have given
Molière the idea of parodying Corneille's heroic style.

Parody in *L'Etourdi* has recently attracted the attention of
Professor Carlo François, who, far from regarding this device
as a disparagement of Corneille, ascribes it to Molière's "nostalgie
du tragique." [2] Although we agree with Professor François'
analysis, we do not intend to discuss, at least for the moment,
whether or not Molière was a frustrated tragedian, but to determine instead what he may have gained by assuming an heroic
style and by introducing a "tragic" element into a farce.

The struggle between the individual and fate plays, as we have
seen, a fairly important part in *L'Inavvertito;* but it is in the
action rather than in expression, for Beltrame chose to write
his comedy in prose and probably never even thought of lending
"tragic" dimensions to Scappino's conversational style. French
alexandrines, on the other hand, need very little encouragement
to fall into heroic patterns. In short, Molière has succeeded in
giving poetic expression to insights which had remained merely
dramatic in the Italian version. The Frenchman's mock-heroic
verse brings out more clearly than Beltrame's lively prose the
contrast between Fulvio-Lélie's impish demon and the idea of
an omnipotent fate, or between Scappino-Mascarille's servile
condition and the pride he takes in his genius for intrigue. The
bare suggestion of a malignant fate, which appears now and
again in *L'Inavvertito,* becomes in *L'Etourdi* a persistent mockery of tragedy itself as well as a consistent devaluation of the

---

[2] Carlo François, *"L'Etourdi* de Molière ou l'illusion héroïque," *RHL,* LIX
(Jan., 1959), 87–93.

heroic. And these essentially literary traits will reappear, in varying forms, in most of Molière's subsequent comedies.

Mascarille definitely takes on more heroic proportions than Beltrame's Scappino. Nothing can slow down his tremendous activity, and he rushes headlong into adventures without ever worrying about the consequences. Molière has given him many of the epic virtues of a true Cornelian hero, of Rodrigue for instance. If anything, he strikes us as more enterprising; and his prowess, no less than that of the Cid, proves the superiority of spirit over matter, of resolute endeavor over all possible obstacles. Although Lélie's surprising blunders make him angry, they never really dishearten him, but must drive him ever onward to greater valor. Even when he discovers that his master's interventions go beyond the bounds of human stupidity and prove beyond a doubt the influence of a supernatural force, he continues to defy fate, vowing that he will triumph over all obstacles:

> Oui, je suis stupéfait de ce dernier prodige:
> On diroit, et pour moi j'en suis persuadé,
> Que ce démon brouillon dont il est possédé
> Se plaise à me braver, et me l'aille conduire
> Partout où sa présence est capable de nuire.
> Pourtant je veux poursuivre, et malgré tous ces coups,
> Voir qui l'emportera de ce diable ou de nous (1692–98).

When Mascarille's latest stratagem fails once again because of another of Lélie's blunders, his Cornelian heroism reaches a climax:

> Je veux, quoi qu'il en soit, le servir malgré lui,
> Et dessus son lutin obtenir la victoire:
> Plus l'obstacle est puissant, plus on reçoit de gloire,
> Et les difficultés dont on est combattu
> Sont les dames d'atour qui parent la vertu (1862–66).

Corneille would have agreed with the maxim: "plus l'obstacle est puissant, plus on reçoit de gloire." And Mascarille's stress on *vertu* and *gloire,* which play so important a part in the serious drama of the period, appears all the more paradoxical because his intrigues invariably put him at odds with law and order. Mascarille evidently has created his own system of moral values. Moreover, he has a reputation to maintain. Annoyed at the miscarriage of one of his most promising stratagems, he deliberates, in a typically Cornelian monologue, whether or not to persist in his heroic enterprise:

> Et que deviendra lors cette publique estime
> Qui te vante partout pour un fourbe sublime,
> Et que tu t'es acquise en tant d'occasions,
> A ne t'être jamais vu court d'inventions?
> L'honneur, ô Mascarille, est une belle chose:
> A tes nobles travaux ne fais aucune pause (911–16).

Molière reveals in this and many other passages his mastery of the mock-heroic style and anticipates Boileau who, in the preface to his *Lutrin,* published nearly twenty years after the first performance of *L'Étourdi,* claimed that he had invented a new and better type of burlesque.

Critics have described Corneille's *Cid* as a series of duels, sometimes real, sometimes verbal. And the idea of a duel gives a semblance of dramatic and metaphorical unity to Molière's first five-act comedy. Indeed, the compilers of the famous Grands Ecrivains edition of the works of Molière insisted on Mascarille's persistent use of terms borrowed from the noble art of fencing, to which the subtitle of the play, "les contre-temps" belongs.[3] This word indicates a sudden change of pace or rhythm intended to fool an opponent, or else an accident in coördination whereby the two adversaries give and receive a hit simultaneously. Clearly, both of these meanings, in addition to the usual one of mischance or mishap, characterize many events or situations throughout the play, and particularly the relationship between Mascarille and his master who never succeed in coördinating their actions. Indeed, Mascarille must perpetually fence against a variety of opponents, including the most treacherous of them

---

[3] Cf. Molière, *Œuvres* (Paris: Hachette, 1873–1900), I, 180. All Molière quotations are taken from this standard edition which will henceforth be referred to as *Grands Ecrivains Ed.*

all, Lélie's invisible imp. He would much rather duel against Lélie's rival, Léandre: "Et contre cet assaut je sais un coup fourré / Par qui je veux qu'il soit de lui-même enferré" (1165–66).

The comedy opens quite appropriately with Lélie challenging his erstwhile friend Leandre, if not to an actual duel with swords, at least to a struggle in which Célie will be the prize. The first line actually provides some sort of key to the entire structure of the comedy: "Hé bien! Léandre, hé bien! il faudra contester." And Molière will contrive a different kind of duel to bring about a happy ending: the battle royal between two old hags, as described by Mascarille. Célie's long lost nurse, recognizing an old gypsy as the evil woman who had abducted her charge, pounces on her. And then follows a "combat furieux, / Qui pour armes pourtant, mousquets, dagues ou flèches, / Ne faisoit voir en l'air que quatre griffes sèches" (1939–40)—a "combat risiblement affreux" (1946).

We see in this ridiculous duel the final and most absurd avatar of Lélie's challenge to Léandre. This *récit,* as well as the leitmotif of the duel, we owe to Molière. Beltrame had thought of an entirely different type of scene to bring his comedy to a close—a scene that many critics regard as superior to the Frenchman's ludicrous recognition. But perhaps Molière needed just one more duel; perhaps an artificial *dénouement* suited his esthetic purpose. And it so happens that Mascarille preludes his narrative of the "combat furieux" by describing the whole thing as "La fin d'une vraie et pure comédie" (1932)—a statement that completely shatters the spectator's suspension of disbelief. Mascarille has suddenly transformed himself into a critic, quite detached from the farce in which he has not only played an overwhelming part, but which he has practically written, directed and staged. Thus the man who was the whole show decides to desert the stage for the contemplation of his own handiwork!

Throughout the performance Mascarille had expressed inordinate pride, not only in his delinquent heroism, but also in his accomplishments as a conscious and highly skilled artist. He never lets the audience forget that his function in life, like that of Molière himself both as playwright and actor, must consist in providing pleasure and entertainment. Early in the first act, he asks his master: "D'un censeur de plaisirs ai-je fort l'encolure, / Et Mascarille est-il ennemi de nature?" (55–56), thus equating nature with the idea of pleasure. His pride closely resembles auctorial vanity: for better or worse, he frequently behaves like a man of letters. In the third scene of the play, he criticizes Lélie's precious, but misplaced, declaration of love to Célie: "Vous le prenez là d'un ton un peu trop haut: / Ce style maintenant n'est pas ce qu'il nous faut" (121–22). In encouraging his master to act in a more practical fashion, Mascarille reminds us of a dramatist finding fault with the rejoinder of one of his characters, or perhaps of a theater director criticizing one of his actors. In fact, Mascarille twice makes Lélie perform a part: first that of a mourning son, which he does quite successfully, and then that of the long-lost offspring of Trufaldin, where he fails disgracefully, in spite of his prompter's warnings: "Votre rôle en ce jeu par cœur doit être su" (1265).

Mascarille insists on maintaining his reputation as a creator. Carried away by his own cleverness, he sees himself crowned with laurel, in the manner of a conqueror or a poet:

> Après ce rare exploit, je veux que l'on s'apprête
> A me peindre en héros un laurier sur la tête,
> Et qu'au bas du portrait on mette en lettres d'or:
> *Vivat Mascarillus, fourbum imperator!* (791–94).

And Molière frequently alludes to literature in one form or another. When Anselme finally discovers that Mascarille has tricked him into believing that his friend Pandolphe has suddenly died, he expresses fear that: "On en feroit jouer quelque farce à ma honte" (620). Previously, the author had put into Anselme's mouth the tritest literary saws concerning death, the high sounding platitudes that poets such as Malherbe and dramatists such as Montchrestien had reveled in half a century earlier, e.g., "Ce fier animal, pour toutes les prières / Ne perdroit pas un coup de ses dents meurtrières: / Tout le monde y passe" (541–43) or: "Des événements l'incertitude est grande" (561), which becomes all the funnier because Pandolphe's death provides just another of the too numerous uncertainties that characterize this particular play. And poor Anselme, who remains all alone on the stage, mechanically pursues his meditation on death: "Le monde est rempli de beaucoup de traverses, / Chaque homme tous les jours en ressent de diverses, / Et jamais ici bas ..." (569–71). But these trite remarks may also allude to the innumerable hindrances that beset the various characters, including the unexpected and terrifying reappearance of Pandolphe, who at that very moment jarringly interrupts Anselme's melancholy thoughts.

Molière never lets us forget the unreality of the various events and *peripeteia* of the play, so much so that we can regard the proceedings as a struggle between two creators: Mascarille's imaginative prowess can never quite vanquish Lélie's own "imaginative," a faculty in which his blundering master takes unjustified pride. Actually, we cannot describe Lélie as stupid, for some of his intrigues, such as the letter from an imaginary Spanish nobleman which he sends Trufaldin, show resourcefulness, and just enough cleverness to foil Mascarille's vastly superior strategy. Molière, even more than Beltrame, insists on the fundamental idea of interference and lack of coördination. Indeed, the subtitle, *contre-temps,* suggests not only mishaps and fencing, but also music. Old Trufaldin himself advises Mascarille and his master: "Mettez pour me jouer vos flûtes mieux d'accord" (186).

The comparison with *L'Inavvertito* shows that Molière, in his first major work, has stressed the poetic aspects of playwrighting at least as much as the purely theatrical, and that we can regard him, at the very beginning of his career, as a highly-conscious literary artist. *L'Etourdi,* a mere adaptation, possesses a definite style as well as an underlying unity. More important still, Molière has revealed his complete mastery of such difficult techniques as parody and literary allusion. And his skill is such that he can project himself as creator into the action of the play and amuse the audience with his cleverness at pulling the strings. Nicolò Barbieri, despite the fact that one of his characters bears his stage name, Beltrame, had remained unobtrusively in the background.

2 *The Metamorphosis of an Increment*

MᴏʟɪÈʀᴇ based his next comedy on Secchi's *L'Interesse—Interest,* or better still, *The Increment,* first published in Venice in 1581, but performed at a much earlier date. In this second adaptation, Molière does much more than improve upon his model, for he completely transforms the play by adding new characters and new incidents, by introducing novel comic techniques, and by supplying a different metaphorical structure. Secchi's *L'Interesse,* no less than Beltrame's *L'Inavvertito,* possesses considerable literary merit, in spite of repetitions and lengthy monologues. Moreover, we can follow the plot with ease. A wealthy Florentine merchant has wagered a large sum of money with his friend Ricciardo that his next offspring will be a boy. When Pandolfo's wife gives birth to a second daughter, he has the child brought up as a boy in order to win his bet and keep the stakes. By the time the play opens, Lelio, *femina,* not only has reached adolescence, but, by assuming her elder sister's identity, has clandestinely married one of the latter's suitors and is already six months pregnant! With consumate skill, Secchi establishes metaphorical and dramatic connections between this rapidly growing pregnancy and the ever accruing sum that Pandolfo owes Ricciardo. Fortunately, Lelio has had the good sense to marry Ricciardo's only son, Fabio, and thus the parties concerned automatically transform the original wager, with its ever accumulating interests, into a fat and handsome dowry. Secchi's central idea may seem preposterous, but it does give rise to a rich fabric of innuendo and equivocation, dubbed by some prudish Molière scholars as unseemly and lewd.

Molière, who had to reckon with *bienséances,* suppressed Lelio-Ascagne's pregnancy, thereby killing the central meta-

8

phor of his Renaissance model. Apparently he had no choice but to let the now meaningless travesty grow unchecked into a labyrinthine imbroglio. Pandolfo-Albert does not even realize that Ascagne is a female! Upon hearing, some fifteen years before the play opens, of the death of his (supposed) son, he had apparently urged his wife to substitute the child of a wet-nurse in order to keep a large inheritance in the family. We discover, in the course of the comedy, that death had come to the wet-nurse's son and that Ascagne is none other than Albert's younger daughter, now clandestinely married to Fabio-Valère, to whom the misappropriated inheritance rightfully belongs. Burdened with this unlikely story, Molière compounds the confusion whenever he follows Secchi too closely, but achieves a measure of success in the scenes of his own invention, notably the famous lovers' quarrel between Eraste and Lucile, and between their clownish servants, Gros-René and Marinette. The Comédie Française still performs *Le Dépit* as a one-act comedy, leaving out the situations borrowed from the inimitable Secchi.

As in *L'Etourdi*, Molière frequently resorts to parody, an eminently literary, not to say intellectual, device which helps relate the fairly low burlesque scenes to passages written in a reasonably elevated style. Although parody does not have the same functional importance as in *L'Etourdi*, Molière uses it effectively in order to satirize the commonplaces of preciosity and mock the pretentious rhetoric then prevalent in the theater. Gros-René pokes fun at his master's habit of speaking of his love in the third person:

> Pour moi, me soupçonner de quelque mauvais tour,
> Je dirai, n'en déplaise à Monsieur votre amour,
> Que c'est injustement blesser ma prud'homie
> Et se connoître mal en physionomie (7–10).

By thus parodying his master's affected language, Gros-René devaluates the latter's passion for Lucile and his impending jealousy. Eraste, Lucile, Valère, and Ascagne, express their love in the loftiest terms possible, but the spectator will follow Gros-René's example and watch their impassioned behavior with amused detachment. And the audience may even enjoy the absurd ramifications of the plot. Indeed, we somehow suspect that Molière wilfully added complications in order to deride the artificiality and obscurity of contemporary tragi-comedies.

Gros-René himself tries to sound like a tragic hero when he gives vent to his temporary and insincere misogyny. He does not, however, find his models in the works of Corneille, Rotrou, or Mairet, for he prefers to imitate the outmoded protagonists of Alexandre Hardy:

> M'oses-tu bien encor parler, femelle inique,
> Crocodile trompeur, de qui le cœur félon
> Est pire qu'un Satrape ou bien qu'un Lestrygon? (330–32).

Archaic language and old-fashioned clothing struck Molière's contemporaries as irresistibly funny. The Sganarelle of *L'Ecole des maris* will insist on dressing in the manner of Henri IV's subjects; one of the illustrations of Scarron's *Virgile travesti,* published in 1648, shows Æneas and his family escaping from burning Troy attired in the sartorial fashions of the League; and the poet in Desmarets de Saint-Sorlin's *Visionnaires* (1637) imitates the highly allusive style of the Pléiade.

Parody, however, matters less in *Le Dépit* than a type of dramatic analogy known as parallelism. Molière uses this old device with telling effect in the scenes where Gros-René and Marinette repeat, on a much lower level, the quarrel and final reconciliation of Eraste and Lucile. Strange as this may seem, only Molière, Marivaux, and Anouilh, at least in French literature, have fully exploited, from a moral or psychological point of view, the contrapuntal behavior of masters and servants faced with similar situations. Marivaux made use of this trite trick in order to dramatize the universality of love, Anouilh in order to reveal the illusory qualities of passion, whereas Molière in *Le Dépit* regarded it as a means to satirize the pretense and superficial bad faith of lovers. As Eraste and Lucile have broken off relations, they simply must start a spirited quarrel in order to get together again. The more they proclaim the end of their engagement, even to the extent of systematically returning their mutual gifts, the more they recall the past and reaffirm their bonds. And they both argue as convincingly as possible in order to persuade each other of the impossibility and absurdity of a reconciliation. Words and rationalizations help most conveniently to keep up appearances while serving as intermediaries for their true feelings. And the two lovers behave as though they had actually succeeded in their deception and self-deception! The humor of the situation results from the patent contradiction between words and gestures on the one hand, and feelings on the other:

> ERASTE: Moi-même de cent coups je percerois mon sein,
> Si j'avois jamais fait cette bassesse insigne,
> De vous revoir après ce traitement indigne.
> LUCILE: Soit, n'en parlons donc plus.
> ERASTE: Oui, oui, n'en parlons plus;
> Et pour trancher ici tous propos superflus,
> Et vous donner, ingrate, une preuve certaine
> Que je veux, sans retour, sortir de votre chaîne,
> Je ne veux rien garder qui puisse retracer
> Ce que de mon esprit il me faut effacer (1328–36).

Eraste, in spite of the fact that he remains in the presence of Lucile, claims that he would kill himself rather than see her again; and in the very act of telling her that he will not utter another word, he of course goes on talking, for he has obviously found the best means to reaffirm his love while indulging his wounded vanity. Marinette and Gros-René, left to themselves after the reconciliation of their masters, will echo, in its various phases, the insincere quarrel they have just witnessed, including the return of all the gifts. In place of the lofty tone of injured innocence which characterized the rejoinders of Lucile, Marinette hurls ludicrous insults at her fiancé. Moreover, the two servants disparage each other's gifts in the very act of returning them. But when it comes to envisaging a real separation, symbolized in true peasant style by the breaking of a straw, they laughingly decide to put an end to this absurd game. Gros-René exclaims: "Ma foi, nous ferons mieux de quitter la grimace" (1453), which proves that neither they nor their masters had meant a single word of what they had said. No doubt, we can regard this type of echo as a peculiar form of parody, replete with satirical implications, a type of parody quite different from the literary pastiches previously discussed.

Marinette and Gros-René's travesty of their masters' quarrel provides merely the most obvious instance of parallelism, for the contradiction between true feelings and outward expression happens to coincide with the central theme of the comedy. Albert, worried about the strange behavior of his "son" Ascagne, who simply refuses to take an interest in girls, consults the philosopher Métaphraste, who does not give him a chance to state his problem. At one point, the pedant promises Albert that he will henceforth refrain from interrupting; but he expresses this reasonable intention in so many ways and at such length that the poor father cannot get in another word. Finally, Métaphraste exclaims, as though he had been listening all along: "Encor? Bon Dieu! que de discours! / Rien n'est-il suffisant d'en arrêter le cours?" (753–54). The obvious contradiction between the philosopher's declared intention not to interrupt and the interruptions he causes thereby anticipates, at least in form, the contradictions inherent in Eraste's brave speeches.

Left to himself, Métaphraste develops, in strict accordance with the canons of rhetoric, the *topos* of contradiction, e.g., "Que les poules dans peu dévorent les renards, / Que les jeunes enfants remontrent aux vieillards" (769–70), in order to reaffirm his privilege as a pedant. Referring to Albert, he complains: "Oh! que les grands parleurs sont par moi détestés!" (765), for he will not admit, or even realize, that his interlocutor never had a chance to utter more than a single sentence at a time. The pedant is no more and no less than a talking and reasoning machine, which Molière had already set in motion in an early farce, *La Jalousie du barbouillé*. But in the present play, this well-oiled and perfectly tuned mechanism provides just another instance of contradiction, just another example of the irrelevance of all argumentation and of the futility of language. Métaphraste's mere presence reduces to absurdity the discrepancies so noticeable in most of his fellow characters. And Gros-René will transpose the pedant's rhetorical exercises in the long chain of mixed-up and mangled arguments with which he will try to prove the unworthiness of all women.

Ascagne, a girl who all her life has had to play the part of a boy and who does not even know her identity, embodies, more than any other important character in the comedy, this spirit of contradiction. As a sort of compensation, she does know her own feelings—much better indeed than her sister Lucile, or Eraste, or even her husband Valère. This knowledge gives her a certain advantage over the other principals. She manages, merely by following her instincts, to reduce all the contradictions inherent in the play, including her father's remorse at having tricked Valère out of an inheritance and his firm intention of holding on to the ill-acquired lucre. Ascagne explains to her confidante Frosine how she happened to fall in love with Valère, whose most passionate protestations had had absolutely no effect on her sister Lucile:

> Je voulois que Lucile aimât son entretien,
> Je blâmois ses rigueurs, et les blâmai si bien,
> Que moi-même j'entrai, sans pouvoir m'en défendre,
> Dans tous les sentiments qu'elle ne pouvoit prendre.
> C'étoit, en lui parlant, moi qu'il persuadoit;
> Je me laissois gagner aux soupirs qu'il perdoit;
> Et ses vœux, rejetés de l'objet qui l'enflamme,
> Etoient, comme vainqueurs, reçus dedans mon âme.
> Ainsi mon coeur, Frosine, un peu trop foible, hélas!
> Se rendit à des soins qu'on ne lui rendoit pas,
> Par un coup réfléchi reçut une blessure,
> Et paya pour un autre avec beaucoup d'usure (429–40).

Love, like a blind machine, gradually transforms Ascagne, the girl without an identity, into a second Lucile—Lucile as Valère would wish to have her! And Ascagne, quite understandably, will appropriate, by borrowing her clothing, her sister's identity and marry Valère in secret. The real Lucile will continue to stand between the two lovers, but as an empty image, as a social identity inimical to Eros. Molière deftly connects this love by indirection to Albert's misappropriation of Valère's inheritance, by describing Ascagne's passion in terms of usury: "Et paya pour un autre avec beaucoup d'usure." Secchi's systematic equivocations may have suggested this comparison to Molière. But the French dramatist, in this remarkable speech, has invented a metaphor of his own, that of the *coup réfléchi* which bounces off one person to reach its mark in another. And poor Valère, who had unknowingly lost a fortune, who had wasted all his efforts to win Lucile, will get everything back by marrying Dorothée, the real name of Ascagne. Through the ministrations of love, everyone wins.

Ascagne's efforts throughout the play consist in freeing positive action and positive feeling from the sham and pretense that clutter up human existence. She plays her sister's part in order to rid herself of a false situation, where she had to behave like a man while possessing the feelings and desires of a woman. And at the end, Valère may not have won the girl of his choice, but undeniably he has acquired love, the irreducible reality that lies beneath if not beyond the *persona*. Molière develops this idea more fully than Secchi. Valère, upon discovering the truth, exclaims:

> Et si cette aventure a lieu de me surprendre,
> La surprise me flatte, et je me sens saisir
> De merveille à la fois, d'amour et de plaisir.
> Se peut-il que ces yeux ... ? (1758–61)

Dorothée-Ascagne's father interrupts: "Cet habit, cher Valère, / Souffre mal les discours que vous lui pourriez faire," which amusingly puts the entire love affair on an appropriate social basis, with all the characters in possession of their real identity and their legal inheritances, but ready, perhaps, to lapse into the errors, falsifications, and bad faith that prevail in human relations.

Ascagne has used illusion to destroy a false situation and to emerge into a real world. In this respect, we can regard her as a character in the baroque tradition, all the more so because, throughout the comedy, the vocabulary contains so many intellectual terms dealing with the relationship between reality and appearance.[1] But these baroque tendencies do not go very far, for Molière, unlike the Corneille of *L'Illusion comique,* or the Rotrou of *Le Véritable saint Genest,* does not attempt to create an inner conflict capable of involving the moral identity of a given character. Illusion, devoid of real tension, ceases to express man's fundamental ambiguity; it thus becomes purely instrumental and, in a sense, superficial. By illusion, first Albert and then Ascagne seek to further their own basic interests; by illusion, Eraste and then Valère force the servant Mascarille to tell all he knows, or thinks he knows, about the real situation. And from the beginning to the end of the comedy, we witness the triumph of unambiguous feelings over such clear-cut obstacles as decorum, rationalization, and plain obtuseness.

[1] Because of the abundance of intellectual terms, this play closely resembles *Dom Garcie de Navarre.*

3   *On the High Cost of Reading*

In the autumn of 1659, Molière, then thirty-eight years old, produced his first masterpiece, a one-act farce in prose, *Les Précieuses ridicules*. Not only did this short play suffice to establish his reputation and his fame, but it set forth, almost in the manner of a manifesto, his conception of literature in general and of comedy in particular. The farce recounts how two suitors avenge their rude reception by two provincial maidens, besotted by stories of love and adventure. Many a writer before and after Molière has achieved success by describing the strange effects which literature can produce on mediocre minds. We do not intend, however, to compare the foolish Magdelon and her equally silly cousin Cathos to Cervantes' magnanimous Don Quixote, whose brains had been addled even more than theirs by countless novels of chivalry. The Don, whom no one will accuse of petty vanity or pretense, possesses all the heroic virtues of the knights he most admires; and he never hesitates to follow his most generous and courageous impulses. Compared to the wondrous adventures unfolding in the recesses of his mind, the real world can only offer a drab and debased existence. The reader suspects that this insane latter-day paladin leads a better life and sees much further than the materialistic vulgarians who deride his accomplishments. Don Quixote definitely possesses the lofty imagination of his creator; and so does the heroic Dorante, the protagonist of Corneille's *Le Menteur*. Obviously, Cathos and Magdelon belong to an inferior species, for their readings and their imagination serve merely to feed their vanity and their affectation. Their inner world, like that of Flaubert's Emma Bovary or the heroine of Maupassant's "La Parure," consists almost exclusively of clichés, of *idées reçues*, of all the banalities and dregs of third-rate literature.

16

As readers, Molière's *précieuses* differ from Madame Bovary in at least one important respect: whereas Emma practically sells her soul to make life conform to the picture-book romanticism of her childhood, Magdelon and Cathos merely deny the outside world in favor of the make-believe universe of current best-sellers. Even the platitudes which they so blithely exchange with the valet Mascarille, disguised as a marquis, deal almost entirely with literature, e.g., "Les madrigaux sont agréables, quand ils sont bien tournés" or "L'impromptu est justement la pierre de touche de l'esprit" (Scene IX).

In rejecting La Grange and Du Croisy as suitors and in preferring the glitter of their disguised servants, the two girls actually show a preference for bad literature over good. Mascarille especially, in dress, manner and expression, is the very incarnation of the salon literature that Molière and his friend Boileau so cordially despised. In fact, La Grange, who stages the play within the play that will soon destroy Magdelon and Cathos, knows immediately what sort of bait to use: "Je vois ce qu'il faut être pour en être bien reçu" (Scene I). Characteristically, Molière uses the word "être," whereas a dramatist of an earlier period might have preferred in this particular instance the term "paraître." But in Mascarille, there can be no demarcation between appearance and essence, affectation and profound personality, public and private image. Divested of his bravery, he stands revealed to our two *précieuses* as a fraud. Indeed, the two porters, who had carried him on stage in a sedan chair, had, in spite of their lack of education and polish, immediately recognized him as such. Mascarille, in his parting words, ambiguously reproaches his erstwhile admirers their lack of regard for "la vertu toute nue" (Scene XVI). And until Du Croisy and La Grange had burst upon the scene, poor Mascarille had embodied for Cathos and her cousin the most desirable features of Parisian literary circles, and his aura had conformed to their every expectation. In the play within the play, arranged by La Grange, but so sincerely performed by Mascarille and Jodelet, Molière has thus externalized a certain type of bad taste.

Molière does much more than attack the unenlightened public whose tastes conform with those of the two girls, for he satirizes the writers and even the actors—those of the Hôtel de Bourgogne—they most admire. Magdelon and Cathos have devoured the interminable novels of Madeleine de Scudéry, as no doubt many of the spectators present themselves had done. But our two *précieuses* have obviously gone much further than any other reader in their rejection of all forms of behavior that do not rigidly follow the pattern of their favorite fictional characters. Molière chose as a perfect foil for the two maidens an obvious nonreader, Gorgibus. To contemporary spectators, he must have seemed just as ridiculous as his daughter and niece, for he behaves as though he had spent his entire existence in some sort of backwoods whose denizens did not even suspect the existence of literature, let alone of preciosity. To Gorgibus' conventional attitude concerning marriage, Magdelon opposes ideas just as conventional if somewhat more fashionable: "Il faut qu'un amant, pour être agréable, sache débiter les beaux sentiments, pousser le doux, le tendre et le passionné, et que sa recherche soit dans les formes" (Scene IV). She apparently wishes to substitute a purely literary convention for a social one, and the expression "dans les formes" reveals the rigidity of her code. She strikes us as a strange sort of pedant, as grotesque in her way as Métaphraste or all the doctors and notaries who will follow in her footsteps. As Magdelon proceeds with her long speech, she transforms these conventions into a rigid, systematic and almost obsessive pattern of behavior: "Après cela viennent les aventures, les rivaux qui se jettent à la traverse d'une inclination établie, les persécutions des pères, les jalousies conçues sur de fausses apparences, les plaintes, les désespoirs, les enlèvements, et ce qui s'ensuit." She thus reduces the stuff and non-sense of contemporary novels to a set of absolutes, that she considers binding in day to day existence. By this reduction, she tends to exclude the reality of human feelings as well as the eventualities of a normal life.

Cathos and Magdelon do not, however, confine their preciosity to literature, but indulge in every conceivable form of artificiality. La Grange had defined their type as a cross between a *coquette* and a *précieuse*. Indeed, they use, in spite of their youth, vast quantities of make-up, as though they wished to transform their countenances into a fixed and permanent mask. Old Gorgibus, at least, conveys that impression: "Elles ont usé, depuis que nous sommes ici, le lard d'une douzaine de cochons, pour le moins, et quatre valets vivroient tous les jours des pieds de mouton qu'elles emploient" (Scene III). With all this pomade, they must look something like Jodelet, who paints his face white in the manner of a clown. The lard mentioned by Gorgibus represents the sordid matrix of their affectation, of their ethereal prudery. The two girls, like any self-respecting *précieuses,* are of course prudes and probably Platonists to boot. Cathos especially expresses her horror of nature in the raw, of undisguised reality: "Comment est-ce qu'on peut souffrir la pensée de coucher contre un homme vraiment nu?" (Scene IV). But does Cathos really hate sex or do her words merely echo the distorted idealism of some members of the *précieux* set? Such hatred might explain why the two maidens wish to escape to a purely imaginary universe: "Laissez-nous faire à loisir le tissu de notre roman, et n'en pressez pas tant la conclusion" (Scene IV). But why look for hidden motivations in a satirical comedy of manners? After all, everything Magdelon and Cathos say or do reflects dramatically and even structurally their ambition to replace the world they live in by literature. These two essentialists might formulate their *cogito* as: "I read, therefore I am." And because they read the wrong sort of books, they must fall for the nonsense of a valet who prides himself on his wit and his creative powers: he who lives by literature, will perish by literature.

Les Précieuses ridicules has, since its first performance, given rise to a controversy. Did Molière intend to satirize a poor imitation of preciosity or the thing itself? Professor Antoine Adam has shown that Molière definitely had in mind Madeleine de Scudéry and her coterie.[1] In fact, La Grange, at the very beginning of the farce, expresses his opposition to the whole

---

[1] Antoine Adam, *Histoire de la littérature française au XVIIe siècle* (Paris: Domat, 1952–1956), III, 258–263.

movement: "L'air précieux n'a pas seulement infecté Paris, il s'est aussi répandu dans les provinces, et nos donzelles ridicules en ont humé leur bonne part." La Grange's strong words—whether or not they express the author's own viewpoint—definitely cast an unfavorable light on preciosity itself, and not only on Cathos and Magdelon. Subsequent scenes will show that La Grange had some justification in referring to preciosity as a contagious disease. Molière, however, attacks the movement in a devious manner, for he flays two vain females who have succumbed to the outward manifestations of preciosity rather than the actual way of life that prevailed at the Hôtel de Rambouillet. And the author uses indirection of a similar kind to make fun of the rival comedians of the Hôtel de Bourgogne, for instead of attacking them directly, he makes Mascarille admire them for their artificiality. Mascarille, played by the author himself, even denigrates the acting of Molière and his company: "... ils ne savent pas faire ronfler les vers, et s'arrêter au bel endroit" (Scene IX). The author will use this same technique in *L'Impromptu de Versailles,* damning his rivals with the exaggerated praise of fools. Pascal, only a few years earlier, had perfected this effective weapon in order to harass the Jesuits. By using indirection against Madeleine de Scudéry and the Hôtel de Bourgogne, Molière could transform into accomplices even fairly staunch admirers of *Le Grand Cyrus* and of Montfleury, for he knew that no one in the audience could possibly identify with such idiots as Magdelon, Cathos, and Mascarille. This explains the general enthusiasm that greeted the farce at its first performance, attended, if we can believe Ménage, by many members of the *précieux* set, who applauded as much as everyone else.[2]

In this as well as in most of his subsequent plays, Molière chooses as victim a gullible or even dedicated person whose tribulations serve to devaluate the system of values in which he or she believes. Normally, this clever method does not obscure the issue, even though it helps protect the author. Sometimes, for instance in *Dom Juan,* we can scarcely determine the play-

[2] Gilles Ménage, *Menagiana,* (Paris: Florentin et Pierre Delaulne, 1693), p. 278.

wright's actual intentions, and interpretation must become a form of conjecture and speculation.

Systematic deflation characterizes *Les Précieuses ridicules.* Cathos and Magdelon imitate a certain conception of preciosity, in the same manner that Mascarille and Jodelet ape two quite different aspects of aristocratic behavior, or that Don Quixote strives to live up to the outmoded, but still admired, ideal of knight errantry. Deflation, in this farce, thus takes the form of parody and caricature: Cathos-Aminthe replaces Catherine-Arthénice of Hôtel de Rambouillet fame, while the two footmen perform the parts of noblemen and wits. Molière cleverly attributes to the four principals, in a most exaggerated form, the actual shortcomings of real *précieuses* and genuine aristocrats. He pokes fun at Mascarille in precisely the same manner that, in *Le Misanthrope,* he will satirize the "petits marquis" whose blue blood is above suspicion. Molière cruelly chastises a relatively poor imitation, but in so doing he deals a tremendous blow at current affectations.

One cannot insist too strongly on the general aggressiveness of the play, on its inherent cruelty. Cathos and Magdelon, by identifying life with the vicissitudes of fiction, have tried to protect themselves from the dull hazards of day to day existence. As they wish to live in an illusory world and indulge their silly vanity, it is fitting that an illusion of a different sort should shatter their dream and bring them down to earth. In thus pulverizing their fondest illusions, their hopes of a brilliant future in Parisian literary and aristocratic circles, Molière actually destroys their very being. The beatings which La Grange and Du Croisy will publicly administer to their servants provide only a slight and purely external indication of the tortures that the two would-be *précieuses* are undergoing at the same moment, almost to the point of annihilation. The more they suffer, the more ridiculous they seem, and the more the audience laughs at them. Freud spoke the truth when he described certain types of laughter as a form of aggression.

Molière very nearly lends a tragic dimension to this cruel destruction of illusion by means of the dramatic device of tragic irony. When Mascarille asks the *précieuses* whether they receive many interesting visits, Magdelon answers: "Hélas! nous ne sommes pas encore connues; mais nous sommes en passe de l'être" (Scene IX). Upon Jodelet's arrival, she exclaims in her elation: "Ma toute bonne, nous commençons d'être connues; voilà le beau monde qui prend le chemin de nous venir voir" (Scene XI). And who can accuse poor Magdelon of having made a false prediction, for fame will soon burst upon the two of them. In the final scene, Gorgibus gives his charges a fairly clear picture of the type of notoriety they have a right to expect: "Nous allons servir de fable et de risée à tout le monde. ..." Irony of a slightly less cruel nature makes itself felt in several of the servants rejoinders, particularly in the Marquis de Mascarille's complaint: "Je ne pense pas qu'il y ait gentilhomme en France plus mal servi que moi" (Scene XI).

When the maidens discover the truth, Magdelon complains to her father: "... c'est une pièce sanglante qu'ils nous ont faite" (Scene XVI), thus revealing the bitter but unconscious irony of one of Cathos' earlier remarks: "Cette journée doit être marquée dans notre almanach comme une journée bienheureuse" (Scene XI). La Grange has not only played a trick on them, but of course staged a theatrical performance in the full sense of the word "pièce." Indeed, Molière, even more frequently than in his two previous plays, amuses the audience with the idea of theatrical illusion. Our *précieuses* are performing their parts to the best of their ability in a play intended to bring about their complete destruction. And at the end, they will suffer mainly as spectators from the absurdity of their own performance. Molière reminds us more than once of this paradox. Mascarille, in discussing the theater, asks the cousins: "Je ne sais si je me trompe, mais vous avez toute la mine d'avoir fait quelque comédie" (Scene IX). Moreover, the author plays with the idea of theatrical illusion by attributing Jodelet's whitened countenance to a recent illness. In order to explain his present lack of creative power, Jodelet says: "... je me treuve un peu incommodé de la veine poétique, pour la quantité de saignées que j'y ai faites ces jours passés" (Scene XI). In *Le Dépit,* Gros-René had referred to his bulkiness in much the same manner. However, such devices take on added significance in a farce dealing with the annihilation of literary illusions. Molière, for that reason, insists several times on the purely histrionic quality of the trick played by the infuriated suitors. He stresses, moreover, the idea of entertainment, indispensable to the performance of a farce, for Mascarille does not hesitate to hire musicians who transform the play into a ludicrous ballet. Thus, the cruel destruction of illusions coincides with the triumph of the theater, where good literature takes the place of trash.

4   *A Comedy of Errors*

Compared with *Les Précieuses ridicules,* where Molière daringly took position against Madeleine de Scudéry and her powerful backers, *Sganarelle* must strike the reader as a simple comedy of intrigue, containing, or so it would seem, little social satire and no politics. This reversion on the part of the author does not necessarily stamp the new comedy as inferior to its immediate predecessor, for *Le Cocu imaginaire* gives evidence of poetic skill and shows a rare mastery of dramatic techniques. This highly intellectual comedy of errors provides a perfect example of what Bergson has described as the snowball technique—the little snowball that swiftly grows into an avalanche merely by rolling down a steep slope. Clélie, told by her grasping father that she must forget her beloved Lélie and marry a wealthier suitor, drops into a dead faint. Her maid shouts for help, and Sganarelle rushes to the rescue. Sganarelle's wife, espying from a distance a strange woman in her husband's arms, jumps to the wrong conclusion. Upon reaching the scene, she finds only Lélie's portrait, which had fallen from Clélie's hands. Sganarelle then surprises his wife in the act of admiring the semblance of a handsome young man, whom he immediately suspects. He rudely forces her to hand over the miniature. Lélie, who has just returned from a trip, discovers his portrait in the possession of Sganarelle and imagines that this unlikely clown must be his wealthy rival, now married to the faithless Clélie! The wildly jealous but timorous Sganarelle tells everyone who will listen about his misfortune, including of course Clélie, who, out of spite, consents to marry her rich suitor. The compounded confusion reaches a climax with all the characters accusing one another. Clélie's levelheaded maid clarifies the situation by making the various people concerned

24

speak in turn. The comedy ends happily with the discovery that Lélie's fearsome rival already has a wife.

Sganarelle, however, has more to offer than a skilfully contrived plot which, after a tremendous build up, suddenly destroys itself. It is, to a large extent, a play about imagination, and as such it richly deserves its subtitle, *Le Cocu imaginaire.* More important still, Molière has fully exploited the farcical consequences of coherent reasoning based on false perceptions. The spectator derives his greatest pleasure from following with the utmost clarity the ever-increasing aberrations of all the characters involved. Reason, ably seconded and abetted by a lively imagination, behaves like a perfectly tuned machine and insists on driving its possessors ever onward to an unlikely disaster. And the merest false perception had sufficed to set this syllogistic monster in motion. Once they have committed their initial error of perception or judgment, the various victims manage to discover in each subsequent event, whatever its nature, ample proof and confirmation that so far at least they have followed the right course. Such a situation would appear humorous enough if it involved only a single individual, but Molière has contrived to make the spirit of aberration spread from one character to the next as though a highly contagious disease had suddenly acquired the predictable uniformity of a machine. Bergson's theory that laughter results from "mécanique plaqué sur du vivant" goes far towards explaining the entire play, all the more so because the initial blunders remain mostly external to the characters who have committed them and can therefore have very little to do with their psychology. In subsequent plays, particularly in those works which come under the heading of "comédies de caractère," the basic error on which the plot is built will arise from a moral or psychological flaw or perhaps a false value judgment. Bergson has shown that the personality traits themselves will operate with the rigidity and predictability of a contraption.[1]

Aberration, which affects each of the principals according to his or her peculiar susceptibilities, takes the form of a sharp

[1] Henri Bergson, *Le Rire* (Paris: P.U.F., 1947), pp. 101 ff.

contradiction between what has actually happened and what the character believes he has seen. This type of aberration can make us laugh by its very precision, for all the shades and nuances of error must necessarily go down the drain, as in that incongruous pedagogical invention, the multiple-choice examination. In two of the characters, Gorgibus and Sganarelle, this external contradiction corresponds ever so slightly to an internal incongruity, of which neither of them has any awareness. Simpler characters, such as Clélie, Lélie and Sganarelle's wife, misinterpret events, merely because they have reverted to that state of basic isolation and mistrust of one another which threatens most of Molière's creatures. This tendency, of which *Dom Garcie de Navarre* and *Le Misanthrope* will provide the most interesting examples, explains the frequency, in his theater, of lovers' quarrels founded on the most superficial misunderstandings. Whereas in later comedies, Molière will endeavor to establish causal connections between internal and external contradictions, in *Sganarelle,* he is quite content to associate them by means of analogy or even juxtaposition.

Gorgibus, who makes his only appearances at the beginning and the close of the farce, is a sententious old codger, prone to confuse moral issues. Although he has solemnly promised Clélie's hand to Lélie, he breaks his word as soon as a more prosperous candidate dawns upon the horizon. He assumes that money must necessarily take the place of all other values. It follows that a rich man cannot fail to be a worthy person and therefore a suitable husband for Clélie: "Allez, tel qu'il puisse être, avecque cette somme / Je vous suis caution qu'il est très-honnête homme" (21–22). Previously, he had rhymed "ducats" with "appas." Such naive materialism immediately stamps Gorgibus as a clod and a clown, but it does not prevent him from describing his sordid avarice as "raison paternelle" or from proclaiming the superiority of his own standards of morality. In a sense, he foreshadows both Harpagon and Orgon as paternal figures. He reproaches his daughter for talking less about God than about her betrothed, and he strongly advises her to read old-fashioned and therefore ridiculous tracts, namely Pybrac's *Quatrains* and Matthieu's *Tablettes,* both of which contain moral precepts in versified form. Moreover, he insists on the importance of ethics at the very moment when he breaks a most solemn pledge! And he praises Matthieu's treatise because so many "beaux dictons à réciter par cœur" can be found therein (36): for lip service only. Gorgibus treats morality as a purely verbal phenomenon—one which helps keep up appearances and sometimes impresses young children. He concludes his speech in characteristic fashion: "Et si vous n'aviez lu que ces moralités, / Vous sauriez un peu mieux suivre mes volontés" (39–40). Like his namesake in *Les Précieuses,* he feels that his daughter reads too many novels, a commodity which, in this instance, becomes a highly desirable element of modern life, for it must stand for all forms of entertainment including, no doubt, the theater. In thus revealing the unconscious contradiction between moral verbalism and selfish action, in thus opposing outmoded moral tracts to modern literature, Molière seems already to be defending his own integrity as entertainer against dishonest attacks. The likes of Gorgibus, far from attending the Petit Bourbon or the Palais Royal, might well accuse dramatists and actors as well as novelists of corrupting society and thus convince themselves, if not others, of their own moral excellence. Orgon, who will wine, dine and lodge Tartuffe, who will, in exchange, share the hypocrite's views on entertainment without in the least modifying his own selfish behavior, can be regarded as a successful avatar of Gorgibus, who publicly identifies himself with ethical standards. Clélie's father does not, however, commit an error of perception or imagination, unless we can so regard his assumption that Villebrequin's son can marry Clélie. Nonetheless, we may consider all the misrepresentations that follow as dramatic externalizations of his moral incoherence.

Sganarelle, on the contrary, gives free reign to his imagination once he has committed his initial mistake. And his growing aberration corresponds, within his own being, to an amorphous mass of confusion. The inordinately vain Sganarelle so prides himself on his good looks and on his personal charm, that the idea that his wife might prefer another man fills him with astonishment. In describing himself, he exclaims: "Cette taille, ce port que tout le monde admire, / Ce visage si propre à donner de l'amour" (166–67). Other people, unfortunately, see him in a different light, and Lélie describes him as "l'homme le plus mal fait" (296). We might expect so vain a person to take his marital honor seriously and to seek immediate revenge. Sganarelle's vanity, however, is hardly a match for his cowardice: the unequal conflict between them will give rise to a protracted monologue apparently suggested by a similar situation in Scarron's *Jodelet soufgleté*. Although this conflict would readily lend itself to a parody of Corneille, Molière preferred to let Sganarelle speak in accordance with his status and use such "low" or popular words as *bedaine, gras, bile, cajoler*. True, the great Corneille used one of those terms in a famous line: "... cajoler Médée et gagner la toison." Nonetheless, Molière's hero occasionally throws in an heroic line to increase, by a contrasting note, the discrepancy between his true nature and the swashbuckler he would like to become, e.g., "Montrons notre courage à venger notre honte" (414), gives way to the more plebeian: "Vous apprendrez, maroufle, à rire à nos dépens, / Et sans aucun respect faire cocus les gens." Actually, Clélie, infuriated by her fiancé's alleged infidelity, had encouraged the cowardly Sganarelle along a bellicose line. Referring to Lélie's apparent betrayal, she had exclaimed: "... ce cœur / Ne sauroit y songer sans mourir de douleur" (399–400). Poor Sganarelle, believing that Clélie has expressed concern for his own injured feelings, makes one of the funniest rejoinders in the play: "Ne vous fâchez pas tant, ma très-chère Madame: / Mon mal vous touche trop, et vous me percez l'âme" (401–02). It would appear that Clélie's sensitivity has become so contagious that it can inspire the thick-skinned and timorous Sganarelle with a thirst for blood quite contrary to his nature. This transformation reminds us of Madame de Sévigné's "humeur empoisonnante" caused by the scattered ashes of la Brinvilliers.[2] Sganarelle's new-found and unsuspected courage really belongs to Clélie, and the task of

[2] Marie de Sévigné, *Lettres* (Paris: Dalibon, 1823), V, 26; letter to Madame de Grignan, dated July 17, 1676.

making this foreign body part and parcel of his own being taxes his powers to the breaking point. Molière has succeeded in transforming a feeling into a material object that can be handed from one person to another, in the same manner that he had previously materialized a false perception.

Sganarelle's espousal of a bellicose attitude thus provides a further instance of contradiction, the main theme of this farce; and Molière derives comic effects from the tendency of such characters as Sganarelle and Gorgibus to switch from one contradictory attitude to the next without the slightest transition. Gorgibus, upon learning that Villebrequin's disobedient son cannot legally marry Clélie, immediately acts as if it had never entered his mind to marry her to anyone save the deserving Lélie! And Sganarelle's parting words hilariously imply that contradictory and erroneous perceptions have suddenly become the universal norm and principle of all human relations: "De cet exemple-ci ressouvenez-vous bien; / Et, quand vous verriez tout, ne croyez jamais rien." Undoubtedly, this intellectual conclusion somehow caps all the absurdities that have just taken place before our eyes. One of the well-springs of laughter in Molière's theater is the creation of an interruption between thought and action; between reason and existence. This kind of imaginary interval lurks no doubt in every human consciousness; but Molière's art consists in widening it until it becomes a gap, where men can perceive their inescapable contradictions and conflicts.

5   *The Incompatible Lovers*

A FEW CRITICS, in discussing *Dom Garcie de Navarre,* have drawn attention to its comic structure. P. A. Chapman saw in the ". . . successive reappearance of a fundamental trait, jealousy, the periodical jack-in-the-box movement so subtly described by Bergson, the effect of which is so irresistibly funny." [1] Chapman, however, in his eagerness to establish a psychological parallel between Molière's only heroic comedy and *Le Misanthrope,* chose not to treat the problem of comic techniques. Moreover, like many another commentator, he regarded *Dom Garcie* not only as vastly inferior to *Le Misanthrope,* but as a fairly dismal failure. One authority, M. Pierre Brisson, goes so far as to claim that *Dom Garcie* contains practically nothing that even remotely resembles the Molière of the unheroic comedies: "Quel mensonge contre soi-même et surtout quel aveuglement!" [2] Although M. Brisson probably expected his readers to take his witty denunciation with the proverbial grain of salt, he states, in an intentionally exaggerated form, an almost universal belief that Molière, in writing this play, committed his only mistake in an otherwise infallibly brilliant career. And it appears that the dramatist aggravated his sin by showing inordinate fondness for the most mediocre of his productions. However, W. D. Howarth has recently proved that *Le Prince*

[1] P. A. Chapman, *The Spirit of Molière* (Princeton, N.J.: Princeton University Press, 1940), p. 143.
[2] Pierre Brisson, *Molière, sa vie dans ses oeuvres* (Paris: N.R.F., 1942). Cf. section on *Dom Garcie.* Professor Antoine Adam's comments on the play, though only slightly more favorable than those of Brisson, suggest however that Molière's "tragédie familière ... côtoyait un certain comique de bon ton" (*Histoire de la littérature française,* III, 271). René Bray, in his *Molière, homme de théâtre,* though more favorable in his appreciation than most critics, appears to regard *Dom Garcie* as a serious play: "... une belle étude de jalousie, dépouillée de ridicule, mais aussi de tragique" (p. 313).

jaloux, in spite of the lofty status of its protagonists, should be read and performed as a comedy. Howarth limited his demonstration to a thorough study of the central character, the jealous prince, and to a discussion of the dramatic structure of the play. He did not, however, pay much attention to that most maligned of Molière's heroines, Done Elvire, whom we intend to rehabilitate, dramatically if not morally.[3]

DRAMATIC STRUCTURE

Dom Garcie, which Molière adapted from a play by Cicognini, has a typical cloak-and-dagger plot: the defeat of the tyrant Mauregat, who had usurped the throne of Leon. This exciting story is dwarfed into insignificance by the vicissitudes of Don Garcie's jealousy. Although we can detect very little interaction of a psychological nature between the protagonist's feelings and the usurper's downfall—such as would mark almost any play by Corneille—the comedy somehow holds together by means of verbal analogies and skilful manipulation of dramatic coincidence. The author did not hesitate to include a subplot: Done Ignès' reconquest of the erring Don Sylve; but, on the whole, he tends to subordinate the plot to more essential considerations, such as the periodical jack-in-the-box movement which Chapman had discerned in the successive reappearances of jealousy. Don Garcie, however, does not behave in the absurd manner of a Sganarelle; and we merely smile in amazement at his aberrant interpretations of innocent events. Indeed, Molière has engineered precarious suspensions of disbelief rather than sudden ruptures of attention.

Don Garcie's jealousy follows a definite not to say mechanical pattern: at each outburst we notice a corresponding increase in dramatic intensity. We learn at the very outset of the jealous prince's dominant characteristic. At his first appearance on stage, he tells us of the unpleasant feelings aroused in him by an ab-

---

[3] W. D. Howarth, "Don Garcie de Navarre or Le Prince Jaloux?" *French Studies,* V (1951), 140–148. This is the only study that does justice to the comedy.

sent rival, Don Sylve. This early manifestation of his "tragic flaw" has absolutely no factual basis; but when his confidant Don Lope brings him a letter torn in two, purported to be addressed to Don Sylve, and written in Elvire's hand, his unfounded suspicions appear, for the first time, to have a solid basis. We can blame his next fit of jealousy on the actual presence of his hated rival—a fact which makes Don Garcie's wildest conjectures pass, in his own eyes, for irrefutable evidence. Moreover, in each of the preceding situations, the hero's jealousy had been fomented by Don Lope, an unsubtle and somewhat pedantic Iago. When the unfortunate prince is finally left to his own devices, he suddenly catches sight of his Elvire in the arms of a man! In each of these increasingly dramatic incidents, we can perceive a corresponding intensification in Don Garcie's conviction; for he progresses from the merest conjectures to strong inference, and from inference to apparently unimpeachable evidence. The last crisis occurs at the *dénouement,* when the Prince of Navarre petulantly, but somewhat pitifully, expresses his despair.

Although Molière in his use of progression and intensification does little more than adapt with slight improvements materials invented by his Italian model, he shows originality in placing each new outburst of jealousy at a moment when the situation promises to take a favorable turn for the hero. The torn letter was addressed, not to his rival, but to himself; and it contained Elvire's first unambiguous declaration of love; Don Sylve has just met with utter defeat in his capacity as suitor when the Prince discovers him in tête-à-tête with Done Elvire; the "man" caught embracing Elvire is none other than Done Ignès, Don Sylve's former flame, who will do her utmost to lead her inconstant lover back to the path of duty; finally, Don Garcie's despair coincides with the revelation of his rival's true identity as brother to Done Elvire. In general, the testimony on which the prince bases his accusations contains within itself the means to refute them.

We might regard Don Garcie's jealousy as an avatar of Lélie's blundering. Moreover, the crescendo-like structure of the Prince's tribulations reminds one of the ever-growing aberrations of *Le Cocu imaginaire*. Like Lélie, Don Garcie can blame his blunders on two quite different but allied forces: his temperament and destiny—a destiny that does not in the least resemble Fate, for it is an impish force which maliciously takes advantage of a psychological weakness or tendency in order to transform a brave prince into a puppet. And a year or so later, Molière will use the same sort of frolicsome Fate to plague a less heroic protagonist, Arnolphe.

In *Dom Garcie*, Molière more closely approximates Rotrou's manner than that of Corneille. The dramatic and comic structure of his heroic play appears to have been patterned after that of *Don Bernard de Cabrère*. Rotrou had created the same type of mechanical destiny and of intensification in depicting Don Lope de Lune's infallible bad luck and his incredibly unsucessful attempts to gain recognition for his prowess, as Molière in Don Garcie's perfectly paced outbursts. Don Lope de Lune suffers just as much from malicious coincidences as the Prince of Navarre.

THE VERBAL STRUCTURE

Molière has welded the plot together and given it a semblance of unity by means of verbal analogies between Don Garcie's fits of jealousy and the conspiracy against Mauregat. Several key words fit with equal felicity into these two quite disparate contexts: *obstacle; cacher* and *secret; monstre* and *tyran.* The first of these, *obstacle,* appears to have no other function than to tie together the various loose ends of the story. In order to obtain the hand of Done Elvire, the Prince of Navarre must overcome, like the knights of old, two obstacles. According to Elvire herself, the easier of the two ordeals consists in vanquishing the usurper on the field of battle, the more difficult in defeating the enemy which lurks within his own mind: jealousy. Don Garcie, however, envisions a very different type of obstacle: Done Elvire's imagined love for another man: "... l'obstacle puissant qui s'oppose à mes feux, / Sans que vous le nommiez,

n'est pas secret pour eux" (241–42). Ironically, a popular revo-
lution in Leon, rather than the might of Don Garcie or his
rival, overcomes Mauregat and eliminates the first obstacle,
whereas the second is conveniently forgotten. Thus, the happy
ending serves to underline the futility of both the internal and
the external struggles: the final hurdle—the expected imposi-
tion by the new king of Leon of a political marriage between his
sister and the apparently triumphant Don Sylve—suddenly collapses when Elvire's long-lost sibling turns out to be none other
than Don Sylve himself! The deflation of the obstacle shows
how much Molière's contrived universe differs from the heroic
world of Corneille, where obstructions stubbornly refuse to
cooperate. In this unheroic but ever so convenient collapse we
have a comic ending, quite typical of the majority of Molière's
dénouements.

Terms which we can describe, rather roughly, as intellectual,
dominate the play. These terms, among which *cacher* and *secret,* as well as *témoin* and its various derivatives, appear most
frequently, refer in one way or another to perception, understanding, knowledge, judgment, and they run the entire gamut
from *aveuglement* to *lumière.* As one might expect in a mid-
seventeenth century play, we find an abundance of words indicating various types of illusion: *apparence, imposture, masque,
déguisement, dextérité, artifice, trompeur, s'abuser* . . . , as
well as the direct results of illusion, namely *méprendre, douter,
perplexité.* . . . However, most of the so-called intellectual
terms offer a more positive meaning: *preuve, rapport, indice,
rayon, éclaircir, garant, véritable, faire foi, certain, intelligence,
expliquer, connoître, savoir, témoin.* . . .

Secret and *cacher* in particular play a preponderant part in
Don Garcie's obsession. Believing fundamentally that Elvire—
who is indebted to him—cannot really love him and must
therefore be insincere, he suspects some dreadful secret on her
part, which through feminine guile she has so far succeeded in
hiding. Now, the Prince, who must unfortunately live in an
atmosphere thick with intrigue, blames Elvire's imagined insincerity instead of politics. His confusion reaches a climax in

the scene where he sees Done Elvire embrace the disguised Done Ignès. In order to refute Don Garcie's apparently well-motivated accusations, the Princess must divulge her persecuted friend's state secret—a revelation almost equivalent to a betrayal. Molière, moreover, introduced a certain number of parallelisms between the various confirmations of Done Elvire's constancy and the unfolding of the cloak-and-dagger plot: when finally her innocence and her sincere love for the jealous Prince stand revealed to everyone concerned, Mauregat has just met with defeat and Don Alphonse, alias Don Sylve, is about to ascend the throne of Leon. In short, the comedy ends at the very moment when Don Garcie's doubts have been dispelled for good. And the words *cacher* and *secret* serve to coördinate the political and warlike aspects of the plot with the increasingly dramatic confrontations of the jealous Don Garcie and the innocent Done Elvire.[4]

Tyran and *monstre* serve a somewhat similar purpose in spite of the fact that they belong to a quite different vocabulary group, containing words which refer to varying aspects of constraint and inequity or, conversely, to freedom and justice. Throughout the play, the author stigmatizes tyranny as a monstrous crime and as the worst form of injustice; and we chose, for that very reason, to place under the same heading words indicating constraint and those expressing guilt. Chief among the former are such words as *dépendance, joug, contrainte, tyran* . . . , or, on the contrary, *liberté, s'affranchir*. . . . Chief among the latter, we notice such legal expressions as *crime, équité, innocent, coupable, injustice, serment, loi, juge,* and the most frequent of all: *arrêt*. Less legalistic, but definitely connected with guilt, are *remords, monstre, sacrifice, pitié*. . . . Of all these terms, *tyran* and *monstre* fit most readily into the dual aspects of the plot—the political and the psychological.

The behavior of both Don Garcie and Mauregat, guilty of quite different crimes, is termed tyrannical and monstrous. For instance, Done Elvire exclaims: "Prince, de vos soupçons la

[4] Molière had already used this type of intellectual vocabulary in *Le Dépit amoureux.*

tyrannie est grande" (283). And much later in the play, she tells him: "Jouissez à cette heure en tyran absolu / De l'éclaircissement que vous avez voulu" (1462–63). She frequently describes her poor suitor's jealousy as a monster. In fact, unjust suspicions and political usurpation tend to have similar effects on her, for both exert a strong constraint on her feelings as well as on her actions. For this reason, Elvire insists that the Prince must overcome his jealousy, before she will consent to marry him, for she regards this fault as an inner tyrant. Although the Prince never does achieve this difficult victory over his instincts, he willy-nilly frees Elvire from the aggressive and tyrannical expression of his passion through his final humiliation and despair; and this apparent change of heart coincides with the complete liberation of her kingdom from the tyranny of the usurper. Moreover, the discovery of Don Sylve's true identity frees her from still another type of constraint: the importunity of the latter's courtship. Taken as a whole, the play shows a general movement from constraint to liberation, from tyranny to freedom.

Earlier in this chapter we singled out, among the intellectual terms, *témoin* and its derivatives *témoignage* and *témoigner*. These words fit as readily into the intellectual as into the legal vocabulary and function as a sort of bridge between them. It takes testimony of one sort or another to prove guilt or innocence. Elvire, accused of embracing Don Garcie's hated rival, insists on showing him: "... l'éclatant témoignage / D'une vertu sincère à qui l'on fait outrage" (1380–81). And in the final scene, the Prince pleads in his despair, albeit a petulant and almost sarcastic despair:

> Donnez-moi, par pitié, deux moments de contrainte,
> Et quoi que d'un rival vous inspirent les soins,
> N'en rendez pas mes yeux les malheureux témoins (1825–28).

At this moment, *contrainte* no longer expresses a form of tyranny, and *témoins* has ceased to be an accusation or an assertion of guilt.

Témoin and its derivatives give a definite direction to the intellectual tendencies of the play, for perception, knowledge, judgment pertain almost exclusively to innocence and guilt in human relations. Don Garcie, by false inferences, repeatedly accuses the Princess who, in each instance, dramatically vindicates her innocence. In accordance with Continental justice of the period, he must consider Elvire as a culprit until she can exonerate herself beyond a shadow of a doubt. But as soon as she can confirm her innocence, the guilt falls back on Don Garcie, whose jealousy then becomes tyrannical, monstrous, iniquitous and criminal. Invariably, the Prince's awareness of guilt paves the way to remorse and to eventual pardon, so much so that it would seem that Elvire uses his repentance as a convenient pretext for reconciliation.

THE BLIND HERO

In spite of the interdependency of the intellectual and legal vocabularies, only the former group gives rise to a major theme: psychological and moral blindness, which will reappear under various guises in a considerable number of subsequent comedies. This type of *aveuglement* usually coincides with overwhelming evidence, evidence that stares the blind or stupid person in the face, but which he alone cannot comprehend. In this respect if in no other, several of Molière's characters act like farcical or burlesque reductions of Œdipus, who ends up by discovering a truth obvious to the audience from the very beginning.

Done Elvire's innocence and her love for the Prince of Navarre are proclaimed in the very first scene, and the author never lets the audience doubt the sincerity of her feelings. As a result, Don Garcie's interpretations of events stand out in each instance as palpably false—as far from the truth as the numerous misinterpretations in *Le Cocu imaginaire*. In many respects, Don Garcie's mistakes have some justification: any normal person in a similar situation might have judged as erroneously. And, to a certain extent, the hero has a perfect right to blame Elvire who, loath to call a spade a spade, or to name her love, has never really given him an unambiguous idea of her feelings.

Indeed, she had even left in the dark her lady-in-waiting, the nimblewitted Elise:

> Cet amour que pour lui votre astre vous inspire
> N'a sur vos actions pris que bien peu d'empire,
> Puisque nos yeux, Madame, ont pu longtemps douter
> Qui de ces deux amants vous vouliez mieux traiter (15–18).

Under these difficult circumstances, how could the Prince have discovered Elvire's love for him? To complicate matters even further, she had shown too much affection to the dashing Don Sylve:

> Ma pitié, complaisante à ses brûlants soupirs,
> D'un dehors favorable amusoit ses désirs,
> Et vouloit réparer, par ce foible avantage,
> Ce qu'au fond de mon cœur je lui faisois d'outrage (33–36).

Her paradoxical conduct goes far towards explaining and even justifying The Prince's initial blindness and subsequent obtuseness. It accounts, at the very least, for his hatred of an absent rival on whom Elvire had showered so many tokens of affection. And Don Garcie, who judges only by externals, cannot help but misinterpret the events he witnesses. Granted this premise, clearly stated in the opening scene, he cannot avoid misunderstanding the torn note, the secret visit of Don Sylve, the sight of Elvire in the arms of a stranger, the happiness of his beloved when Don Sylve reveals his identity. And to this premise, from which every misrepresentation must follow, we may add Don Garcie's strange lack of confidence in his own merits.

Although the Prince's jealousy does not result from an obsession, he remains blind to Done Elvire's true feelings until the final scene, repeated confirmations of her innocence notwithstanding. Perhaps the Prince's mistakes and misconceptions are meant to show the subjective not to say instinctive nature of evidence, and man's propensity to project on external events the fantastic shape of his own insecurity. In short, emotional premises tend to distort reality. Don Garcie is repeatedly convinced of Elvire's affection for him; but this conviction cannot last, because his underlying mistrust, similar in this respect to La Rochefoucauld's self-love, constantly lurks in the shadows:

> Ce n'étoit pas en vain que s'alarmoit ma flamme;
> Par ces fréquents soupçons, qu'on trouvoit odieux,
> Je cherchois le malheur qu'ont rencontré mes yeux;
> Et malgré tous vos soins et votre adresse à feindre,
> Mon astre me disoit ce que j'avois à craindre (1277–81).

He rejects, by such irrational means, all previous assurances of Done Elvire's innocence, and considers his ill-founded and frequently refuted suspicions as premonitions of the absolute, the eternal, the awful truth! In this speech, external evidence and irrational conviction combine in such a manner that they make the Prince utterly certain of Elvire's betrayal and, at the same time, completely blind.

In later comedies, this type of certainty will become obsessive, so much so that the blind protagonist will instinctively and automatically refuse to see the truth. The best example appears in *Tartuffe*, where Orgon, even after the impostor has revealed his real nature to the point of embarrassment, will not budge from his hiding place. Imperviousness to truth definitely constitutes a major theme in Molière's theater. Conversely, creators of false appearances such as Tartuffe and even Don Juan eventually succumb to the forces of illusion: to Elmire's play-acting and to the statue's invitation.

DONE ELVIRE'S SELF-DECEPTION

The Princess shows as much reluctance to reveal her feelings in unequivocal terms as any of Madeleine de Scudéry's heroines. If Molière had given her the choice, she would have picked as lover some consummate Platonist trained at the Hôtel de Rambouillet. But her ill-starred fate selected instead a swashbuckling, insecure hero who turns out to be the sorriest tyro at courtship. Under such circumstances, she cannot really help becoming a *précieuse ridicule,* as silly, despite her princely manners, as the

bourgeoises Magdelon and Cathos. Because she thoroughly
knows her own feelings, she expects that the gentleman she
happens to prefer will perceive them just as clearly as she does.
And she demands, at the very least, a high degree of intuition
on his part—two hearts, two minds, with a single idea and a
single purpose:

> Au moindre mot qu'il dit, un cœur veut qu'on l'entende,
> Et n'aime pas ces feux dont l'importunité
> Demande qu'on s'explique avec tant de clarté.
> Le premier mouvement qui découvre notre âme
> Doit d'un amant discret satisfaire la flamme ... (284–88).

Don Garcie, however, demands much more than this modest
first movement; in fact, he requires nothing less than perpetual
motion—constant reiteration of affection. Moreover, Elvire's
words explain why she can so easily discount her false show of
affection to Don Sylve: only her inner reality is worthy of consideration. The Prince should have known how to distinguish
between such paltry appearances and her real being. In short,
she expects him to be ever so much more perceptive than even so
famous a character as the shepherdess Astrée.

As a result of this strange philosophy of love, she necessarily
resents Don Garcie's jealousy, which reveals an abysmal misunderstanding of her deepest feelings and aspirations. His displays
of jealousy fill her with amazement. She has never doubted the
sincerity of his love for her, and she hopes to find in him the
same certainty of her affection; in other words, she seeks the
deepest kind of understanding, based not on crude demon-
strations of passion, but on some mysterious form of communion, of intuition. In this light, the Prince becomes the
perfect foil, on a comic level, for the subtleties of a *précieuse;*
and his outbursts of jealousy strike us as the only fitting punishment for her platonic aberrations, which retard ever so slightly
the processes of nature. She is ridiculous because she so desper-
ately hangs on to a false conception of love. If she had the
power, she would reduce sex to a form of knowledge quite devoid of passion or any other inconveniences.

Played by an accomplished actress, the part of Done Elvire could easily become one of the most remarkable in Molière's theater, very nearly on a par with that of Célimène. In her own special way, the Princess of Leon is as frustrated as Don Garcie himself, or as Lélie, or Horace, or even Arnolphe: the perpetual victim of *contre-temps;* a heroine who has chosen as partner a hopeless blunderer, one who invariably misses his cue and who, instead of playing the soul-satisfying game of innuendo, as a civilized aristocrat should, behaves in the crude and childish manner of a jack-in-the-box.

Done Elvire, however, has a much more serious grievance than mere misunderstanding. By his very suspicions, Don Garcie shows his lack of proper esteem. Instead of accusing her, a true lover would uphold her honor and champion her cause against the entire universe:

> ... dans mes sentiments, assez bien déclarés,
> Vos doutes rencontroient des garants assurés;
> Vous n'aviez rien à craindre; et d'autres, sur ce gage,
> Auroient du monde entier bravé le témoignage (650–53).

The other men referred to in Elvire's rejoinder populate practically all the tragicomedies and novels of the period. Far from taking so direct a hint, the Prince shows a lack of tact unparalleled among seventeenth-century heroes, were it not for Alceste's misanthropic rantings:

> J'ai cru que dans ces lieux rangés sous ma puissance,
> Votre âme se forçoit à quelque complaisance,
> Que déguisant pour moi votre sévérité ... (660–62).

Done Elvire interrupts him. Her indignation would not be disowned by Emilie, Laodice, Eurydice, or any other of Corneille's embattled heroines:

> Et je pourrois descendre à cette lâcheté!
> Moi prendre le parti d'une honteuse feinte!
> Agir par les motifs d'une servile crainte!
> Trahir mes sentiments! et, pour être en vos mains,
> D'un masque de faveur vous couvrir mes dédains!

> La gloire sur mon cœur auroit si peu d'empire!
> Vous pouvez le penser, et vous me l'osez dire! (663–69).

Her indignation, though moving in the presence of a Mauregat, appears ridiculous under the circumstances, for it can express little more than frustration at Don Garcie's persistent blundering.

Done Elvire naturally expects to find in the Prince of Navarre the normal Cornelian virtues which she most admires. She even expects to discover them in Don Sylve, whom she does not love:

> Vous n'avez que les maux que vous voulez avoir,
> Et toujours notre cœur est en notre pouvoir:
> Il peut bien quelquefois montrer quelque foiblesse;
> Mais enfin sur nos sens la raison, la maîtresse ... (962–65).

By an amusing paradox of Molière's invention, this *précieuse,* this would-be Cornelian heroine, has chosen to love a brave and no doubt handsome young prince, full of the best intentions, but who happens to be a living denial of all literary gallants, a misfit in the world of *Le Grand Cyrus* or of *Le Cid.*

In Elvire's Cornelian ethos, in her Platonism, in her preciosity, however deeply imbedded they may appear, we can detect pretense and affectation. This does not necessarily imply a fundamental lack of sincerity on her part; for she has to take seriously a certain public, social, and cultural image of herself which she can conveniently discard as soon as a more genuine and natural feeling asserts itself. However royal her birth and lofty her status, she resembles in this respect the bourgeoise Mariane who tries to play a Cornelian part in the face of adverse circumstances only to be crushed by Dorine's famous rejoinder: "Non, vous serez, ma foi! tartuffiée." Unfortunately, Elvire happens to be a princess, and her lady-in-waiting cannot allow herself to interpret so bluntly the voice of nature. Elise disagrees with her mistress in regarding jealousy less as lack of esteem than as proof of affection: "C'est par là que son feu se peut mieux exprimer; / Et plus il est jaloux, plus nous devons l'aimer" (97–98). On the strength of this psychological truism, she predicts that, in spite of Elvire's momentary annoyance,

Don Garcie will always receive a full pardon: "... je sais quel pouvoir, malgré votre menace, / A de pareils forfaits donnera toujours grâce" (780–81). And Elise does not hesitate to advise the Prince in guarded terms to consider Elvire's jealousy as little more than an idiosyncrasy: "Mais nous avons du Ciel ou du tempérament / Que nous jugeons de tout chacun diversement" (1182–83). In short, she states most politely that Elvire's platonic convictions and Cornelian idealism are no more than an irrational and irrelevant nuisance.

The wise Elise, however, would never think of showing bitterness or even astonishment at such diversity of temperaments nor would she wish to change humanity. This *raisonneuse*—the first in Molière's theater—believes that people should tolerate the foibles of others and do their best to conform to them:

> Et puisqu'elle vous blâme, et que sa fantaisie
> Lui fait un monstre affreux de votre jalousie,
> Je serois complaisant, et voudrois m'efforcer
> De cacher à ses yeux ce qui peut les blesser.
> Un amant suit sans doute une utile méthode,
> S'il fait qu'à notre humeur la sienne s'accommode;
> Et cent devoirs font moins que ces ajustements
> Qui font croire en deux cœurs les mêmes sentiments
>   (1184–91).

From a courtly, platonic, or Cornelian viewpoint, such a tolerant, skeptical, and fundamentally disillusioned attitude represents a capitulation. Elise's advice to Don Garcie contains satirical implications. It definitely pricks the bubble of current heroic conceits regarding love and throws an unfavorable light on the Princess, whose demand of esteem and communion of souls it reduces to a "fantaisie." Such underlying irony tends to transform the play into a gigantic *dépit amoureux* with endless ramifications, including of course the almost forgotten cloak-and-dagger plot.[5]

[5] As we have already stated, this comedy has a vocabulary fairly similar to the play entitled *Le Dépit amoureux*.

LOVE AND APPEARANCE

Elise states, and the entire play reveals, that at least on the level of emotions people should not expect a true communion of souls. In spite of their love, or perhaps because of it, Elvire and the Prince live in separate, not to say private, little worlds. Expecting perfect understanding from the person least likely to provide it, she instinctively does her utmost to prevent any outward or, for that matter, inner formulation of her love. And Don Garcie is so blinded by circumstancial evidence and so anguished by his imaginary lack of merit that he makes no real effort to observe Done Elvire.

In a world where lovers must live isolated within themselves, within their own fantasies and emotions, the distinction between appearance and reality becomes increasingly arduous.[6] Elise alone has found a practical, if not morally valid, approach in human relations—an approach that can easily lead to hypocrisy: *ajustements*. May one claim that the world of *Le Prince jaloux* remains a thoroughly baroque universe, full of disguises, where appearance only rarely corresponds to reality, where human understanding is no more than a false impression that skill and guile can fabricate, a pleasing illusion that may result at certain moments from deceptively conciliatory attitudes "Qui font croire en deux cœurs les mêmes sentiments?" (1191).

These baroque aspects of the play are themselves misleading; for Molière, in thus dramatizing the difficult distinction between reality and appearance, has attempted to unmask certain contemporary forms of pretense. Communication and communion, difficult in themselves, can be rendered almost impossible by affectations and blindness. And the author obviously prefers to stress the humor of misunderstanding rather than the tragedy of incommunicability. In *Dom Garcie,* the audience never loses sight of the true feelings of the protagonists and, as a result, can follow them with amused detachment through the labyrinthine ways of their misrepresentations. The baroque spirit

[6] Hence the intellectual nature of the vocabulary.

would, perhaps, consist in losing oneself in the perplexities of the characters; the classical spirit, in a clear appraisal of their aberrations. In this regard, neither Molière nor his public would quarrel with La Rochefoucauld's maxim: "La souveraine habileté consiste à bien connoître le prix des choses." [7]

Neither Elvire nor Don Garcie is in any manner *habile*, let alone *souverainement habile;* neither possesses a discriminating perception of values. However, beyond her pretense and her *idées reçues,* beyond his blindness and his blunders, we can discern a sensible but unreasoning power which will eventually set everything right: Nature. When the time comes, Elvire will unhesitatingly throw aside her Cornelian ideals, her peculiar sense of honor or *convenances,* in order to reciprocate the Prince's passion. His remorse at the *dénouement* may be heartfelt, but were it patently an *ajustement,* the Princess would have accepted it gladly at its face value in order to gain her own and Nature's ends: love and sex.

The uneven struggle between the Cornelian persona and Nature finds dramatic expression throughout the play in Elvire's facile rejections of her solemn pledges to banish Don Garcie from her presence at the very next manifestation of his jealousy. Such oaths have no more reality than so many words: like several other of Molière's characters, Elvire *se paye de mots.* For the same reason, she does not take very seriously, in spite of her irritation, the Prince's accusations, for they confirm, albeit in a redundant manner, the intensity of his passion. Does it really matter if her persona be weaned from its wordy diet? After all, it is no more than a mask.

Love triumphs despite the separateness of the lovers, whose passion, for lack of a better diet, must thrive on misunderstanding. La Rochefoucauld will go even further than Molière in stressing this fundamental lack of communion: "N'aimer guère en amour est un moyen assuré pour être aimé." [8] Molière, how-

---

[7] This maxim, no. 244 of the 1678 edition, first appeared in the 1664 (Dutch) edition. See *Œuvres complètes* (Paris: Pléiade, 1957).

[8] Maxim no. 301 of the 1665 edition. A similar misunderstanding will mark the relationship between Alceste and Célimène in *Le Misanthrope,* which contains several passages lifted from *Dom Garcie.*

ever, regards love as a manifestation of Nature capable of over-coming all obstacles; in comparison, platonic ideals and courtly essences are no more than cobwebs which lovers must sweep aside together with such an irrelevant notion as a communion of souls. Nonetheless, the author would probably agree with La Rochefoucauld in detecting in love the presence of *amour-propre* —a presence which Don Garcie reveals in the strangest of wishes:

> Oui, tout mon cœur voudroit montrer aux yeux de tous
> Qu'il ne regarde en vous autre chose que vous;
> Et cent fois, si je puis le dire sans offense,
> Ses vœux se sont armés contre votre naissance;
> Leur chaleur indiscrète a d'un destin plus bas
> Souhaité le partage à vos divins appas,
> Afin que de ce cœur le noble sacrifice
> Pût du Ciel envers vous réparer l'injustice,
> Et votre sort tenir des mains de mon amour
> Tout ce qu'il doit au sang dont vous tenez le jour (217–26).

Professor Adam regards these words as merely *précieux*.[9] But behind the apparent disinterestedness of his passion, there lurks not only an anguished feeling of insecurity, but also the dangerous ambition of becoming the master of Elvire's destiny. What happiness, what egotistical pleasure if only the Princess could owe her very being to him! That alone might insure absolute possession. Perhaps it is her very independence—her otherness—which he resents and fears, an independence which gives rise to his jealousy. By this act of unconscious arrogance, Don Garcie foreshadows Arnolphe's demand of complete submission on the part of a wife.

The Prince's speech helps explain the inevitable incompatibility of the two lovers—for absolute possession is as impossible as perfect communion or the reduction of sex to knowledge. Both of these exorbitant wishes reveal a tendency to negate the

[9] Adam, *op. cit.*, III, 272. The author regards Elvire as "une précieuse, et de la pire espèce." But perhaps Molière intended her to be just that. Why assume that he wished to create a compelling "romantic" heroine instead of a pathetically absurd woman in a comic situation?

very being—the otherness—of the person loved. It would appear that each lover strives, in one way or another, to play the dominant part in the projected relationship. The insecure Prince seeks to destroy Elvire's liberty, which he fears and to which he responds by jealousy; the Princess, whose approach to love is more essentialistic than existential, takes refuge in a sentimental form of Platonism which, by transforming love into an intellectual conceit, makes it both attractive and safe. In short, the hero and the heroine are so completely incompatible that they require the bountiful help of Nature.

But why did so remarkable a comedy fail to attract the public or to impress the critics? We suggest that Molière tried too hard to reach perfection by putting too much subtlety into the language and too many refinements into the characterization, even to the point of forgetting his usual preoccupation: that of entertaining the audience.

6

Battledore &
Shuttlecock

*A*FTER HIS unsuccessful venture into the
refinements of heroic comedy, Molière returned to an earthy
type of humor and wrote one of his most entertaining plays.
L'Ecole des maris, from a theatrical point of view, has few if
any rivals in his entire repertory, for it contains an abundance
of ludicrous situations expressed in witty verse and capped by
a flawless *dénouement.* As the title suggests, intellectual considerations, reduced, for obvious reasons, to a form of pedantry,
play a dominant part: it seems that Molière started the fashion
of using the word "école" in the title of a comedy. And this
word reveals not only the author's preoccupation with reasoning
or discourse as a source of laughter, but perhaps the intellectual
nature of comedy itself, if not of most forms of humor.

THE DEFENSE OF ENTERTAINMENT

The opening scenes oppose antithetical systems of education:
the permissive attitude of Ariste, who believes in entertaining
young people, and the strict disciplinarian methods of Sganarelle,
who insists on keeping them busy. Not that Molière wrote this
comedy to prove the superiority of Ariste's educational philosophy! In fact, this gentleman does not deign to expound a definite system of pedagogy, for he merely rejects all rules and pre-
conceived notions: "Et l'école du monde, en l'air dont il faut
vivre / Instruit mieux, à mon gré, que ne fait aucun livre"
(191–92). Even his younger but less youthful brother hardly
advocates a specific educational system, although we can safely
assume that he has never deviated from some sort of precon-
ceived plan.

To a seventeenth century audience, neither Ariste's extreme

48

permissiveness, nor Sganarelle's workhouse techniques would have seemed realistic or even theoretically tenable positions. But the author, for dramatic reasons, needed to establish between the two brothers as strong an opposition as possible, even to the point of absurdity. Moreover, he chose to make the siblings different in other respects. Ariste insists on following the latest fashions so long as they do not conflict with good taste, and on attending all the plays, ballets, and other celebrations that Paris has to offer. One can hardly imagine him missing a first-night performance at the Théâtre du Palais-Royal or applauding, like the Marquis de Mascarille, for the wrong reasons. He appears to represent not so much the author's own views as a discriminating and worldly attitude, with which the pleasure-seeking public could sympathize, even to the extent of becoming Molière's willing accomplices. Now, the most paradoxical thing about Ariste is not his so-called philosophy but his age! His tactless brother insists several times at the beginning and towards the end of the farce on Ariste's advanced years—he is close to sixty. Molière thus throws comic traditions to the winds by entrusting to so decrepit a man-about-town the defense of life, love, and happiness. That Ariste should proclaim the rights of old age to have a gay old time will in no way astonish a modern reader, but it may have shocked some of Molière's devout contemporaries, who regarded *divertissement* as tolerable at best for young adults. A generation later, La Bruyère will express surprise at the strange behavior of N . . . , a sickly and heirless oldster, who squanders his last breath on building a stately mansion which he cannot possibly live to see completed. We can surmise that if N . . . had asked his advice, the author of the *Caractères* would have recommended solemn thoughts on somber resting places rather than conspicuous construction.

Sganarelle rejects the contemporary world with all its attractions and dresses for comfort in the style of Henry of Navarre's subjects. This refusal to belong to the present as well as his stubborn isolation must have struck the public as the height of abnormality. Molière, however, does not bother to tell us why Sganarelle behaves in so unpopular a manner, combining tyranny with a contemptuous but fearful rejection of all social amenities. Did the author wish to create a character with whom the spectators could have nothing whatever in common—a person who, almost by definition, would never be caught dead in a playhouse?

At the end of the comedy, Léonor, who has a blanket permission to indulge in every whim and who rarely misses a show, gladly consents to marry the still dashing Ariste, some forty years her senior, in preference to the immature dullards with whom she openly consorts; whereas her sister Isabelle deftly turns the tables on Sganarelle, only twenty years her senior, in order to elope with the still more youthful Valère. Youth must be served, and old age as well. The comedy thus demonstrates the educational value of entertainment as well as its capacity to smooth over the asperities of advancing years. And Molière's happy patrons may have left the Palais-Royal feeling that entertainment can sometimes have greater ethical value than many priests would care to admit. Ariste's justification of his worldliness suggests that the author calculated his moral effects and consciously tried to assure the triumph of a carefree, mundane attitude:

> C'est un étrange fait du soin que vous prenez
> A me venir toujours jeter mon âge au nez,
> Et qu'il faille qu'en moi sans cesse je vous voie
> Blâmer l'ajustement aussi bien que la joie,
> Comme si, condamnée à ne plus rien chérir,
> La vieillesse devoit ne songer qu'à mourir,
> Et d'assez de laideur n'est pas accompagnée,
> Sans se tenir encor malpropre et rechignée (57–64).

From a secular standpoint, Ariste could hardly have spoken more wisely and convincingly, or his brother shown less tact and more foolishness; but an uncompromising Christian might have assigned the urbane Ariste to a prominent place aboard the Ship of Fools, where he would have found himself in good if crowded company: "...il vaut mieux souffrir d'être au nombre des fous, / Que du sage parti se voir seul contre tous" (53–54).

M. Paul Bénichou noted the growing discrepancy between the worldly attitude of the court and of Molière's comedies, and the Christian viewpoint.[1] No doubt an "honnête homme" could at one and the same time behave like a sincere Christian and misbehave like a stagestruck Epicurean without attracting undue attention; and Molière, in catering to the pleasure-seeking side of human existence, could assume, without falling into "libertinage," that the secular view should prevail within the confines of his theater. After all, why should a skilled cook concern himself artistically with days of fasting? Molière seems to have made this assumption in full awareness, for rarely does he miss an opportunity to rise to the defense of entertainment. This militant attitude appears to be peculiar to him, even though Pierre Corneille, in *L'Illusion comique,* Quinault, in *La Comédie sans comédie,* had broken a lance or two in favor of entertainers.

CONVENTION AND DRAMATIC STRUCTURE

We can regard the antithetical assumptions of Ariste and Sganarelle as a sort of dramatic convention, all the more so because the action of the comedy unfolds with all the rigor of a demonstration. And the tremendous power which each of the brothers holds over his ward partakes of this convention, for it enables Molière to assure complete freedom to Léonor while reducing her sister to a state of total constraint. By the unlikeliest of whims, the girls' father had entrusted the brothers with the combined moral authority of a parent, a schoolmaster, and a husband! Molière may have borrowed this clever trick from contemporary tragedians who, by attributing absolute power to a king or emperor, strove to create the impression that action, within the play, must depend on one man's passion. The dramatist, sole arbiter of relevance within the closed universe of the theater, can freely reduce the number of causes in order to increase the intensity of the proverbial tragic moment. Molière limits the number of potential causes for quite different reasons; for instead of hypostatizing some terrifying force or transcendent

[1] Paul Bénichou, *Morales du Grand Siècle* (Paris: N.R.F., 1948), pp. 157 ff.

ideal, he brings forth a mechanical device hardly more threatening than a toy. Fate, in his universe, gives way to the dangling
contraptions used in puppet shows; and that power which dwarfs
even Roman emperors in a tragedy becomes a sort of gadget.
Thus, Molière's art frequently consists in replacing the supernatural by the "subnatural," the mystical by the conventional.

Whereas Léonor enjoys, as we have seen, all the freedom and
independence she wants, Isabelle is Sganarelle's prisoner in every
sense of the word—a prisoner condemned to a life of hard labor,
for her guardian, who will trust no one, refuses to employ servants. This alone stamps the wealthy Sganarelle as abnormal
in the eyes of a seventeenth-century audience, all the more so
because the maiden to whom he assigns the most menial chores
belongs to a noble family (cf. line 927). Her imprisonment
gives rise to a novel dramatic situation: Isabelle can reach the
outside world only through Sganarelle himself—through a mis-
anthropist who fears all human contacts.[2] To the foregoing
devices, Molière adds still another dramatic convention: the
audience must not know or even care about the nature of Ariste's
or Sganarelle's actual feelings towards their charges, in spite of
the fact that the play ends with the formal engagement of Ariste
and Léonor. True, Sganarelle does show affection towards Isabelle, but only at those specific moments when he rejoices at the
apparent success of his educational policy. It would seem therefore that the author has focused attention on the public image of
the two brothers, to the exclusion of their personal lives.

Convention leads almost directly to dramatic structure. The
comedy recounts how Isabelle manages to turn the tables on
Sganarelle by transforming him into a docile intermediary between Valère and herself. As Professor Adam has pointed out,
the play moves with every scene towards a veritable crescendo.
And this ascending movement depends, to a large degree, on a
theme dominant in most of Molière's comedies: the interplay
between blindness and obviousness. Sganarelle will never suspect
until the end that he alone has served to bring Isabelle and
Valère together, whereas the audience can follow without the

---

[2] For Molière's indebtedness to Boccaccio, see *Grands Ecrivains Ed.*, II, 340.

slightest effort the skilful machinations of the lovers. Molière has entrusted Sganarelle with a dual function: he must act simultaneously as Isabelle's oppressor and as her unsuspecting agent. Isabelle had no other choice, for Sganarelle suspects the entire human race, with one notable exception, namely himself. And the closer the two lovers move towards an understanding, the more the self-confident guardian gloats over his marvelous success as an educator. He even takes pity on the young man whom he regards as a paltry and innocuous rival. In this manner, the relationship between Valère and Isabelle follows an almost mechanical progression, corresponding to the ever-increasing cecity of Sganarelle which he makes clear to the audience by the ever-growing intensity of his optimism. At first, upon Isabelle's request, he advises Valère to cease importuning his ward, for she has fully understood his amorous intentions. He then brings the young man a gold box containing a letter, received but left unopened by Isabelle. Sganarelle, in order to convince Valère of the hopelessness of his cause, invites him to the house; for the first time the lovers find themselves together, and even manage to exchange a kiss when Sganarelle looks the other way. Finally, Sganarelle, mistaking Isabelle for Léonor, sends her packing to her lover's house and arranges their marriage before he realizes the awful truth. One could hardly imagine a smoother dramatic progression, punctuated only by Sganarelle's exultations: a silent flirtation, a vicarious exchange of words, a letter, a furtive kiss, and suddenly complete possession!

Throughout the comedy, Sganarelle performs to perfection his part as messenger, for Molière has endowed him with a remarkable talent: that of repeating verbatim and without the slightest hesitation everything he hears! He repeats, much better than a parrot, entire speeches of Isabelle and Valère. Moreover, the majority of these speeches have a double meaning: one intended only for himself, the other for the lovers and, of course, the audience. Repetition, as Bergson has shown, tends to provoke laughter, particularly when it transforms an unsuspecting human being into a mechanical contrivance; and Sganarelle's continuous shuttling back and forth between the lovers serves

to heighten the audience's growing impression that they are
watching a machine bent on self-destruction rather than a free
agent acting in behalf of his interests. While the play moves on
like a well-oiled mechanism, Sganarelle functions with such
clock-work perfection that he very nearly triumphs in the end!
Carried away by his admiration for Isabelle's ladylike conduct,
he advances the date of their wedding to the very next day.
This unforeseen crisis forces the lovers to act even more quickly
than before in order not to succumb to the mechanical monster which, merely by its *vis inertiæ,* has gotten out of hand.

Sganarelle's blindness closely resembles the erroneous perception of his namesake in *Le Cocu imaginaire,* for he automatically misinterprets every word he repeats and every action
he witnesses in order to make everything conform to his pre-
conceived ideas about the actual situation. Already in his first
message to Valère, the discrepancy between the meaning he
attributes to his own utterances and their significance for the
audience almost reaches the breaking point:

> ... ayant vu l'ardeur dont votre âme est blessée,
> Elle vous eût plus tôt fait savoir sa pensée,
> Si son cœur avoit eu, dans son émotion,
> A qui pouvoir donner cette commission;
> Mais qu'enfin les douleurs d'une contrainte extrême
> L'ont réduite à vouloir se servir de moi-même (423–29).

Sganarelle goes so far as to define his own function as messenger.
He cannot realize, of course, that "contrainte extrême" must refer to his own tyranny rather than to the importunities of Valère.
He even scrutinizes the youth's expression in order to discover
the ravages that his fateful message has produced. Naturally,
he manages to see precisely the sort of thing he expects:

> Que sa confusion paroît sur son visage!
> Il ne s'attendoit pas sans doute à ce message.
> Appelons Isabelle. Elle montre le fruit
> Que l'éducation dans une âme produit (443–46).

Whatever Sganarelle happens to say, do or observe serves merely
to confirm him in his error. His imagination leaves no room for

experience. Racine will use an analogous device in *Bajazet,* but with the most tragic intentions: Roxane will interpret Bajazet's forebearance and even his coldness as indications of love, for her own overwhelming passions blind her to reality. There exist few comic devices which do not have their parallels in a tragic context.

THE PRICE OF FANCY

Sganarelle has isolated himself from his fellow men and from the present. He has made himself inaccessible, but in the process he has shut himself off from any understanding of the world around him. Molière emphasizes this separateness in Sganarelle's first encounter with his rival. Valère wishes to establish relations with Isabelle to whom he has never spoken; he therefore tries to make friends with her Argus by offering to inform him of the latest gossip he has heard at Court. Worse still, he mentions with appreciation the pleasures of Parisian life. Obviously, he could scarcely have chosen a gambit less likely to succeed with a person who lives in a past of his own imagining. Isabelle, on the contrary, after years of coexistence, knows precisely what method to follow. She bases each one of her tricks on her guardian's prejudices and assumptions, and especially on his long standing habit of trusting only his own judgment.

Sganarelle always knows better than his contemporaries, a frivolous pack of idiots who insist on dressing in uncomfortable clothes. To this silliness and artificiality, he opposes his *fantaisie,* a word that had at that time a somewhat stronger meaning than it does today. Far from suggesting that Sganarelle bases his conduct on a whim or caprice, it implies a deliberate intention on his part. As he consistently prefers his *fantaisie* to the opinions of the rest of humanity, he very nearly affirms his own infallibility or at the very least the superiority of his pedagogical and moral principles. He probably regards Isabelle's upbringing as complete, for at the moment the play begins, he has just decided to marry her himself within the week and reap the rewards of his wisdom. Although he fears to some extent the corrupting influence of Léonor, he undoubtedly regards marriage with Isabelle a safe venture. In a sense, he is predisposed in her favor, for he tends to see her as a product of his educational system, and therefore endowed with solid, old-fashioned virtues. Herein lies a paradox, for Sganarelle's *fantaisie,* far from consisting of unorthodox ideas of his own invention, coincides with the sternest pedagogical clichés of the old guard. Isabelle knows how to take advantage of this attitude in order to send Valère her first note. Upon being shown the unopened letter that Isabelle claims to have received from her suitor, Sganarelle immediately wants to find out what the young man has written. His ward, however, advises him not to break the seal, because proper young maidens should return such missives without deigning to read them. In recognizing the type of conduct he has always advocated, he can only concur with her decision and admire her for it. This trick, more clearly perhaps than any other, shows how Isabelle succeeds in turning her guardian's most trusted weapons against him. In fact, she predicts his reactions so accurately, that we have the impression that even if she had had Sganarelle built according to her own specifications she could not have obtained any better results.

Although Sganarelle regards Valère as quite innocuous, he does have a rival whom he takes seriously: Ariste. It would almost seem that sibling rivalry blinds him to other perils. And nothing would please him more than some escapade on the part of Léonor. He naturally expects the worst from a girl left to her own devices, spoiled and corrupted by the permissiveness of his superannuated brother. When Isabelle, pressed for time, suddenly tells him the cock-and-bull story about Léonor's unhappy and illicit love affair with Valère, he eagerly believes it, for it provides him with a golden opportunity to gloat over Ariste. He assembles the necessary officials and then rushes over to his brother's house to bring him the good tidings. Before the ultimate revelation, he even repeats an entire speech, uttered by Ariste very early in the play, to drive home the absurdity of a lenient attitude in education. Naturally, Sganarelle is hoisted by his own petard or, rather, deafened by his own echo; and the play ends with Isabelle safely married to Valère and Sganarelle publicly exposed as a fool. That the comedy should come to a close with Sganarelle surrounded by torches in the night exteriorizes in the most dramatic fashion the theme of blindness. Upon discovering the bitter truth, he consigns all women to perdition without expressing, at least in words, the pangs of betrayed love. He had wanted all along to make Isabelle part of his own little universe, separated from the rest of humanity. At one stage, he had paid her the supreme compliment of telling her that at last she had made herself worthy of becoming his spouse, all of which goes to show that *fantaisie* by no means precludes vanity.

His final curse, which contains such terms as *malice, Satan, damner, diable,* as well as the sentence "j'y renonce à jamais"— as though, in the manner of a good Catholic, he intended to renounce the devil for all eternity—happens to be the only passage in the play that has definite religious implications and which hints that Sganarelle, the enemy of *divertissement,* may belong to that group of vociferous Christians who plagued Molière during most of his career. There is irony in the fact that this enemy of entertainment should himself become a wondrous spectacle for his neighbors and for the audience. The author has put him, so to speak, in the limelight.

In renouncing all women, Sganarelle merely completes his isolation. He retreats to a world where he will soon be joined by such people as Arnolphe, Harpagon, Alceste, and Armande, who have only one thing in common: their self-exclusion. Such is the ultimate consequence of *fantaisie.* But unlike these other characters, Sganarelle does not exclude himself from humanity because of some passion, but rather because of his "intellectual" conception of the world. He has figured out human existence once and for all, and so his life consists in applying ready-made principles. Sganarelle, a creature without complexity, becomes utterly predictable and thus the designated prey of the first person who takes the trouble to understand him. But in a sense, he does not really exist, for he has systematically transformed all his drives into a set of essences and he has removed himself from actuality. It remained for Molière to relate this mechanical form of essentialism, whereby an individual tries to take refuge in dogmatism, to a driving passion or at least to a definite psychological motivation. Apart from his self-love and his vanity, Sganarelle does not indulge in any vices capable of determining his conduct, in spite of the fact that, unlike the various characters in *Le Cocu imaginaire,* he must assume "moral" responsibility for his mistakes. For this type of essentialism to become completely internalized, it must result from an emotional involvement rather than from a myopic world vision.

7 *The Plot's the Thing!*

$\mathcal{M}$OLIÈRE, in order to entertain the young king at Fouquet's palatial estate, hastily strung together a remarkably successful comedy of episodes, interspersed with *scènes de ballet*. He inserted at a later date a particularly amusing episode, that of the frustrated hunter, suggested by the Sun King himself. And he could no doubt have lengthened the play still further, had it been His Majesty's good pleasure, for this sort of show, like our pre-war reviews, has no other limitation than the amount of entertainment an audience can absorb in one evening, or the number of entertainers that the director has at his disposal. However, unlike modern showmen who provide a variety of routines for the stars of the moment and, with the help of the thinnest of threads, give their spectacle a semblance of continuity, Molière made use of the plot itself as the basic analogy and thus created an organic and even unified work of art.

Les Fâcheux received its first and greatest performance out of doors in an enchanting setting. Molière took this factor into account, for he expresses the keenest awareness that he must face a rather special audience under unusual circumstances. And he realized that he would have to invent new methods in order to win over these spectators and particularly the most redoubtable of them all, Fouquet's royal guest. Before the play can get under way, he suggests that nature—a nature ever so submissive to skilful gardening—has created the spectacle:

> D'abord que la toile fut levée, un des acteurs, comme vous pourriez dire moi, parut sur le théâtre en habit de ville, et s'adressant au Roi, avec le visage d'un homme surpris, fit des excuses en désordre sur ce qu'il se trouvoit là seul, et manquoit de temps et d'acteurs pour donner à Sa Majesté le divertissement qu'elle sembloit attendre. En même temps,

> au milieu de vingt jets d'eau naturels, s'ouvrit cette coquille
> que tout le monde a vue, et l'agréable Naïade qui parut
> dedans s'avança au bord du théâtre, et d'un air héroïque
> prononça les vers que M. Pellisson avoit faits, et qui servent
> de prologue (Avertissement).

The author, by this clever trick, avoided a very serious danger,
for the natural splendor of Vaux-le-Vicomte threatened to destroy the last vestiges of theatrical illusion. Molière thus sac-
rificed one form of illusion, that of the usual suspension of disbelief that prevails in a theater, in order to set up another one. By
letting nature take his place as director, he makes the many-
fountained park actively participate in the show which otherwise it might have ruined!

The poet Pellisson, a friend of La Fontaine and a protégé of
Fouquet, stresses with dramatic and lyric skill the idea of spectacle. Paradoxically, the water-nymph, played by Madeleine
Béjart, an actress of Molière's company, magically transforms
the chief spectator, namely the Sun King, into the only spectacle worth seeing: "Pour voir en ces beaux lieux le plus grand
roi du monde, / Mortels, je viens à vous de ma grotte profonde."
And the clever compliments continue apace: "Lui-même n'est-il
pas un miracle visible? / Son règne, si fertile en miracles
divers, / N'en demande-t-il pas à tout cet univers?" Louis XIV,
thus transformed by flattery into a visible miracle, will call forth
an equally perceptible miracle on the part of nature. Pellisson can
then bring about still another metamorphosis: the King suddenly becomes the "meneur du jeu," the master of ceremonies,
and not merely the first spectator of the ensuing entertainment
—the very entertainment that Molière did not have time to arrange:

> Ces Termes marcheront, et si Louis l'ordonne,
> Ces arbres parleront mieux que ceux de Dodone.
> Hôtesses de leurs troncs, moindres divinités,
> C'est Louis qui le veut, sortez, Nymphes, sortez (Prologue,
>   17–20).

The next few lines suggest even more clearly the idea of theatrical illusion:

Je vous montre l'exemple, il s'agit de lui plaire:
Quittez pour quelque temps votre forme ordinaire,
Et paroissons ensemble aux yeux des spectateurs,
Pour ce nouveau théâtre, autant de vrais acteurs (Prologue,
21-24).

And after a stage miracle has metamorphosed these nymphs
and satyrs into entertainers in modern dress, the play itself can
begin. Thus the park with the help of its mythical denizens provides, purely out of admiration for France's miraculous ruler, a
theater, performers, and a comedy. A less competent playwright
than Molière would merely have set up a makeshift stage in the
midst of the splendid landscape, without even trying to blend
the artificiality of the theater with the natural charm of a gar-
den.

After an initial ballet, the play begins in earnest. But the first
fâcheux never appears on stage. Eraste, the hero, describes in
a long narrative how an aristocratic bore practically ruined a
theatrical performance:

J'étois sur le théâtre, en humeur d'écouter
La pièce, qu'à plusieurs j'avois ouï vanter;
Les acteurs commençoient, chacun prêtoit silence,
Lorsque d'un air bruyant et plein d'extravagance,
Un homme à grands canons est entré brusquement,
En criant: "Holà-ho! un siége promptement!"
Et de son grand fracas surprenant l'assemblée,
Dans le plus bel endroit a la pièce troublée (13-20).

By this noisy interruption, the bore enters into conflict with the
play and already tends to become the center of interest. In fact,
his own dramatic importance depends upon the destruction of
theatrical illusion. In spite of the fact that this nuisance does not
appear on stage, his brutal intervention thrusts into the background the actors whom Eraste wishes to hear and see. Even
after he has located a place on the stage, the bore does his utmost
to eclipse the entire performance: "Au milieu du devant il a
planté sa chaise, / Et de son large dos morguant les spectateurs, / Aux trois quarts du parterre a caché les acteurs" (32–

34). Recognizing Eraste among the spectators, he noisily changes his seat and, for the benefit of his embarrassed friend, really takes charge:

> La-dessus de la pièce il m'a fait un sommaire,
> Scène à scène averti de ce qui s'alloit faire;
> Et jusques à des vers qu'il en savoit par cœur,
> Il me les récitoit tout haut avant l'acteur (55–58).

The substitution has now become complete, for the bore has succeeded in making himself the whole show in every sense of the word. Earlier in his narrative, Eraste had complained about the bad habits of his compatriots: "... faut-il sur nos défauts extrêmes / Qu'en théâtre public nous nous jouions nous-mêmes?" (23–24), a rhetorical question which stresses the fact that this first bore has played a part as will his successors in the scenes that follow. And in a sense, we scarcely have the right to describe this overwhelming spectator as the first of the *fâcheux,* for this honor really belongs to Molière himself, who had appeared on stage in city clothes to make his lame excuse to the King, as though to spoil Madeleine Béjart's entrance in the scant attire of a water-nymph. Thus, both in the prologue and the opening scene, Molière, by stressing the vulnerability of a theatrical performance, creates a new type of suspense.

In the following scenes, the author plays with threats and dangers of a different type: the various obstacles which insist on coming between Eraste and his beloved Orphise. And naturally, the first nuisance who comes between the two lovers happens to have theatrical connections or ambitions, for Lysandre adores the ballet and counts Lulli among his good friends. Thus poor Eraste, recently frustrated in his attempt to enjoy a play, falls into the opposite predicament, for Lysandre forces him to participate in a performance. His situation appears all the more ironical because his friend has imagined a ballet which subtly suggests the hero's pursuit of the elusive Orphise:

> Vois-tu ce petit trait de feinte que voilà?
> Ce fleuret? ces coupés courant après la belle?
> Dos à dos; face à face, en se pressant sur elle? (194–96).

Both Lysandre and Eraste's previous persecutor originate from the basic theatrical analogies established in the prologue: dramatic illusion; the blending of comedy with ballet; the fusion of a performance with the impressive spectacle of Vaux-le-Vicomte. Moreover, all these scenes contained some sort of conflict, if only the underlying struggle between art and nature.

Molière, after setting this complex pattern, did not need to integrate in so skilful a fashion the remaining tableaux. Nonetheless, the duelist, who interrupts the hero in the very next scene, brings to a head the idea of conflict while enabling the author to heap a few more compliments on Louis XIV who had recently proscribed all duels. The pair of *précieuses* who ask Eraste's opinion about jealousy ironically mirror his preoccupations of the moment, for he has just seen his beloved in the company of a strange man. This conversation, by its very artificiality and unreality, securely maintains the audience within the confines of literature and art: like Lysandre's dance steps, like the interrupted play, it belongs to the world of entertainment. And to this category will also belong the hunting scene as well as the game of piquet. Actually, the hunt provides us with two *fâcheux:* the man who tells the story and the bumpkin who frustrated him. In this tableau, Molière develops the old conflict between blindness and evidence: Dorante does not realize that Eraste wants to get away; and the country squire, who prides himself on his competence as a hunter, commits the crime of shooting the stag with a pistol.

The card game develops another structural aspect of the play by stressing an important theme: chance. Alcippe tells Eraste how he lost a near perfect hand despite the fact that he had all the odds in his favor. This loss has so astonished him that he insists on transforming it into a spectacle: "Je le veux faire, moi, voir à toute la terre" (344), which is the ambition of a playwright rather than of a gambler. But his bad luck cannot even compare with the misfortune of Eraste who must contend with an endless succession of bores. The odds against so continuous a persecution, precisely at this inauspicious moment, stagger the imagination. In the literature of the period, only Rotrou's Don Lope de Lune and Molière's own Arnolphe must endure so persistent a siege by the forces of chance and coincidence.

Eraste realizes from the beginning that Fate has turned against him:

> Sous quel astre, bon Dieu, faut-il que je sois né,
> Pour être des Fâcheux toujours assassiné!
> Il semble que partout le sort me les adresse,
> Et j'en vois chaque jour quelque nouvelle espèce (1-4).

Eraste specializes in bores. Even in love, he chooses a girl whose guardian, obviously the most dangerous *fâcheux* of them all, opposes their marriage. But it so happens that Fate, in spite of this endless persecution, has really put his omnipotence on the side of Eraste. All the bores have one common characteristic: they delay the hero, first in his encounter, then in his tryst, with Orphise. Now, these frustrating delays enable Eraste to burst upon the scene at the critical moment in order to save the guardian's life and by this brave act win Orphise's hand. Had he arrived a minute earlier or a minute later, he would have accomplished nothing. Unwittingly, the bores have done him a good turn, merely because the twisted arm of coincidence wanted to strike its heaviest blow in his favor. Dramatically, the *dénouement,* however contrived it might appear, shows in retrospect that the incredible procession of bores must have served a meaningful purpose as though some occult force, such as the mythical beings of Vaux-le-Vicomte or Molière himself, had planned everything in advance. The haphazard quality of *Les Fâcheux* hardly results from unpremeditated art.

A definite pattern emerges as the play proceeds. With the exception of the swashbuckling duelist, the various characters who plague Eraste during the first two acts concern themselves, in one way or another, with games—in the broad sense of the term. Moreover, at the end of each of these two acts, Eraste must contend with people playing pall-mall or bowls, or rather with dancers who try to represent this sport, whereas the interruption at the end of the comedy comes from a troupe of mummers wearing masks. Thus the last group of *fâcheux* brings us right back where we started. Moreover, these mummers bring to a climax the idea of fancy, so much more important in the final act than in the first or second. Caritidès and Ormin are crackpots who live in an imaginary universe. The former questions the grammar in Parisian signs: a preoccupation which we may regard as a *reductio ad absurdum* of the artistic ambitions of the other bores. The latter, upon discovering that a seaport increases the wealth of a nation, brightly suggests that the King transform the entire French coast into a chain of harbors. The third nuisance, Filinte, has a bee of a quite different sort in his bonnet: he assumes that Eraste intends to fight a duel for which he needs a second. This trinity of visionaries makes the surprise ending appear less incredible. And we discover that the spectacle that Nature had so auspiciously started ends up as a triumph of the artificial and the theatrical. Quite fittingly, Molière's *comédie-ballet* gave way to a tremendous display of fireworks— of *feux d'artifice*.

8

A Burlesque
Tragedy

$\mathcal{A}$LTHOUGH ARNOLPHE shares many of Sganarelle's views concerning the education of women, he hardly resembles the ridiculous hero of *L'Ecole des maris*. Apart from his obsessive fear of "horns," he behaves like an "honnête homme." Moreover, he truly loves Agnès; and his jealous passion increases with each act. Finally, he must contend with a veritable army of coincidences. In short, Molière has combined in a single individual the salient features of his three previous protagonists: Don Garcie, Sganarelle, and Eraste.

L'Ecole des femmes has given rise to conflicting interpretations. Simone Weil states that "La misère humaine est mise à nu, à propos de l'amour, dans *L'Ecole des femmes,* dans *Phèdre.* ...."[1] And the French mystic does not make this strange comparison for the sake of paradox, for she insists elsewhere on Arnolphe's misery. The line: "Mais je sens là-dedans qu'il faudra que je crève" (1024), where Louis Jouvet, with appropriate gestures, would make the public titter, sounds, according to Simone Weil, the very depths of suffering. Most modern critics would share the actor's view of the matter, but cast a somewhat apprehensive look in the direction of the mystic. And what if both Jouvet and Weil were right in their apparently conflicting interpretations? Such an eventuality would probably destroy all the neat distinctions between comedy and tragedy, between laughter and Aristotle's fear and pity. Indeed, Ramon Fernandez had attempted this reconciliation long ago: "La comédie et la tragédie se rejoignent, s'harmonisent, au bénéfice de la comédie. Mais sans que la tragédie perde un pouce de ses

---

[1] Simone Weil, *La Source grecque* (Paris: N.R.F., 1942), p. 42. Cf. also *La Pesanteur et la grâce* (Paris: Plon, 1950); *L'Attente de Dieu* (Paris: La Colombe, 1950).

droits sur l'expression du réel."[2] During the play's very first run, an enemy of Molière, Boursault, had criticized the mixture of comic and serious traits.[3] Perhaps a discussion of *L'Ecole des femmes* will lead to a fruitful comparison between comedy and tragedy at least from the standpoint of literary technique.

THE SUFFERING OF ARNOLPHE

Few tragic heroes have suffered more excruciatingly than Arnolphe. Not only does he endure the tortures of the damned, but he never refrains from letting the audience know all about it. One of his favorite expressions: "je crève," has more vigor than nobility. He first uses it in line 327 upon learning of Horace's affair with Agnès. But as often as not he reveals his suffering in a more elevated manner, for instance in the monologue which opens the second act: "Car enfin de mon cœur le trouble impérieux / N'eût pu se renfermer tout entier à ses yeux: / Il eût fait éclater l'ennui qui me dévore" (373–75). These lines, as well as the alexandrine which ends the scene: "Eloignement fatal! voyage malheureux!" (385), would sound quite appropriate in a tragedy, for instance in Racine's *Mithridate*. But Molière took good care to interrupt these elevated tones with discordant notes: "Mais je ne suis pas homme à gober le morceau / Et laisser un champ libre aux vœux du damoiseau" (377–78). Although classical canons proscribed the juxtaposition of serious and farcical traits, Molière did not hesitate to alternate grandiloquence with popular speech, as though Arnolphe could not decide whether to play the part of a tragic hero or that of a bourgeois of Paris. This ludicrous contrast creates a feeling of discontinuity replete in comic effects.

As Fernandez has suggested, Molière suppresses the imaginary demarcation between tragedy and comedy. Arnolphe, after his first meeting with Horace, flies into a towering rage; but

---

[2] Ramon Fernandez, *La Vie de Molière* (Paris: N.R.F., 1929), p. 123.
[3] Boursault, *Le Portrait du peintre ou la Contre-critique de l'Ecole des femmes* (Paris: 1663). Reprinted in V. Fournel, *Les Contemporains de Molière* (Paris: Didot, 1863), I, 127 ff.

the audience cannot take him seriously or consider him dangerous, for he vents his anger on the two servants Alain and
Georgette instead of on Agnès herself: "Ouf! je ne puis parler,
tant je suis prévenu: / Je suffoque, et voudrois me pouvoir mettre
nu" (393–94). This powerful expression of indignation and
torment serves only to frighten out of their wits two peasants
purposely chosen for their stupidity. Their ludicrous reactions
merely degrade Arnolphe's genuine suffering. Moreover, the
hero attracts attention to his body rather than to his feelings. An
actor can heighten the absurdity by pulling at his clothing as if
he intended to undress on the stage! Molière uses a similar device in the following monologue where Arnolphe refers to
Horace whom he has known as a child: "Aurois-je deviné
quand je l'ai vu petit, / Qu'il croîtroit pour cela? Ciel! que mon
cœur pâtit!" (405–06). This reflection might perhaps have
aroused pathos in a different situation, for instance if it were
King David deploring the revolt and death of Absalom, or even
a less regal father complaining about the betrayal of a son. But
as these words express the jealousy of an eccentric they can
hardly fail to make an audience laugh. Moreover, Arnolphe attracts our attention for the second time (cf. lines 256–59) to
the growth of the child Horace, and thus a familiar and trite
image interferes with the idea of destiny, clearly implied in
"uncle" Arnolphe's somber reflections. For this reason, his
tormented "Ciel! que mon cœur pâtit!" far from arousing our
pity, makes his misfortunes even more laughable.

No less amusing are Arnolphe's efforts to hide his anger in
order not to frighten Agnès with his questions. His true feelings, however, burst forth in such asides as: "Je souffre en damné"
(577), or better still: "O fâcheux examen d'un mystère fatal /
Où l'examinateur souffre seul tout le mal!" (565/66). These
exclamations could easily fit into a tragic context, where knowledge signifies suffering. But in the present context, they can
only elicit laughter. And Arnolphe's grimaces as well as his
rapid alternations between inner wrath and external urbanity,
between eloquence and clownish exclamations such as "ouf!",
serve only to increase the humor of his predicament. Moreover,

he tries to hide his jealous wrath, not from a beleaguered tragic heroine such as Desdemona, but from a naïvely sentimental school girl. Because of these diverse and conflicting tonalities, Arnolphe's most anguished complaints appear disconnected, isolated, and, in a sense, irrelevant.[4]

Probably the most dramatic example of fragmentation in the entire play occurs in the famous notary scene. Separated from the solicitor's answers, Arnolphe's reflections would not strike an audience as the least bit funny. Indeed, they express his deepest preoccupations and torments. The solicitor, by assuming that these reflections are meant for his ears and must involve his legal competence, unwittingly plays the part of a mocking echo in his endeavors to reply. His interruptions naturally reduce Arnolphe's despair to pure farce.

The hero's despondency reaches the breaking point at the end of the play, when Chrysalde tells him:

> Je devine à peu près quel est votre supplice;
> Mais le sort en cela ne vous est que propice:
> Si n'être point cocu vous semble un si grand bien,
> Ne vous point marier en est le vrai moyen (1760–63).

Now, the audience that all along has shared Chrysalde's commonplace views and sided with the two lovers, will delight in this cruel witticism and laugh at Arnolphe's almost mute departure from the stage, despite the fact that his final "Ouf!" expresses as intense and genuine a torment as the sorrowful "Hélas!" with which Antiochus ends *Bérénice*. If, at the very moment when he realizes the full extent of his failure, Arnolphe strikes us as supremely ridiculous, it is because his parting gestures of despair merely repeat earlier expressions of suffering in the most stereotyped fashion possible. The spectators have been conditioned, like Pavlov's drooling dogs, to burst out laughing at each renewal of Arnolphe's lamentations, and the more intense the merrier. Moreover, Arnolphe's internal not to say spiritual suffering, by the mere fact that it gushes forth so frequently, closely resembles the purely physical bumps and aches

[4] For the importance of discontinuity, see Georges Poulet, *Etudes sur le temps humain* (Paris: Plon, 1950), pp. 79 ff.

featured in slapstick comedy. He reminds us of the irascible stooge, in one of Chaplin's early masterpieces, whose gouty and heavily bandaged foot insisted on getting in everybody's way, to the detriment of its unhappy owner, but to the huge delight of the spectators, who would laugh uproariously at each repetition of his agony.

Historically, we can situate Arnolphe's grandiloquent complaints as well as his less dignified exclamations within a burlesque framework. Molière's technique approximates more closely the heroic-comical burlesque style which Boileau systematized a few years later in his *Lutrin* than the type of writing that Scarron and Dassoucy had popularized a dozen years earlier, and which had already gone out of fashion. Whereas Boileau's method consists in describing in the most heroic and elevated terms possible the merest trivialities, Scarron's technique consists in depicting heroic actions in trivial and almost slangy words. Molière had imitated Scarron and anticipated Boileau in earlier plays, for instance in *L'Etourdi;* but the discrepancy between Arnolphe's actual situation and his exaggerated language, as well as his habit of switching from one style to another without transition, greatly increase the effectiveness of the two types of burlesque in *L'Ecole des femmes.* As Molière's contemporaries would automatically regard a middle-aged eccentric's passion for his ward as a commonplace of comedy and as a subject totally unfit for serious drama, Arnolphe's tragic tones, suitable for one of Corneille's or Rotrou's storied heroes, must have surprised the audience by their very incongruity. In addition, this misplaced grandiloquence has an important psychological function, for it reflects his overweening vanity. And this vanity, which tends to decuple his sufferings, finds its truest expression in an obsessive fear of becoming a cuckold:

> Et quel affront pour vous, mes enfants, pourroit-ce être,
> Si l'on avoit ôté l'honneur à votre maître!
> Vous n'oseriez après paroître en nul endroit,
> Et chacun, vous voyant, vous montreroit au doigt (1096–99).

Don Diègue, insulted and slapped by the Count, might reasonably utter such words, but for a man in Arnolphe's situation to express such sentiments could only amaze seventeenth century spectators who took their class distinctions seriously. Arnolphe's obsession prevents him from distinguishing between his own person and that of his household, for at this stage he believes that everyone close to him must share his feelings. Molière goes so far as to put into his hero's mouth a line actually borrowed from Corneille's *Sertorius*. When Agnès hesitates to carry out her guardian's command to drop a large stone on the offending head of her beloved Horace, he shouts: "C'est assez. / Je suis maître, je parle: allez, obéissez" (641–42). These are the words uttered by Pompey the Great when, at the end of the tragedy, he sends Sertorius' assassin, Perpenna, to his death. And the great Roman, unlike the bourgeois Arnolphe, immediately excuses himself for having spoken so imperiously.[5]

LA FORZA DEL DESTINO

Suffering is not enough. A self-respecting tragedy requires the malignant influence of an occult power: "C'est Vénus tout entière à sa proie attachée." Now, the idea of Fate, of Destiny, of predestination permeates, under one guise or another, the entire plot of *L'Ecole des femmes* and stands out as the dominant theme of the comedy. Chance and destiny make their presence felt in the very first scene, for Chrysalde jokingly refers to human horns as the infallible mark and attribute of cuckolds; and he adds: "Ce sont coups du hasard, dont on n'est point garant" (13). Chrysalde, however, does not really believe in chance, for later on he will humorously ascribe the infidelities of wives to a superhuman force: "Ainsi, quand à mon front, par un sort qui tout mène, / Il seroit arrivé quelque disgrâce humaine ..." (59–60). Arnolphe himself takes into account the power of destiny in the little matter of his impending marriage:

Contre cet accident, j'ai pris mes sûretés;
Et celle que j'épouse a toute l'innocence
Qui peut sauver mon front de maligne influence (78–80).

[5] Cf. Frédéric Hillemacher, quoted in *Grands Ecrivains Ed.*, III, 208.

In the light of this astrological context, a clever girl must obviously strike Arnolphe as an evil omen (cf. line 84). Thus, at the very beginning of the play, our burlesque hero seems to defy a malignant destiny whose omnipotence he has yet to experience. For the ensuing struggle, he has as weapons his lengthy meditation on the ruses of women and the alleged stupidity of his ward. Against the persecution of an hostile destiny, he will oppose his purely human intelligence. Arnolphe thus faces, in an infinitely degraded form, the situation of many a tragic hero. He finds himself in the predicament of Œdipus whose limited wisdom had triumphed over the resourceful Sphinx (or so he thought) and would, he hoped, allow him to muddle through his present difficulties.

Dramatically, the various incidents of *L'Ecole des femmes* show how the hero, in spite of the fact that he holds all the trumps in his struggle against an inexperienced girl and a blunderer, will meet defeat at the hands of an impish destiny, which manifests its power through a series of incredible coincidences.[6] Arnolphe's inevitable fate crops up even in his name —in both of his names. Saint Arnolphe, according to some authorities, had a special tenderness, even in Molière's day, for the unfortunate cuckolds who invoked him. This threatening association may have determined the hero to change his name to the more aristocratic de la Souche, where of course he fared no better, for in the seventeenth century the word *souche,* in addition to its botanical implications, could signify among other things a particularly virulent form of foolishness.[7] In

[6] Molière was very proud of this invention: "Pour moi, je trouve que la beauté du sujet de *l'Ecole des femmes* consiste dans cette confidence perpétuelle; et ce qui me paroît assez plaisant, c'est qu'un homme qui a de l'esprit, et qui est averti de tout par une innocente qui est sa maîtresse, et par un étourdi qui est son rival, ne puisse avec cela éviter ce qui lui arrive" (Uranie, in *La Critique de l'Ecole des femmes,* Scene 6).

[7] The change from Arnolphe to de la Souche also reveals our hero's vanity. Molière could scarcely have chosen a more suitable name, for *souche* can also mean the origin of a race or family, Arnolphe being the first and probably the last of his line. Moreover, the term *souche* signifies not only stupidity but lack of sensitivity, a meaning which becomes ironical when applied to the morbidly sensitive Arnolphe. By the way, Pierrot describes his Charlotte as "eune vraie souche de bois," *Dom Juan* (II, 1), in order to show her lack of response to his advances.

that sense, it is very nearly synonymous with the word *sot*.

Fate makes its presence felt throughout the five acts, and particularly at that critical moment when Arnolphe, overwhelmed by his love for Agnès, finally forgets his pride:

> Ciel, faites que mon front soit exempt de disgrâce;
> Ou bien, s'il est écrit qu'il faille que j'y passe,
> Donnez-moi tout au moins, pour de tels accidens,
> La constance qu'on voit à de certaines gens! (1004–07).

And like many a tragic protagonist before him, he becomes increasingly aware of the mysterious forces which insist on persecuting him: "Quoi? l'astre qui s'obstine à me désespérer / Ne me donnera pas le temps de respirer? (1182–83).

Arnolphe, however, does not have to come to grips with the dangerous and ineluctable type of fate which we find in tragedy; rather, he must face a mechanical goblin who repeatedly makes him bump into Horace. His imp seems to specialize in farfetched coincidences, particularly at the end of the play. One might even describe him as the incarnation of futility, for we discover that Horace would have married Agnès even without their chance encounter—even if Arnolphe's pedagogy had succeeded—for their parents had decided their marriage long before the play began. Horace, quite fittingly, refers at the conclusion of the comedy to chance: "Le hasard en ces lieux avoit exécuté / Ce que votre sagesse avoit prémédité" (1766–67). This unobtrusive statement reveals, more perhaps than any other, that the tremendous display of activity we have just witnessed, including Arnolphe's intense suffering during the last few hours and his dedicated efforts of the last thirteen years, has been an utter waste. Molière had used this trick in *Le Cocu imaginaire* without, however, giving it any emotional impact.

The author has thus systematically degraded the very idea of Fate along with Arnolphe's suffering. Now, we can regard degradation as the chief purpose, whether they acknowledged it or not, of the burlesque poets.[8] Molière does not push this devaluation as far as Scarron or develop mock-heroic inflation to

---

[8] Boileau, in "Epitre VII," uses the term burlesque in praising *L'Ecole des femmes*: "... ta plus burlesque parole / Est souvent un docte sermon."

such extremes as Boileau, not only because he uses these literary techniques alternately, but especially because he insists on preserving the authenticity of his characters, and particularly of Arnolphe, who certainly does not lack psychological complexity. Scarron's *Virgile travesti* as well as Boileau's *Lutrin* actively negate, each in its own way, the epic spirit. In a similar manner, the poetry of Voiture and of the other *précieux* writers reduces to innocuousness anything that might resemble a genuine emotion or a spontaneous feeling. Molière, at least in *L'Ecole des femmes,* far from denying the existence of tragedy, has succeeded in deforming, transforming, and transvaluating it into comedy and sometimes into farce without impairing its emotional impact. He has thus metamorphosed fear or at least pity into laughter.

GUILT AND KNOWLEDGE

Suffering caused by a mysterious and hostile destiny is still not enough. Tragedy requires in addition the presence of knowledge and, perhaps, of guilt. In *L'Ecole des femmes,* as in the majority of Molière's comedies, mental considerations, including such essentials as knowledge and judgment, play a preponderant part, sometimes to the detriment of the so-called intellectual or pedant. In the first scene, which sets up antithetical views of women and marriage, both Chrysalde and Arnolphe argue their case as convincingly as possible. Although the events that follow will confirm the wisdom of the former and the foolishness of the latter, we cannot affirm that Molière created Chrysalde in order to expound his own ideas on the subject.[9]

[9] One of Arnolphe's "heresies," which he shares with Scarron's *Don Pèdre,* his literary prototype, is his choice of an ignorant wife. According to seventeenth-century standards, a stupid girl could never pass as lovable, for esteem played an important part in love. But unlike Don Pèdre, Molière's hero has selected, perhaps unwittingly, a bright child: "Un air doux et posé, parmi d'autres enfants, / M'inspira de l'amour pour elle dès quatre ans" (129–30). Poise in a four-year-old usually indicates intelligence. In thus picking for emotional or esthetic reasons the most attractive child, Arnolphe shows a certain lack of consistency. But perhaps this sudden passion for a little girl was intended as a travesty of that old literary cliché: love-at-first-sight.

Arnolphe too readily trusts his own judgment and, at least in this respect, he reminds us of the Sganarelle of *L'Ecole des maris*. But self-confidence is frequently a characteristic trait of a tragic hero, and particularly of the most famous of them all, Œdipus. Unlike Sophocles, Molière did not intend to prove the limitations of the human mind, but to exploit for comic purposes the degradation of judgment and reason through its transformation into pedantry. Arnolphe, who usually behaves like an "honnête homme," eschews the jargon of a Métaphraste or a Caritidès; nonetheless, he is at heart a pedant of the worst type:

> En sage philosophe on m'a vu, vingt années,
> Contempler des maris les tristes destinées,
> Et m'instruire avec soin de tous les accidents
> Qui font dans le malheur tomber les plus prudents (1188–91).

Later in the same monologue he will insist once again on his "vingt ans et plus de méditation" (1202), all of which goes to show that his pedantry consists in substituting an apparently rational scheme, an intellectual construct, for existence. In the farcical dialogue between Arnolphe and the solicitor, two ready-made systems confront each other. The notary persists in reducing the vagaries of life to a set of legal formulas, whereas his client, who has just now gained some awareness of the failure of his own ready-made scheme, but who still cannot reject his ingrained intellectual habits, continues to affirm, as an imperative, his inveterate ambition: "Il se faut garantir de toutes les surprises" (1044). Under the circumstances, the hero's motto appears even more absurd than the notary's efforts to assure some sort of financial and legal security in this particular marriage which, fortunately, will never take place. Arnolphe, in his rude rejection of the worthy notary's services, unwittingly condemns his own intellectual ambitions, his own frame of mind, as though he had at last realized the illusory nature of precautions. Paradoxically, the solicitor's remarks, which Arnolphe has not even heard, echo the latter's deepest preoccupations.

The hero's anguish pertains directly to intellect; and indeed he has no other way to pay for his moral and metaphysical aberrations than by his intense mental suffering. In fact, the other characters appear to condemn him, and Chrysalde regards him as a raving maniac (cf. line 195). His madness and his aberrations have not only led him to reduce Agnès to a state of ignorance and slavery, but to waste the rest of his time in publicly exposing and satirizing the unoffending cuckolds of the town. And these strange acts can easily jeopardize the well-being of both the individual and society. Alienation, in the seventeenth century, by no means precluded the idea of sin or guilt, and it was frequently confused with diabolical possession. Molière, who probably did not believe in all the old-wives tales that so impressed most of his contemporaries, might still associate madness with perversity.[10]

To Arnolphe's specialized madness corresponds a strange scale of values, where the only evil consists in wearing horns, the only good in possessing a faithful and submissive wife. Worse still, the wife's fidelity and obedience need not result from her own sense of responsibility or from her love for her husband, but from the latter's skill in training her. Moreover, Arnolphe's mania coincides with his burning desire to achieve some sort of superiority over the rest of mankind. And whether or not we regard this alienation as immoral by definition or by association, it remains closely tied in with moral corruption in the form of vanity and pride. Thus Arnolphe, like almost any other tragic protagonist, has a definite moral flaw, however distorted and burlesque it may appear. Unlike a tragic hero, he cannot, for all his human weakness and his suffering, arouse the sympathy of the audience, for this tragic flaw strikes us as too preposterous and eccentric for any other human being to share it. In this manner, the spectators can remain totally aloof from Arnolphe, in spite of the fact that his "tragic" flaw hardly lacks universality: it merely seems outlandish. As Molière has, in a moral sense, cut him off from humanity and conditioned the audience

[10] In plays performed about 1630, alienation frequently results from excessive sensuality. Some twenty years later, at the height of the burlesque vogue, dramatists tend to use insanity for its spectacular qualities.

to laugh at his suffering, the tremendous emotions which storm within him inspire not terror but amusement.

Arnolphe's distorted self-love leads him, as we have already mentioned, to persecute husbands of unchaste wives. He sets himself up as their nemesis, as the supreme witness of their shame. And he believes that all women, and particularly the clever ones, will go to any lengths in order to deceive their husbands, unless you can prevent them from attaining the age of reason. He tactlessly casts suspicion on Chrysalde's worthy spouse. Indeed, his chief pleasure in life consists in discovering and publicizing the hidden misfortunes of husbands. One gathers, from the early stages of his conversation with Horace, that he not only makes fun of cuckolds, but that he will gladly help any likely young man who feels like increasing the numbers of that uneasy fraternity. It is only just that such a person should become the lucid spectator and witness of his own misfortune, or rather of the disgrace of Monsieur de la Souche, his alter ego. Poor Arnolphe squeezes into a single day all the suffering that he had inflicted on his neighbors in the course of twenty-odd years of railing. Molière chose as his tormentors a naïve young maiden who does not know how to hide her feelings to avoid offending the susceptibilities of others, and a blunderer who unwittingly shows him the variegated spectacle of his failure and of his aberrations.

Agnès' ignorance, for which Arnolphe must obviously take full responsibility, becomes the chief source of his torments.[11] Her ignorance does not, however, preclude natural intelligence: in the course of a few hours, she realizes her shortcomings and passes from childish innocence to a cleverness almost equal to that of Isabelle in *L'Ecole des maris*. Horace who, in this respect if in no other, shares Valère's attitude towards women, loves her for her feminine cunning—for wrapping a note around the stone she had to throw at his head. And were it not for Horace's consistent blundering, she would have had little trou-

[11] In *La Critique de l'Ecole des femmes*, Molière insists that Arnolphe is being punished by "les choses qu'il a cru faire la sûreté de ses précautions" (Scene VI).

ble in turning the tables on her guardian. Her ignorance takes the form of a complete lack of inhibition or, conversely, of utter frankness in human relations. Her lack of affectation disarms Horace, who had intended to seduce her, and may well be the source of Arnolphe's passion. But this apparently charming lack of reserve serves to inflict the cruelest wounds on her guardian. A more sophisticated maiden would not have dared reveal her love in so clear a manner; she would have described her feelings more impersonally by using the trite language of preciosity. Her uninhibited account of her discovery of love wounds Arnolphe to the quick: "La douceur me chatouille et là-dedans remue / Certain je ne sais quoi dont je suis toute émue" (563–64); and he bitterly says to himself: "O fâcheux examen d'un mystère fatal, / Où l'examinateur souffre seul tout le mal." Arnolphe has reaped the reward of his system of education which has made Agnès unfit to live in polite society. Later in the scene, when he asks her: "Mais pour guérir du mal qu'il dit qui le possède, / N'a-t-il point exigé de vous d'autre remède?" (583–84), he receives an astounding answer, which simultaneously reassures and tortures him: "Non. Vous pouvez juger, s'il en eût demandé, / Que pour le secourir j'aurois tout accordé" (585–86).

Horace does his best to assure Arnolphe's triumph. He chooses him as the confidant of his love and tells him in advance of all his schemes. But as the protagonist has the full force of Fate arrayed against him, nothing can possibly save him. Consequently, Horace's misplaced trust serves only to increase Arnolphe's suffering by revealing to him a hideous caricature of himself. From the fourth scene until the end of the comedy, he sees himself, through the eyes of his rival, as a stupid fellow full of the most ludicrous eccentricities. Little by little, he witnesses the disappearance of the satirical and worldly Arnolphe of old and the emergence, under the name of de la Souche, of a stock character whose emblem is a pair of horns. And this unflattering likeness, sharpened by each new encounter with the hated Horace, pricks the bubble of his self-conceit. His most secret actions, for instance his impotent rage in Agnès' chamber, are minutely described to him by his young rival. Never since Œdipus' persecution by the Sun God has a character scrutinized his own being in so pitiless a light. Even in these moments of intense humiliation and anger, he must hide his feelings and play a part in order not to reveal his identity. His mute despair, his vision of his own disgrace provide a fitting punishment for his merciless persecution of cuckolds. He becomes, in every sense of the word, his own nemesis.

THE SIN OF HUBRIS

If Molière had limited Arnolphe's punishment to this hideous spectacle of himself and to this bitter awareness of intellectual as well as emotional failure, one of the dimensions of tragedy, or rather of tragic pride, would be wanting, and *L'Ecole des femmes* would provide no more than a highly original and subtle variation on the old theme of the *voleur volé*—of poetic justice. True, this theme coincides with self-discovery on the part of the protagonist; and poetic justice appears to take on a new, tragic dimension by virtue of Arnolphe's overweening pride. His pride, however, like that of Œdipus, does not stop at a mere affirmation of superiority over *men*, but unfortunately encroaches upon Nature's design and God's prerogatives. In this manner, *hubris*, in a degraded form, plays a part in this comedy.

Arnolphe suffers from a psychological or perhaps even a metaphysical ailment which, for lack of a more suitable term, we might describe as a Pygmalion complex. With the help of his purely human intelligence or, rather, his pedantry, he unwittingly takes the place of God and Nature by endeavoring to create at any cost a woman in his own image—a wife who will devote her entire existence to the exclusive cult of Monsieur de la Souche. For this reason, he describes marriage as woman's perpetual adoration of man:

> Faites la révérence. Ainsi qu'une novice
> Par cœur dans le couvent doit savoir son office,
> Entrant au mariage il en faut faire autant (739–41).

The opening scenes of the third act contain parodies of devotional texts and of religious attitudes. Arnolphe starts the ball rolling when he praises Agnès for having thrown the stone at Horace, adding: "Et voilà de quoi sert un sage directeur" (646). Now, Arnolphe may have a right to call himself Agnès' guardian or even her future husband, but he is scarcely entitled to describe himself as her "directeur," her spiritual director, a prerogative that belonged almost exclusively to the priesthood. No doubt Arnolphe uses this term somewhat loosely; still, in the very next line, he states that he fully intends to give her spiritual guidance: "Votre innocence, Agnès, avoit été surprise," for he expertly alludes to a category of sins known to theologians and casuists as "péché de surprise." He then proceeds, in the manner of an experienced director, to remind his charge of the wages of sin: "Vous enfiliez tout droit, sans mon instruction, / Le grand chemin d'enfer et de perdition" (649–50), and adds that young men without exception "sont vrais Satans" (655). In the following scene, the parody becomes even more daring. Our self-styled spiritual director exhorts his ward to "contempler la bassesse où vous avez été" (681), for he will deign to raise her from her condition of poor peasant girl to the lofty status of "honorable bourgeoise" (684). The presence of such words as *contempler* and *bassesse,* so frequent in religious writings, shows more than anything else Arnolphe's pathological need of adoration. In fact, his exhortations sound like a typical prelude to self-examination and confession. Later in the speech, Arnolphe stresses the importance of humility: "Vous devez toujours, dis-je, avoir devant les yeux / Le peu que vous étiez sans ce nœud glorieux" (689–90). In other words, Agnès should, in marrying him, imitate the attitude of a nun pronouncing her final vows. From a comic standpoint, religious parody reaches a climax in Arnolphe's sweeping assertion: "Votre sexe n'est là que pour la dépendance: / Du côté de la barbe est la toute-puissance" (699–700). Two of the terms, *dépendance* and *toute-puissance,* definitely have religious connotations; and their crashing association with *barbe*—a word that would no doubt have sounded out of place in contemporary tragedy—somehow brings to mind the stock image of God the Father, wearing the flowing white beard so typical of Renaissance or Baroque paintings and engravings. The "office de la femme" puts the final touch on this parody by completely identifying the duties of a married woman with religious and ceremonial obligations. In fact, the word *office* fits perfectly in both contexts.

Arnolphe's Pygmalion-complex becomes explicit after Agnès' reading of the maxims of marriage:

> Ainsi que je voudrai, je tournerai cette âme;
> Comme un morceau de cire entre mes mains elle est,
> Et je lui puis donner la forme qui me plaît (809–11).

Not only does he encroach upon the functions of God as creator, but he tries to abolish Agnès' freedom. He sincerely believes that he can form, with his sole intellect, a being in his own image, a soul entirely dependent on his will! Although this ambition involves only his immediate family circle, it somehow goes way beyond the bounds of human power and therefore cries out for divine vengeance, or rather for its burlesque equivalent. Few tragic heroes have expressed so clearly their desire to make themselves absolute. Arnolphe strives to play the part of God in at least one aspect of his existence: a domain where he stands some chance of exerting his control and where he possesses a measure of power. In a king or a conqueror, ambition of this type has frequently led to disaster, but a small-time capitalist is somewhat restricted in his assumption of divine power.

Arnolphe does not limit his encroachment on God's preserves to demiugic ambitions. If an impish destiny has made him the butt of an incredible array of coincidences, it is because our hero, in his attempt to rise above his human condition, has tried to suppress chance. Horns, according to his friend Chrysalde, are no more than "coups du hasard" (13). But Arnolphe believes that man, by the methodical use of his intelligence, can banish accidents from his existence. He therefore tries, after twenty odd years of meditation, to impose a rigid system of his own invention in the unstable realm of feeling and emotion, where spontaneity and adaptability should prevail.

Man's most Promethean ambition consists in the attempt to eliminate chance and act with perfect efficiency—he becomes almost the equal of the gods. In a philosopher such as Descartes, this ambition often has a tragic grandeur, for it eventually leads to failure of one sort or another. But in Arnolphe, this titanic urge appears merely ludicrous. His sin—or his aberration— consists mainly in his foolhardy attempt to transform himself into an absolute on whom a normally free human being must become totally dependent. It is an unheard of manifestation of self-love that simply invites disaster. Forced by circumstances to abandon his neat system of tyranny and enslavement as well as his vision of a world of which he alone would be the center, he loses, as the curtain falls, the only possession that might give value to his tight little universe. The sense of absolute power which he expects from the complete possession of Agnès is suddenly transformed into a cruel and passionate love which finally gives way to deprivation. By attributing a super-human value to this possession he makes his predicament appear as potentially tragic; but the discrepancy between this absolute value and his actual situation transforms him into a figure of fun. Molière has thus reduced man's thirst for the absolute and his Promethean tendencies to a triviality—to the abortive marriage of an eccentric. And he accomplished this tremendous feat by borrowing and of course transfiguring the burlesque technique of systematic degradation.

AGNES' EDUCATION AND THE RELIGIOUS ISSUE

L'Ecole des femmes was violently attacked by disgruntled playwrights, envious of its popularity. They quickly seized upon the religious issue and described Arnolphe's speech concerning the duties of marriage as a sermon—a term used by Molière himself when he refers to this scene in his *Critique de l'Ecole des femmes*. But did Molière intend to flout, as De Visé and Boursault maintained, religious institutions and practices? He definitely does attribute to his Arnolphe certain priestly attitudes. But then, how else could he have dramatized his tyranny as a distortion of spirituality? Allusions to religion appear almost everywhere in the play. We learn, for instance, that Agnès has spent most of her existence in a convent among particularly unsophisticated nuns. But here Molière merely follows Scarron, who had described Agnès' prototype in the following terms:

> Elle avoit esté mise dans un Couvent dés l'âge de quatre ans, & en pouvoit avoir alors seize ou dix-sept. Il la trouva belle comme tous les Anges ensemble, & sotte comme toutes les Religieuses qui sont venuës au monde sans esprit, & en ont esté tirées dés l'enfance pour estre enfermées dans un Couvent.[12]

Scarron very obviously does not think highly of the type of education that then prevailed in convents, Spanish or French. Scarron's heroine, however, was born stupid, whereas Agnès has stupidity thrust upon her, a fact which, existentially at least, changes the entire picture. Don Pèdre has carefully selected a nitwit, and no amount of education can change her, basically. Arnolphe, on the contrary, has acted almost criminally in preventing his charge from developing into an intelligent human being. For this alone, he deserves her reproaches and her subsequent revenge.

As the quotation from Scarron seems to imply, the type of upbringing which Arnolphe has so minutely arranged for Agnès has nothing strange or really unusual about it according to seventeenth-century standards. Jacqueline Pascal's ideas concerning the education of young girls scarcely differ from those of Arnolphe. Instead of studying Greek, as did the young Racine, girls, at Port-Royal, even in adolescence, learned only how to pray, to sew and to knit. One may wonder why Molière wished to make a common practice of his time appear as the

[12] Paul Scarron, "La Précaution inutile," in *Œuvres* (Amsterdam: Pierre Mortier, 1697), IV, 59.

insane scheme of an eccentric in both *L'Ecole des femmes* and *L'Ecole des maris.* Thus, in their revolt against their guardians, both Isabelle and Agnès are opposing, not the whims of madmen, but well-established values often stated in religious terms. Arnolphe proudly tells Chrysalde:

> Dans un petit couvent, loin de toute pratique,
> Je la fis élever selon ma politique,
> C'est-à-dire ordonnant quels soins on emploîroit
> Pour la rendre idiote autant qu'il se pourroit (135–38).

Actually, these good nuns did not need encouragement to maintain Agnès in a state of innocence. If Arnolphe had asked them to transform his ward into an accomplished young lady, he would certainly have run into difficulties and he might even have shocked them. It would seem, therefore, that Molière has attributed this "politique" to his protagonist for satirical reasons: the sisters treat their pupils *as if* they intended to make them abysmally stupid from a worldly as well as from an intellectual standpoint. And Arnolphe praises heaven when he finds out that the nuns have obeyed him and thus remained faithful to their traditions as educators. Characteristically, he opposes his ward's innocence to the literary sophistication of many of her contemporaries—a sophistication they could not possibly have acquired in a convent. And when Agnès, towards the end of the play, rebels against his authority, he naturally threatens to confine her to a "cul de couvent" (1611). It would appear, therefore, that our hero, who has nothing of the *dévot* about him and who probably enjoys all the secular pleasures that Sganarelle despised, uses religion as a convenient means to attain his own ends. In this respect, we can hardly accuse Arnolphe of madness or even eccentricity, for many men of his class shared this attitude towards religious institutions. Under different circumstances, the self-seeking Arnolphe might easily become a Tartuffe.

The protagonist of *L'Ecole des femmes* has, however, greater complexity and more depth than Molière's hypocrite, who is little more than a histrionic criminal who overplays his part.

Although the situation in which he suddenly finds himself forces Arnolphe to become an actor and even, when need be, a theater director—for instance, he makes Alain and Georgette rehearse their reception of Horace—he actually resembles a creative artist, as one might expect of a person suffering from a Pygmalion complex. Indeed, he suffers, as a spectator, from his vain attempt to make life, or at least a living being, conform to his own system and follow without deviation a plot of his own invention. Thus, *L'Ecole des femmes* is, among other things, a play about artistic creation, about imagination, and its hero an avatar in degraded form of Molière himself, of Molière the author, certainly not of Jean-Baptiste Poquelin the husband, as partisans of the biographical approach to literature would have us believe.[13]

[13] For further discussion of the religious aspects of the play, see Gaston Hall's important note: "Parody in *L'Ecole des femmes*: Agnès's Question," *MLR*, LVII, 1 (Jan., 1962), 63–65. The question: "Si les enfants qu'on fait se faisoient par l'oreille" (164) parodies the Annunciation, as expressed by such poets as Racan and Du Perron, e.g., the latter's "Cantique à la Vierge," where we find the lines: "C'est celle dont la foi pour notre sauvement / Crut à la voix de l'Ange et conçut par l'oreille."

9

The Horns of the Dilemma

Dᴇꜱᴄʀɪʙᴇᴅ ɪɴ Loret's *Muse historique* as an impromptu, *Le Mariage forcé* answers Panurge's thorny question about matrimony. In this hurriedly written farce, Molière again exploits the futility of deliberation, the absurdities inherent in reasoning. When Panurge first asked Pantagruel his famous question, he had not yet made up his mind about marriage or selected a likely candidate. Moreover, his question led to an endless series of perplexities and equivocations. But in *Le Mariage forcé,* the audience can immediately answer Sganarelle with a resounding "No!", for he obviously shows promise as a cuckold: "Tel qu'en lui-même enfin l'éternité le change." His friend of long standing, Géronimo, whose frank opinion he has repeatedly requested, strongly advises him to stay single. But we soon discover that Sganarelle's perplexity was purely rhetorical and that he actually craved his friend's enthusiastic endorsement: "Je suis résolu de me marier ... c'est un mariage qui se doit conclure ce soir, et j'ai donné parole" (Scene 1). Thus, the entire deliberation concerning Sganarelle's hypothetical marriage suddenly collapses, and his demand for complete frankness on the part of Géronimo conflicts with his own lack of sincerity. When his friend does find out the truth, he politely lapses into insincerity and ironically applauds Sganarelle's decision or rather the *fait accompli.* Naturally, the remainder of the farce will show that the hero should, in perfect good faith, have asked Géronimo's advice long before committing himself.

In the the very first scene, Molière gives two cogent reasons why Sganarelle had better live and die a bachelor. In the first place, Sganarelle has his age against him; in the second place, his bride has already established a somewhat questionable reputation. Géronimo, upon hearing that his friend will marry "cette jeune Dorimène, si galante et si bien parée," daughter of Alcantor and sister of the swashbuckling Alcidas, can only exclaim: "Vertu de ma vie!" Moreover, Sganarelle confirms the audience's expectancy when he states: "Ce mariage doit être heureux, car il donne de la joie à tout le monde, et je fais rire tous ceux à qui j'en parle." Like so many of Molière's ridiculous characters, our fiancé cannot recognize the truth when it stares him in the face.

The humor of reasoning stands out in Géronimo's efforts to demonstrate to his friend, who for obvious reasons would prefer to forget his age, that he, Sganarelle, has already spent some fifty-two years on this earth. He forces his friend to agree that he was twenty-years old when they met, that he has lived eight years in Rome, seven in England, five and one-half in Holland, before returning to Paris some twelve years ago in 1656. By this round about approach, covering four countries, Géronimo corners the hero and makes him face the ineluctable truth. The comic disproportion between the simple fact of Sganarelle's age, known to both of them, and Géronimo's lengthy calculation expresses arithmetically the discrepancy between the protagonist's wilful blindness and a true appraisal of his situation. The mathematics involved lend a farcical precision to his predicament and especially to his obtuseness. Indeed, numbers can provoke laughter whenever they express a confusion between quantitative and qualitative reality, and particularly when they reveal an invasion of the latter by the former.

After amusing the audience with this initial tussle between blindness and obviousness, Molière traces Sganarelle's evolution from complacency to doubt, and from doubt to an agonizing reappraisal of his position. In short, he slowly discovers what everyone had guessed at the start. From a practical standpoint, it scarcely matters whether Sganarelle should anticipate his marriage as a blessing, whether he should apprehend its consequences, or whether he should realize that he is rushing towards disaster, for knowledge cannot set the clock back and help him avoid his destiny. Thus, Fate plays a farcical part in this comedy, just as it did in *L'Ecole des femmes;* but whereas

Arnolphe seemed to hold all the trumps, Sganarelle is practically disarmed from the beginning. In a sense, he must face the same sort of predicament as La Fontaine's logical lamb; and his belated discovery will turn out to be no less futile than his initial rhetorical question and his attempt to escape his age. The wolf will get him even if he does watch out, even if he has unimpeachable reason on his side. In fact, his awareness serves only to increase his misfortunes, for in addition to marrying the spendthrift Dorimène who will shortly make him wear a pair of horns, he receives a beating at the hands of the soft-spoken but murderous Alcidas. His cogitations help him only to measure the full extent of his catastrophe.

In passing from complacency to doubt, and from doubt to an exact assessment of his disaster, Sganarelle displays considerable energy. Sganarelle's pilgrimage from imagination to reality resembles in certain respects Panurge's endless peregrinations, for it leads him far afield: he consults two antithetical types of philosopher, a couple of dancing gypsies, a magician, and, worst of all, he overhears his fiancée talking to her lover. Thus, the further he wanders, the more obvious becomes his misfortune; and it would seem that the comic structure of the play—a loop which terminates in a precipice—was already implied in Géronimo's circuitous calculations of Sganarelle's age.

The hero's eager questioning of the two philosophers, the two gypsies, and the magician strikes us as even more ludicrous than Panurge's expeditions into the realm of possibility, for Sganarelle's future is already very much upon him and his impending shame stands out in his countenance no less clearly than warlike glory in the valiant wrinkles of Corneille's Don Diègue. His encounters with an Aristotelian dogmatist and with a skeptic add to his frustration for, try as he may, he cannot communicate with either of them. Molière had already used this device, typical of Italian farce, in *La Jalousie du barbouillé* as well as in *Le Dépit amoureux* where it had remained somewhat extraneous to the plot if not to the fabric of the play. But in *Le Mariage forcé,* the futility of the two philosophers provides just another variation on the central theme: the uselessness of discourse. And Sganarelle does justice both to the philosophers and to himself by making the dogmatist shut up at least temporarily and by beating the skeptic with a real stick. The gypsies and the magician, for their part, easily guess what the audience has seen all along. The second gypsy compliments Sganarelle on his goodly countenance: "... physionomie d'un homme qui sera un jour quelque chose" (Scene VI). And in the very next scene Lycaste, his fiancée's lover, confirms this prognostication when he congratulates Dorimène on her choice: "Vous ne pouviez pas mieux trouver, et Monsieur a toute la mine d'être un fort bon mari."

As in *L'Ecole des femmes,* "fate" involves, directly or indirectly, suffering and punishment—the punishment and suffering of a stooge who of course lacks the psychological and moral depths of Arnolphe. Although the beating which his brother-in-law administers with such exquisite tact must have made him feel rather uncomfortable, his real torment lies in his complete awareness of what the future holds in store for him: a shotgun marriage without benefit of sin. He even hears Dorimène tell her lover that he, Sganarelle, "... n'a tout au plus que six mois dans le ventre," a prospect more frightening than that of publicly wearing horns. Thus, she sees the protagonist, a man who chooses to ignore his age, as a doddering and stupid old man who will soon leave her his fortune. Previously, she had told him quite frankly that she intended to spend his money freely. Thus, the cowardly, vain and stingy Sganarelle, who had wanted to settle down to a peaceful and healthy family life, suddenly sees his very existence in jeopardy. He, the wealthy and not too scrupulous merchant, has met his match and will undoubtedly be bled white, both figuratively and literally, by his wife's killing pace. His first speech in the play gives the audience an inkling of his grasping nature: "Si l'on m'apporte de l'argent, que l'on me vienne quérir vite chez le Seigneur Géronimo; et si l'on vient m'en demander, qu'on dise que je suis sorti et que je ne dois revenir de toute la journée." Clearly, all he needs is to marry a lavish spender. Nonetheless, he regards his marriage as a business deal. In the presence of Géronimo, he alludes first to "une affaire que j'ai en tête" and then to "une chose de conséquence, que l'on m'a proposée" instead of stating outright his intention to marry the young Dorimène. Molière may have wanted to show, by this equivocation, that Sganarelle's prudence and astuteness in business have failed him in his choice of a wife. At present, it is his turn to pay. Indeed, Dorimène and her impoverished family have consented to this marriage only because of Sganarelle's wealth. From her standpoint, the entire arrangement appears as nothing more than a profitable transaction: she defeats the plutocratic Sganarelle, who has financial interests all over Europe, at his own game.

10

Hypocrisy as Spectacle

Tartuffe received its first performance at Versailles during the festivities known as "Les Plaisirs de l'Isle enchantée," for which Molière had expressly written the purely spectacular *Princesse d'Elide,* adapted from the vigorous Spanish play *El Desdén con el desdén,* by Moreto. Molière's comic opera concerns the comedy of intellect in two respects. In the first place, the Prince, in order to win the hand of a reluctant Princess by indirection, not only plays the part of a disdainful, self-infatuated prig, but ably directs the clever clown Moron. And in the second place, action, which usually takes the form of entertainment or spectacle, invariably produces positive results, whereas words must remain completely ineffectual. Euryale who, despite his passion, succeeds in keeping quiet, triumphs in the end, while his rivals, who have declared themselves in so many words from the very beginning, must willy nilly marry the ruler's less attractive daughters. Moreover, Tircis, a minor character, appeals to the shepherdess Philis through his singing, but that enterprising chatterbox Moron fails completely in his suit. As for the Princess herself, she does her utmost to conquer Euryale by shining in all the performing arts. However, the Prince puts on the best performance of all, for he not only excels as an actor, but he wins the chariot race. And naturally the two stars will marry and live happily ever after. The star in Molière's very next play will not fare as well.

PERFORMANCE AND PERCEPTION

Tartuffe will concern us less as a moral and psychological entity than as a spectacle. We may indeed regard him as a professional performer who overplays his part. The show he

puts on receives the enthusiastic applause of Orgon and his
mother, but it fails to impress anyone else. Molière of course
has unmasked his hypocrite even before he has a chance to appear in person on the stage; but at the same time he has succeeded in illuminating, with the help of Tartuffe's reflected glory,
the other characters in the play and perhaps even the audience
itself. In fact, the author so consistently puts his impostor,
present or absent, in the limelight, that all the other personages
are more often than not reduced to the state of spectators. Indeed, we can regard as spectators Cléante, Damis, Orgon, Madame Pernelle, Mariane, and even such active characters as Elmire
and Dorine, or so lofty a person as the King, who sends the
Exempt to Orgon's house in order to bring the whole performance to a close. Of course, several of these characters emulate
Tartuffe by putting on shows of their own. In the interests of
poetic justice, Tartuffe must indeed be defeated by performances
more successful than his own. Elmire stages two of them and
the Sun King a third: instead of having the impostor thrown
into prison immediately, he arranges his arrest in the most
spectacular manner possible in order to see just how far his
delinquency will lead him. Thus Tartuffe the actor is, to everyone's edification, thrice transformed into a spectacle which he
had never intended to show. Paradoxically, this master of histrionics proves to be as uncritical and as gullible as his victim
Orgon.

The type of human relationship that prevails in *L'Imposteur*
is the purely theatrical rapport between play and audience. As
humanity, in the world of the impostor, exists only as an audience, esthetic appreciation becomes a most important factor.
But to exert an influence on this strange universe, made up only
of spectators like himself, the individual must succeed in pro-
ducing a spectacle of his own—the spectacle of his own awareness. And for this reason, Louis XIV becomes the true hero of
the play—the most lucid spectator of them all. Here, Molière
flatters not only the King but also those more modest patrons
who all along had seen through Tartuffe's disguise and laughed
at Orgon's obtuseness.

It may seem foolhardy on the part of a critic to attempt to grasp the dramatic structure of this play, for it appears that the author had to add on a certain number of more or less extraneous scenes. Professor Cairncross has recently confirmed, at least to our satisfaction, Michelet's brilliant guess that *Tartuffe* in 1664 was a comedy complete in three acts, similar in structure to *L'Ecole des maris,* and much more outspoken than the play we know today. It would seem that this *Ur-Tartuffe* corresponded roughly to the first, third and fourth acts of *L'Imposteur.* This means that we should regard the famous scene of *dépit amoureux* as well as the *dénouement* in which the King plays a prominent part as late additions dictated by prudence rather than by inspiration.[1] Although *L'Imposteur* may lack the coherence of the lost *Ur-Tartuffe,* it definitely has unity, for Molière has skilfully integrated the later additions into the general fabric of the play. Dramatically, the only extant version has a definite weakness: Cléante's discursive comparisons between true and false devotion. But if Cléante had been less verbose and argumentative, perhaps the third version would have gone the way of the other two.

The comedy opens with a series of portraits drawn by Madame Pernelle. In 1667, after the only performance of *Panulphe,* (second version, in five acts, of *Tartuffe*), the perceptive author of *La Lettre sur l'Imposteur* pointed out the importance of these etchings not only as a means of acquainting the audience with the characters therein described, but of exposing Madame Pernelle herself.[2] In her attempt to unmask the faults she attributes, perhaps falsely, to others, she reveals her own outmoded attitudes and her stupidity. No doubt, she must have appeared more ridiculous to the author of *La Lettre* by her manner of speaking and of dressing than by her actual words, which an unsuspecting reader might possibly regard as providing a true picture of the various members of Orgon's household. This does not mean that Madame Pernelle's remarks completely

---

[1] Cf. John Cairncross, *New Light on Molière* (Paris: Droz, 1956), pp. 1–53.
[2] *Lettre sur la comédie de l'Imposteur* (Paris: 1667). Reprinted in *Grands Ecrivains* Ed., IV, 529–566. For the comments on the portraits, cf. pp. 531 ff.

fail to hit their mark, but rather that the light she tries to throw on others serves mainly to illuminate her as a prejudiced and stubborn old dragon. Her admiration for such obvious hypocrites as Daphné, Daphné's "petit mari," and Orante shows her lack of perception. Dorine's satirical account of these people's devotion to morality and religion reveals that they criticize others in order to cover up their own turpitudes. Their censure of others becomes in this manner a sort of *décor* and their devoutness a performance having little to do with their actual behavior and feelings: the couple wants to hide its wickedness whereas Orante wishes to cover up the ravages of old age with a mask of piety. Dorine's satirical sketches prepare us for the portrait of Tartuffe himself and his belated appearance on the stage. Her sketches produce a much more powerful effect on the audience than the grandmother's conventional comments on her family, for Dorine dwells on the hidden causes of their hypocritical behavior. The spectators therefore have the impression of discovering the truth; and the pleasure of discovery not only puts them on the side of Dorine but whets their appetite for further revelations.

These satirical portraits definitely steal the grandmother's thunder; and when she praises Tartuffe, the arch-performer, for having banished all forms of entertainment from her son's house, the audience somehow anticipates an immediate refutation of her words. The rebuttal starts in the very next scene when we learn that Tartuffe, the self-styled enemy of pleasure, far from behaving like an ascetic, devours great quantities of food and gulps down several glasses of wine. Dorine naturally stigmatizes him as a hypocrite: "Lui, qui connoît sa dupe et qui veut en jouir, / Par cent dehors fardés a l'art de l'éblouir" (199–200). But his hypocrisy, by Dorine's use of such terms as *art, fardés,* and *éblouir,* reminds us of the theater; and we gather that the impostor has been putting on a performance.

Molière has provided numerous portraits of his hypocrite, so much so that the public, long before Tartuffe appears on stage, repeatedly sees this religious man in all his fleshiness as a belching, swilling, and sleeping glutton: "Gros et gras,

le teint frais, et la bouche vermeille" (234). The contrast between his fraudulent asceticism and his sensuality reaches a
climax when he makes his first appearance in Act III, scene 2.
After ordering his servant Laurent to put away his hair shirt
and his scourge, he orders Dorine to cover her breasts with a
handkerchief. The latter retorts: "... je vous verrois nu du
haut jusques en bas, / Que toute votre peau ne me tenteroit
pas" (867–68). This statement, because of the various portraits
which precede, functions as a sort of litotes. Indeed, Molière
has conditioned the audience to anticipate disgust at Tartuffe's
first appearance, and the vision of the impostor in all his
physical and moral nakedness abundantly fulfills these expecta-
tions. In this manner, Molière adds to the spectator's percep-
tivity an emotional response and involvement.

Paradoxically, Orgon himself unwittingly traces the clearest
picture of Tartuffe's falsity. In trying to convince Cléante, he
reveals Tartuffe for what he is: an actor who consistently overplays his part—"Il attiroit les yeux de l'assemblée entière"
(285). Even his servant Laurent plays a part, for he imitates
his master in every detail. But Orgon takes their shabby performances for genuine religiosity, whereas Cléante—and the
audience—without ever having laid eyes on these two men,
recognize them immediately as frauds. Orgon reminds us of a
critic who, merely by quoting with admiration a particularly
repugnant piece of literature, convinces his more discerning
readers of his own lack of taste. Indeed, Tartuffe appears in this
scene not only as an impostor, but as a combination author, actor
and stage director, whose efforts do not quite succeed in im-
pressing the audience. Cléante justifiably refers to hypocrisy in
traditional theatrical terms such as *masque, dehors plâtré, grimace,*
and he describes hypocrites as *charlatans*—mountebanks who
attract customers by their histrionic antics.

The blind and tasteless Orgon admires Tartuffe precisely
because he overplays his part. He would probably take no notice
of a saintly person in need of help. But in Tartuffe he sees a
choice possession, one that will undoubtedly enhance his prestige in this world and his chances in the next. In fact, Orgon

behaves just like an appreciative proprietor, but hardly like a
devout Christian. This side of his nature stands out clearly after
his discovery of Tartuffe's hypocrisy: "C'en est fait, je renonce
à tous les gens de bien: / J'en aurai désormais une horreur ef-
froyable, / Et m'en vais devenir pour eux pire qu'un diable"
(1603–05). Orgon's violent change of heart enables the eloquent Cléante to come to the defense of these "gens de bien"
and thus prove Molière's unimpeachable intentions. Orgon's
about-face implies, moreover, that he has never really identified
himself with devout Christians, but rather that he has remained
throughout an admiring spectator and sponsor of an imitation
saint. The Sun King's lucidity contrasts sharply with Orgon's
blind admiration: "D'abord il a percé par ses vives clartés, / Des
replis de son cœur toutes les lâchetés" (1919–20). It would
seem that our hypocrite, in denouncing his benefactor before the
King, had gone unwittingly to his Last Judgment, for his soul
is laid bare and his criminal past exposed almost in a flash.
Rarely has a "ham" met with as cruel and as richly deserved a
fate or fallen on a less appreciative or more miraculous audience!
Perhaps the author of *La Lettre sur l'Imposteur* was not entirely
wrong in praising the *dénouement* as the high point in the play.
After all, the dominant theme, that of discernment, reaches a
climax in His Majesty's radiant gaze.

Molière has connected with the theme of perception a traditional comic device or routine, whereby a purblind dullard cannot recognize the most obvious truth. Now Tartuffe, at least
within the framework of the play, never tells a direct lie. Even
when he denounces Orgon in the presence of Louis XIV he
has in his possession all the necessary evidence. In the scene
where Damis catches him red-handed, he tells Orgon the truth
about his unworthiness, but in such a manner that his confession sounds exactly like the self-criticism of an ascetic. Orgon, quite naturally, pays attention to Tartuffe's pious manner,
to his *persona,* instead of concerning himself with what he
has to say, and he therefore persists in regarding him as a saint.
The impostor does not even have to deny Damis' allegations
against him:

Oui, mon frère, je suis un méchant, un coupable, *(nasty)* *(guilty)*
Un malheureux pécheur, tout plein d'iniquité,
Le plus grand scélérat qui jamais ait été;
Chaque instant de ma vie est chargé de souillures;
Elle n'est qu'un amas de crimes et d'ordures;
Et je vois que le Ciel, pour ma punition,
Me veut mortifier en cette occasion.
De quelque grand forfait qu'on me puisse reprendre,
Je n'ai garde d'avoir l'orgueil de m'en défendre (1074-82).

Once he has assured himself that Orgon has remained stead-
fastly on his side, Tartuffe impudently confesses his hypocrisy.
It would seem that Molière intended thereby to reveal the full
extent of Orgon's blindness rather than Tartuffe's daring vir-
tuosity:

Ah! laissez-le parler: vous l'accusez à tort,
Et vous ferez bien mieux de croire à son rapport.
Savez-vous, après tout, de quoi je suis capable?
Vous fiez-vous, mon frère, à mon extérieur?
Et, pour tout ce qu'on voit, me croyez-vous meilleur?
Non, non: vous vous laissez tromper à l'apparence,
Et je ne suis rien moins, hélas! que ce qu'on pense;
Tout le monde me prend pour un homme de bien;
Mais la vérité pure est que je ne vaux rien (1091-1100).

Now, the only false statement we can find in either of his
speeches—including his subsequent exhortation to Damis to
call him *perfide, infâme, homicide* . . . —is that "tout le
monde me prend pour un homme de bien," for actually all the
characters concerned, with the exception of Orgon and Madame
Pernelle, have seen through his little game. But Tartuffe tells
the truth about himself as though he were reciting a speech
learned by heart, or rather a prayer meant to instill into the soul
of a saintly person a sense of sin. The most innocent begging
friar will accuse himself of having crucified the Lord single-
handed with his hideous sins. From the standpoint of Orgon,
who judges only by externals, by gestures, Tartuffe, in accusing
himself of all the sins in the calendar, in humbly turning the
other cheek, in refusing to defend his conduct, provides just

another proof of his holiness.[3] Thus, merely by continuing to overplay his part, Tartuffe manages to fool his dupe under the most adverse circumstances. Indeed, this part has become second nature; and we have the feeling that Tartuffe could not express his thoughts in a secular manner even if he tried. In short, Orgon only sees a performance—a performance which he craves and to which he must necessarily react in his accustomed manner. His admiration for Tartuffe has become a conditioned reflex; and the latter can boast to Elmire: "... je l'ai mis au point de voir tout sans rien croire" (1526). When Orgon finally does see the light, he must immediately contend with his mother's persistent blindness, a frustrating situation which gives rise to his proverbial: "Je l'ai vu, dis-je, vu, de mes propres yeux vu, / Ce qu'on appelle vu" (1676–77). Although he now knows that the saintly Tartuffe has fooled him with pious words and gestures, he probably still regards holiness as a form of external behavior, as a part that, unlike his false friend, a good Christian should play sincerely. We find at least partial confirmation of this attitude in his strong reaction against "gens de bien" referred to earlier in this chapter—a reaction which seems to imply that any person whose deportment happens to remind him of Tartuffe must necessarily be, at bottom, a scoundrel. Through his lack of perception, Orgon identifies reality with appearance, being with *persona*, face with mask. He cannot even imagine that spiritual values might exist apart from specific manifestations of piety. And perhaps his love for Tartuffe reveals not only an intellectual deficiency on his part but a lack of moral and spiritual value. After all, Louis XIV's radiant gaze, as we have already stated, demonstrated spiritual as well as intellectual penetration.

Tartuffe, Elmire, and the King are not the only people who play a part or stage a performance; or Orgon and his mother the only characters who fall for a *persona*. The entire second act, which we may regard in many respects as extraneous to the general structure of the play, develops in its own particular

[3] In this respect at least, Tartuffe resembles Montufar in Scarron's "Hypocrites," cf. *Grand Ecrivains Ed.*, IV, 352 ff.

manner the theme of perception as well as the idea of a relationship between audience and performance. Mariane, who sees through Tartuffe's falsity, gets into difficulties because of her own false *persona*, which may result from having attended too many tragedies and tragi-comedies by such dramatists as Corneille and Rotrou. When her father suggests that she should marry Tartuffe, her reaction, to say the least, lacks vigor; and Dorine must willy-nilly answer Orgon in her stead. When asked by the *suivante* why she has behaved in so passive a manner: "Avez-vous donc perdu, dites-moi, la parole? / Et faut-il qu'en ceci je fasse votre rôle? (585–86), she replies: "Contre un père absolu que veux-tu que je fasse?" (589). To hear the silly Orgon referred to as "un père absolu" causes some surprise, for throughout the play he behaves like the traditional dupe whom anyone can fool. In her next reply, Mariane goes even further: "Un père, je l'avoue, a sur nous tant d'empire, / Que je n'ai jamais eu la force de rien dire" (597–98). Total obedience to such a father as Orgon strikes us as almost pathological; but later in the scene, she gives us an inkling of her true motivation. Indeed, when Dorine wants to know what her mistress will do if forced to marry Tartuffe, Mariane answers: "De me donner la mort si l'on me violente" (614), which shows that she has cast herself in the part of a tragic heroine. Outside the theater, people, especially maidens of good Parisian families, just did not commit suicide. Dorine, who violently objects to Mariane's self-dramatization, makes fun of her: "Fort bien: c'est un recours où je ne songeois pas; / Vous n'avez qu'à mourir pour sortir d'embarras" (615–16). But it will take more than irony to make the timid Mariane cut short her performance:

> Mais par un haut refus et d'éclatants mépris
> Ferai-je dans mon choix voir un cœur trop épris?
> Sortirai-je pour lui, quelque éclat dont il brille,
> De la pudeur du sexe et du devoir de fille?
> Et veux-tu que mes feux par le monde étalés ... (631–35).

She sounds very much like a coy but embattled princess referring to the dashing young prince she wishes to marry. Dorine in-

terrupts in quite a different style: "Non, non, je ne veux rien.
Je vois que vous voulez / Etre à Monsieur Tartuffe" (636–37).
And her daring enjambment breaks the rhythm of Mariane's
elevated tones. Sickened by the girl's inappropriate performance,
she decides to shatter her pretense once and for all by dramatizing the more unpleasant aspects of a marriage with Monsieur
Tartuffe. She shows no mercy even when her mistress exclaims:
"C'en est fait, je me rends, et suis prête à tout faire" (653),
for she uses Mariane's own arguments against her: "Non, il faut
qu'une fille obéisse à son père, / Voulût-il lui donner un singe
pour époux" (654–55). This gives an unexpected twist to the
absoluteness of fathers. Dorine, however, really destroys Mariane's Cornelian performance with the vision of a somewhat less
sophisticated type of entertainment:

> Vous irez visiter, pour votre bienvenue,
> Madame la baillive et Madame l'élue,
> Qui d'un siége pliant vous feront honorer.
> Là, dans le carnaval, vous pourrez espérer
> Le bal et la grand'bande, à savoir, deux musettes,
> Et parfois Fagotin et les marionnettes,
> Si pourtant votre époux ... (661–67).

This time, it is Mariane's turn to interrupt: "Ah! tu me fais
mourir", for how can one really live without the performances
of such stars as Montfleury at the Hôtel de Bourgogne or
Molière at the Palais-Royal? In certain respects, she finds herself in the same predicament as Tartuffe, for she sees her own
theatricals squelched by a performance of another color, ending
with the memorable: "Non, vous serez, ma foi! tartuffiée"
(674). But in other respects, she resembles her father because
of her instinctive preference for a false *persona*, a preference
which could easily lead to disaster if Dorine did not step in to
put things in their true perspective.

    In spite of her squelching, the incorrigible Mariane reverts
to type in the very next scene. She cannot resist playing an inappropriate part as soon as Valère enters the picture; and, by

her attitude, she forces her astonished fiancé to perform as best he can. In the course of the quarrel, both Mariane and Valère say things which they do not really mean. They of course realize, in spite of the earnestness of their acting, that their love has by no means abated. Dorine becomes a spectator and decides to derive as much enjoyment as possible from their atrocious bad faith: "Voyons ce qui pourra de ceci réussir" (704). When she, and the audience, have had their fill of this particular show, she consents to intervene, just as though she had been directing their performance all along:

> Pour moi je pense
> Que vous perdez l'esprit par cette extravagance;
> Et je vous ai laissé tout au long quereller,
> Pour voir où tout cela pourroit enfin aller (753–56).

The Exempt, in the name of his Majesty the King, will play the same sort of cat-and-mouse game with Tartuffe at the end of the comedy, in his capacity as absolute spectator, in order to see "l'impudence aller jusques au bout, / Et vous faire par lui faire raison de tout" (1931–32). Only Dorine and the King combine the functions of theater director and spectator. Damis, hidden in the closet, and Orgon, concealed beneath the table, merely watch a show which they did not put on. Orgon becomes so completely a spectator that he can no longer react and manifest his presence. At the crucial moment, he behaves as though Elmire's plight did not really concern him or involve his honor. As for Cléante, he functions as an observer whose purely verbal interventions scarcely influence the action of the play. Critics have sometimes regarded him as the author's spokesman, as the voice of wisdom. We prefer to consider him as an intermediary between author and public. His moderation acts as a sort of buffer zone against the attacks of the so-called *cabale des dévots,* for Molière seems to have cast him in the part of an ideal spectator, capable of involving himself emotionally in the play while maintaining from beginning to end his intellectual objectivity. One of the author's cleverest tricks in *Tartuffe* con-

sists in forcing the audience to participate in the action and
therefore to take sides—for action in this particular comedy is
indistinguishable from discernment and penetration.

MEDLEYS

Although those complementary themes, perception and performance, dominate *Tartuffe,* they can by no means explain
the entire play from a structural standpoint. Unstable mixtures
of incompatible attitudes appear quite frequently throughout
the comedy. Such a blending characterizes Daphné's and her
husbands efforts to camouflage their own misconduct: "Des
actions d'autrui, teintes de leurs couleurs, / Ils pensent dans le
monde autoriser les leurs" (111–12). They endeavor to smear
their neighbors in order to fade unnoticed in a lurid, mono-
chrome background. But as soon as we understand their game,
we perceive that their own shortcomings stand out in sharp relief.

Mixture plays a more subtle part in the portrait of Orante:

> Elle a fort bien joui de tous ses advantages;
> Mais, voyant de ses yeux tous les brillants baisser,
> Au monde, qui la quitte, elle veut renoncer,
> Et du voile pompeux d'une haute sagesse
> De ses attraits usés déguiser la foiblesse (127–30).

Orante definitely has recourse to theatrical techniques in transforming the coquette of yesteryear into the prude of the present. She tries to make her acquaintances identify her completely
with spiritual values, but a discriminating public will perceive
nothing more than a superanuated coquette wearing the mask of
prudery. Moreover, the idea of separation or incompatibility
stands out clearly in the line: "Au monde, qui la quitte, elle
veut renoncer," where the expression "renoncer au monde" has
purely spiritual connotations, but where her abandonment by
the world, or rather by high society, reveals the shallowness of
her so-called conversion. And the instability of this mixture is
especially evident in the subdued pun on "monde."

Instability of a somewhat different type characterizes Orgon's unassimilated religiosity. Referring to Tartuffe's spiritual direction, he tells Cléante:

> Il m'enseigne à n'avoir affection pour rien,
> De toutes amitiés il détache mon âme;
> Et je verrois mourir frère, enfants, mère et femme,
> Que je m'en soucierois autant que de cela (276–79).

Orgon adds a new twist to the Christian practice of detachment as set forth in Christ's exhortation to his disciples to leave their families for a better life. Indeed, he transforms religious detachment into callousness and lack of charity towards others. Cléante reacts in the expected manner: "Les sentiments humains, mon frère, que voilà!" (280). The clownish Orgon's idea of religion hardly differs from inhumanity because of his unjudicious use of such expressions as "affection pour rien," his detachment, not from temptation, but from friendship, and especially his unfeeling anticipation of death and destruction in his own family. Manifestly, Orgon does not have a religious attitude, but merely an unstable mixture of indifference and selfishness. Like the Sganarelle of *L'Ecole des maris*, he ceases to belong to humanity. And we know that he is no more than a puppet in the hands of Tartuffe.

In the next act, he attempts to justify in Christian terms his decision to marry-off his daughter to Tartuffe:

> Enfin avec le Ciel l'autre est le mieux du monde,
> Et c'est une richesse à nulle autre seconde.
> Cet hymen de tous biens comblera vos désirs,
> Il sera tout confit en douceurs et plaisirs (529–32).

He manages to transform religion into wealth and even into a career. The mixture of secular and spiritual values, or rather their utter confusion, is ludicrous in a particularly repulsive manner, for it would suggest the utter debasement of spirituality even if the speaker were not referring to Tartuffe. The marriage between the fleshy impostor and poor Mariane, which of course will never take place, promises to become particularly vicious and revolting. The line: "Il sera tout confit en douceurs et plaisirs" suggests, by the use of the word "confit" and the subdued pun on "douceurs," a nauseating sweetness, especially when we remember Tartuffe's well-nourished body. And the expression "confit en douceurs," which recalls "confit en dévotion," evokes the impostor's mealy-mouthed hypocrisy. Later in the comedy, Orgon will discover an even better justification for this marriage. He exhorts his daughter: "Mortifiez vos sens avec ce mariage" (1305), for she had just expressed her intention of entering a convent. In this particular instance, the mixture becomes almost explosive.

As unstable blendings of incompatible attitudes stigmatize practically all forms of fraudulence, whether it be Orgon's bad faith or Tartuffe's hypocrisy, we naturally can expect to find similar mixtures in the two seduction scenes. The villain, in making his proposals to Elmire, rarely departs from the language of devotion, e.g.:

> Ce m'est, je le confesse, une audace bien grande
> Que d'oser de ce cœur vous adresser l'offrande;
> Mais j'attends en mes vœux tout de votre bonté,
> Et rien des vains efforts de mon infirmité;
> En vous est mon espoir, mon bien, ma quiétude,
> De vous dépend ma peine ou ma béatitude ... (953-58).

Removed from the present context, Tartuffe's words could readily fit into a religious play, such as *Le Véritable saint Genest,* or even into a purely secular tragedy, where an impassioned prince might be so transported with love as to transform his beloved into an object of adoration. But we know that the impostor uses such spiritual terms as *offrande, infirmité, béatitude* insincerely, even from the standpoint of profane love, for he seeks only to satisfy his lust. We sense that fundamentally his desire for Orgon's young and attractive wife scarcely differs from his gluttonous anticipation of, let us say, more mutton for dinner. His attempted blending of spirituality with sex resolves itself into insincerity and grossness, a duality to which Tartuffe himself gives expression in the famous line: "Ah! pour être dévot, je n'en suis pas moins homme" (966). Paradoxically, Tartuffe has hardly anything of the *dévot* about him. Even his manliness seems questionable, for he strikes one as a slimy, subhuman creature who mechanically spouts pious words. Thus, Tartuffe by his hypocrisy, Orgon by his stupidity and his selfishness, practically exclude themselves from humanity or at least society. In the great scene where Tartuffe turns the tables on Damis merely by admitting the truth, the mixture of sanctimonious language with villainy produces a single impression in Orgon's mind, that of saintliness, whereas, for the audience, it merely adds to the impostor's repulsiveness. An analogous blending of opposites manifests itself in Monsieur Loyal's general attitude, for he combines brutal expropriation with the sweetest language, particularly in his parting words: "Le Ciel vous tienne tous en joie!" (1809), an antiphrasis where *joie*, replete with its religious connotations, clashes with his function.

In these blendings or mixtures, perception must play an important part, for it consists in separating all these fraudulent and unstable medleys into their component parts: e.g., the King will see through the false image of a patriotic Christian who sacrifices his best friend for reasons of duty and perceive a criminal who uses devotion to king and country for personal gain and revenge. Molière, however, may have had a special purpose in repeatedly attacking hypocrisy and bad faith as fraudulent mixtures. Professor Adam has shown that Molière was attempting to keep religion in its place by separating it from secular behavior.[4] Indeed, we have the impression that whenever a *dévot* attempts to meddle with worldly activities he automatically becomes suspect. Cléante gives as sterling examples of religious fervor only those people who restrict their attention to their own private salvation and who, without any conscious effort on their part, serve as models for the rest of humanity: "C'est par leurs actions qu'ils reprennent les nôtres" (394). Cléante describes their devotion to God as "humaine" and "traitable" (390). In short, Elmire's wise brother advises

[4] Antoine Adam, *Histoire de la littérature française* (Paris: Domat, 1952–1956), III, 312.

his spiritually-inclined contemporaries to mind their own business. Religion has charm as long at it does not exceed the boundaries of pure spirituality.

In this manner, *Tartuffe* provides, among other things, another instance of Molière's consistent defense of secular attitudes, of worldly pleasures, and, ultimately, of his own professional activities as actor, director, and playwright. Indeed, the comedy assures the unparalleled triumph of good theater over the evil histrionics of religious shamming. In the same manner that Jehovah attracted Athaliah into his eternal temple, Molière entices religious pretense into his playhouse, transforms it into a vulgar performance, and then destroys it. This secular attitude does not necessarily mean that Molière was an atheist or even a libertine. After all, his attack against certain forms of religiosity can be construed as a justifiable act of self-defense.

DIGRESSION ON LA LETTRE SUR L'IMPOSTEUR

This anonymous letter, to which we have referred on several occasions in the course of the chapter, contains the first critical appreciation of *Tartuffe,* or rather of *Panulphe.* It appeared in 1667, soon after the first performance of the second version of *L'Imposteur,* and it remains even today one of the most penetrating studies of Molière's art. As literary criticism, it has few if any peers in the seventeenth century. The author so eloquently defends the play, and he brings so many brilliant ideas to bear in his analysis of character and in his elucidation of esthetic problems, that many scholars believe that if Molière did not write the letter himself, he must at least have inspired the ideas it contains. M. Georges Poulet bases his remarkable interpretation of Molière's thought on this letter, and Professor Adam by no means minimizes its importance.[5] The style of the letter would seem to preclude direct authorship by the dramatist who, fortunately or unfortunately, never made a habit of writing essays. In fact, he has left us only dramatic works,

---

[5] Georges Poulet, *Etudes sur le temps humain* (Paris: Plon, 1950), pp. 79–89.

a few scattered poems, many prefaces, and we know that he translated the *De natura rerum*. In short, we have nothing by Molière that might serve as a valid standard of comparison with the letter. *La Lettre sur l'Imposteur* immediately strikes the reader as eloquent, discursive and ornate. Its author could have read it, with very few changes, as a paper at the French Academy. The frequent, and ever so slightly pedantic, allusions to Aristotle and other standard gods of the academic world, would have made the forty immortals feel perfectly at home. Although Molière could have quoted Greek and Roman philosophers almost as ably as the most learned members of the Académie, one just cannot imagine the author of *Les Femmes savantes* doing it seriously, particularly in an anonymous pamphlet couched in an epistolary form. And writers of Molière's generation rarely wrote such learned epistles, fashionable in the days of Guez de Balzac. If the author of *Tartuffe* had had to write an epistle, he would perhaps have preferred to imitate the manner of Louis de Montalte.

Several of the ideas expressed in the letter scarcely conform to Molière's intellectual or, rather, anti-intellectual approach, for they give evidence of too great a faith in reason, in systematic thought, in rational explanations of vital phenomena. Whether or not the definition of religion as "une raison plus parfaite" (p. 555) restricts, as Professor Adam claims, the importance of religious thought in human existence, it certainly gives a very high place to reason. But actually, this definition has nothing unorthodox about it, otherwise theology itself would become irrational. In this connection, we can quote M. Jacques Maritain's remark about theological knowledge:

> Procédant selon le mode et les enchaînements de la raison, mais enracinée dans la foi, dont elle reçoit ses principes, empruntés à la science de Dieu, sa lumière propre n'est pas la lumière de la raison toute seule, mais la lumière de la raison éclairée par la foi.[6]

[6] Jacques Maritain, *Les Degrés du savoir* (4th ed.; Paris: Desclée de Brouwer, 1946), pp. 492–493.

If faith illumines reason, we can certainly define religion as a more perfect reason.

We can find in the letter numerous statements that seem to clash with the usual trend of Molière's thought, e.g., "le sentiment du ridicule est le plus choquant, le plus rebutant et le plus odieux de tous les sentiments de l'âme" (p. 563); "l'antiquité, si sage en toutes choses ..." (p. 557); "brider l'impétuosité du torrent d'impureté qui ravage la France" (p. 565); "Le désordre ne procède d'autre cause que de l'opinion impie où la plupart des gens du monde sont aujourd'hui que ce péché [la galanterie] est moralement indifférent, et que c'est un point où la religion contrarie directement la raison naturelle" (p. 565). The author goes so far as to praise Molière for having made seducers ridiculous: from now on, women will tend to associate them with Tartuffe. Indeed, this particular argument verges on the ridiculous and somehow jars with the incisive reasoning which characterizes most of the letter. It may, however, have appeared to contemporary readers as an effective defense of the play.

For these and other reasons we feel that Molière could not have written this work, even though he may possibly have suggested some of the ideas it contains. And then why would the dramatist make a serious pastiche of the style of the King's physician, the noted Cureau de la Chambre, and borrow several of his most characteristic ideas? Cureau may perhaps have written the letter himself. We know that a copy of the first edition bears in print the signature "C" after the usual polite ending. But this fact carries less weight than one would expect, for it so happens that the names of many Gassendists of the period begin with this letter: Carel de Sainte-Garde, Chapelain, Chapelle, Charpentier. . . . Indeed, even a cursory reading of the work would indicate that its author belonged to the Christian wing of the Gassendist camp, as did Gassendi himself. Monsieur C . . . , who explains moral values in the light of the pleasure principle, regards the soul as "naturellement avide de joie" (561). He does not consider truth and reason as purely mental or spiritual: "Quoique la nature nous ait fait naître capables de connoître la raison pour la suivre, pourtant ... elle a voulu donner à cette raison quelque sorte de forme extérieure et de dehors reconnoissable" (p. 559). Previously, in referring to both truth and reason, he had stated: "... comme elles ne sont, à proprement parler, vérité et raison que quand elles convainquent les esprits, et qu'elles en chassent les ténèbres de l'erreur et de l'ignorance par leur lumière toute divine, on peut dire que leur essence consiste dans leur action ..." (p. 555). In spite of the religious preoccupations involved, the author appears to regard truth and reason as operational in nature and as having mainly a practical purpose. He also explains laughter in functional terms: "Le ridicule est donc la forme extérieure et sensible que la providence de la nature a attachée à tout ce qui est déraisonnable, pour nous en faire apercevoir, et nous obliger à le fuir" (p. 560). The expression "providence de la nature," which implies that nature and religion have a common purpose and common bonds, would seem to exclude Jansenist authorship in the same manner that the direct relationship between mental and external manifestations would preclude the attribution of this work to a Cartesian thinker.

It might seem strange that Cureau de la Chambre, a physician, should rise to the defense of the author of *L'Amour médecin*. But Cureau did not practice medicine in the usual sense, except perhaps for important people such as Séguier and Louis XIV. Instead, he preferred to write most eloquently about the psychological, ethical and physical aspects of passion, about the souls of animals, about physiognomy and chiromancy. He held an important position at court, and it appears that Louis XIV relied on his judgment and on his competence as a physiognomist in the selection of his ministers and other important functionaries. He frequented literary salons where he was known as a "bel esprit." And he was a friend of Le Vayer de Boutigny, himself a close friend of Molière. Even Boileau admired him! We cannot prove that Marin Cureau de la Chambre (1594–1669) actually wrote the letter, but we intend to show that he must at least have exerted a strong influence on its author, whether it was Molière himself or any other follower of Gassendi.

Cureau's most impressive work, *Les Charactères des passions,*
contains a chapter on laughter, which he regards as a passion.
Strangely enough, he does not include laughter among the passions in a subsequent work, *L'Art de connoistre les hommes.*
He maintains that laughter results to a large extent from self-
love:

> Neantmoins si l'on considère que l'Homme est naturelle-
> ment amoureux de soy-mesme, qu'il prétend toûjours à
> l'excellence & à la superiorité; on ne trouvera pas estrange si
> en voyant les defaus des autres, il tasche de tesmoigner qu'il
> en est exempt, & s'il veut faire croire par la surprise &
> l'estonnement que leurs imperfections luy donnent, qu'il est
> plus parfait qu'eux.... Quoy qu'il en soit, cette raison est
> generale pour toutes les difformitez Ridicules, & pour toutes
> les choses que l'on mesprise.[7]

Cureau shows originality in describing laughter as a social
phenomenon whereby the individual actively strives to prove to
himself and to others his superiority. A few pages later, he expresses a similar idea in terms of motivation: "... il n'y a que
deux Motifs qui obligent l'Homme à faire voir la surprise que
les objets Ridicules luy causent, sçavoir est sa propre Excellence,
& la Societé civile."[8] We note that laughter quickly becomes an
action. Indeed, passions, throughout the treatise, are almost invariably forms of action with scarcely a trace of passivity. He
states unequivocally that "les Passions & les Vertus sont des Actions Morales."[9]

We find in *La Lettre sur l'Imposteur* fairly similar views concerning the motivation of laughter:

> Or cette connoissance d'être plus qu'un autre est fort
> agréable à la nature; de là vient que le mépris qui enferme
> cette connoisance est toujours accompagné de joie: or cette
> joie et ce mépris composent le mouvement qu'excite le

---

[7] Marin Cureau de la Chambre, *Les Characteres des passions* (Amsterdam:
Antoine Michel, 1658–1662), I, 152–153.
[8] *Ibid.,* I, 158.
[9] *Ibid.,* I, 3.

ridicule dans ceux qui le voient; et comme ces deux sentiments sont fondés sur les deux plus anciennes et plus essen-
tielles maladies du genre humain, l'orgueil et la complaisance
dans les maux d'autrui, il n'est pas étrange que le sentiment
du ridicule soit si fort et qu'il ravisse l'âme comme il fait, elle
qui se défiant, à bon droit, de sa propre excellence depuis le
péché d'origine, cherche de tous côtés avec avidité de quoi la
persuader aux autres et à soi-même par des comparaisons qui
lui soient avantageuses, c'est-à-dire par la consideration des
défauts d'autrui (p. 565).

Cureau de la Chambre and Monsieur C . . . were by no means
the first thinkers to attribute laughter to a feeling of superiority.
They show however more originality in stressing man's efforts—
"tasche de tesmoigner" in Cureau; "cherche avec avidité de quoi
la persuader aux autres" in the letter—to prove his superiority.
The two passages differ in several respects. The author of the
letter insists on the importance of contempt in laughter, whereas
Cureau stresses the idea of surprise. The latter, however, far
from rejecting contempt as a form of ridicule, discerns its presence in certain types of laughter. Moreover, religion plays a
part in Monsieur C . . . 's explanation of laughter, for he refers to original sin. Cureau, on the contrary, never alludes to
religion as such in his treatise. Nonetheless, the two passages
seem to move in the same direction, and the discussion in *La
Lettre sur l'Imposteur* might possibly be a development of
Cureau's fundamental ideas. Indeed, the two writers agree in
many respects, for instance, they both agree on the importance
attributed to external manifestations which they call "charactères," and in the stress they place on the "unconscious." The
author of the letter claims that the soul "ne s'avoue jamais à
soi-même la moitié de ses propres mouvements" (p. 565);
Cureau distinguishes two types of knowledge, of *connoissance*:
"l'une est claire et distincte qui appartient aux sens, à l'imagination & à l'entendement; l'autre est obscure & confuse qui se
trouve dans l'appétit & dans toutes les autres puissances, qui ont
une connoissance naturelle de leurs objets & de ce qu'elles

doivent faire." [10] In the final analysis, only action, only these *charactères,* have the mark of infallibility. And thanks both to Providence and to "providence de la nature" everything in the world, everything in man's deportment somehow becomes functional and useful. Both works advocate a philosophy of action, of efficacy, close, in some ways, to pragmatism, but quite opposed to dogmatism. In short, their ideology corresponds, roughly, to that of Molière's plays.

[10] *Ibid.,* I, 35. The "unconscious" also plays a part in the paradoxical action of laughing at one's self: "Que si l'on rit souvent de ses propres defaus, c'est la mesme chose que quand l'on se met en cholere contre soy-mesme; car le trouble que ces passions jettent dans l'ame, empesche qu'elle ne puisse discerner les objets qui l'esmeuvent, & luy fait prendre pour estranger ce qui est à elle-mesme" (I, 155).

II

The Seducer as Catalyst

*D*om Juan stands out as Molière's most controversial play. Like *Tartuffe,* it struck the *parti dévot* as an abominably irreligious work. Unlike *L'Imposteur,* it has appeared to many critics, irrespective of their religious convictions, as an artistic failure in spite of a certain number of redeeming scenes. A few admirers of Molière, however, regard this comedy his masterpiece, superior even to *Tartuffe* and *Le Misanthrope.* This controversy probably arose from the fact that *Le Festin de Pierre* differs so greatly from any other play by Molière or his contemporaries. Instead of providing his usual neatly contrived dramatic machine, Molière appears to have strung together a certain number of tableaux. Even the central character, Don Juan, who, by his mere presence, gives a semblance of unity and continuity to the play, behaves at times inconsistently, if not incoherently. But perhaps we should not judge this strange comedy according to so-called classical standards, for it may, after all, possess its own peculiar unity, comparable to the poetic coherence of some of Shakespeare's plays. Professor Doolittle, in an important article, has shown that *Dom Juan* by no means lacks this unity and coherence.[1] We agree with his interpretation according to which the exposure of convention is a central theme. We feel, however, that it is the Don himself, and not only his victims, who behaves in a conventional manner.

Critics have generally placed too much emphasis on Don Juan's belief or disbelief in the same manner that they have over-emphasized the psychological aspects of Tartuffe's hypocrisy. And they assume that Molière intended only to create a convincing hypocrite and an equally convincing seducer with

[1] James Doolittle, "The Humanity of Molière's *Dom Juan,*" PMLA, 68 (June, 1953), 509–534.

atheistic leanings, and therefore that character study preoccupied
him more than any other aspect of dramaturgy. Recently however, M. Simon has stressed the importance of Sganarelle, who
serves as an intermediary between the isolated seducer and the
audience.[2] His theory corroborates, in some respects, that of
Professor Doolittle, for it transforms the Don into a different
sort of creature, set apart from the general or conventional run
of humanity. Still, this isolation—a feature of many of Molière's
characters—does not make Don Juan any the less conventional,
as we shall presently see. Rather, his separation from the rest of
the world puts him at times in the same category as Tartuffe
himself, or Arnolphe, or even Alceste.

Enough has been said about Don Juan as a realistic portrait
of a seventeenth century libertine and aristocrat, but perhaps too
little about the effect he produces on others. After all, his very
existence as a legend, and even as a dramatic figure, depends
primarily upon the reactions of his victims—and in Molière's
version, upon the behavior of Sganarelle. If, in *Tartuffe,* the
gullibility of Orgon and Madame Pernelle matters at least as
much as the artifices of the impostor, why then should not
susceptibility to temptation count as much as the personality
of the seducer? To Orgon's eagerness to play the part of dupe
corresponds the enthusiasm with which Don Juan's victims
succumb to the first temptation that happens to come their
way. After all, Faust did invite the devil; and, as readers, we pay
less attention to Mephistopheles than to Faust himself. In *Le
Festin de Pierre,* Don Juan plays on occasion the part of devil,
which does not mean that we can consider him as evil incarnate
or as the spirit of deprivation. Only on one occasion does the
truly diabolical side of his nature come to the fore—in his
jealousy of an obviously happy couple:

> La tendresse visible de leurs mutuelles ardeurs me donna de
> l'émotion; j'en fus frappé au cœur et mon amour commença
> par la jalousie. Oui, je ne pus souffrir d'abord de les voir

[2] Alfred Simon, *Molière par lui-même* (Paris: Editions du Seuil, 1957) pp.
103–117.

si bien ensemble; le dépit alarma mes désirs, et je me
figurai un plaisir extrême à pouvoir troubler leur intelligence,
et rompre cet attachement, dont la délicatesse de mon cœur
se tenoit offensée (I, 2).

In most instances, however, he acts as a catalyst of evil as well
as of good, and his attempts at seduction serve mainly to test
the mettle of others. In short, we may regard Don Juan's role
as primarily functional and as analagous in this respect to that
of Tartuffe. Nonetheless, we consider both the seducer and the
repulsive hypocrite as convincing, lifelike characters, even
though this aspect of dramaturgy need not concern us in these
pages. The Don, however, is much more complex than Tartuffe,
perhaps because we can see in him not only the portrait of a
courtier, but because he combines within himself the traits of
two quite different characters: that of the Spanish Don Juan
Tenorio and that of Hylas.[3] Indeed, this composite nature of
Molière's seducer might explain an apparent lack of coherence
in his behavior.

MOVEMENT

Molière has neglected at least one of the three classical uni-
ties in *Le Festin de Pierre:* that of place, which changes more
frequently than in almost any other play of the period. In this
respect, Molière was merely following tradition, for the original
version by Tirso de Molina as well as the various Italian and
French imitations, contained a wealth of entertaining incidents.
But in Molière's play, the perpetual agitation of the hero happens to be merely one aspect of a conflict between motion and
immobility. The key word in this antithesis is *demeurer.* Don
Juan succeeds in exerting a strong attraction on people who remain confined to a village or to a convent, but who would love
to escape and go to an imagined paradise. He seduces all those
who show discontent with their lot, such as Elvire, a nun im-

[3] Don Juan's speech about his conquests, where he develops the theme of in-
constancy, has reminded critics of similar pronouncements by the inconstant
Hylas, one of the chief characters of Honoré d'Urfé's *L'Astrée.*

prisoned in a convent, or Charlotte, a peasant girl engaged to a
rustic whom she does not even like. Characteristically, Don
Juan tells Charlotte: "... vous n'êtes pas née pour demeurer dans
un village," (II, 2) whereas Sganarelle, upon his master's departure, gives the two peasant girls a piece of advice diametrically
opposed to his: "... demeurez dans votre village" (II, 4). Previously, the seducer had confessed to Done Elvire: "... je vous
ai dérobée à la clôture d'un couvent," before telling her to return "à vos premières chaînes," or, in other words, to her previous immobility and *engagement* (I, 3). And the Don, whom
Sganarelle describes as "le plus grand coureur du monde," refuses to stay in one place and limit his endeavors to the chains
of a single love. His eloquent and lengthy speech about his
amorous conquests opens with a question worthy of Honoré
d'Urfé's Hylas: "Quoi? tu veux qu'on se lie à demeurer au
premier objet qui nous prend?" Concerned only with pursuit
and conquest, he speaks in the name of all seducers when he
exclaims: "... nous nous endormons dans la tranquillité d'un
tel amour, si quelque objet nouveau ne vient réveiller nos
désirs." Refusing all limitations in time, space, or numbers, he
seeks, like Alexander the Great, new worlds "... pour y pouvoir
étendre mes conquêtes amoureuses" (I, 2).

In his conquests, Don Juan sees himself as moving from one
seduction to another with so much speed that none of his victims will ever manage to catch up with him; but, unfortunately
for him, he no longer moves quite as rapidly as he imagines.
We first realize that the Don has slowed down when Elvire "en
habit de campagne" unexpectedly catches up with him—an
event which greatly annoys him. Worse still, in his pursuit of
the young couple whose love had so offended him, he is badly
outdistanced and very nearly drowned for his pains, after having miserably failed to separate the lovers by his seductive
words. Thus, in his first two encounters, he moves too slowly
to maintain his reputation as a *coureur,* in spite of the fact that
his heart, according to Sganarelle, is "le plus grand coureur du
monde" (I, 2). Moreover, his enemies (the brothers of Done
Elvire) do not give him enough time to damage the reputations

of the two peasant girls who have so readily succumbed to his charm and to his promises. In spite of these failures, he maintains throughout the first half of the comedy, a high degree of mobility and the dashing pace of a seducer. While fleeing his pursuers, he encounters the beggar, frustrates the bandits in their attempt to kill Don Carlos, and finally wanders into the cemetery where he finds the statue of an erstwhile victim: the Commander.[4] And he attributes to chance almost everything that happens to him.

During the second half of the play, the situation is reversed: everybody seems to wander into Don Juan's house, from Monsieur Dimanche to the marmorean statue of the Commander. In a sense, the hero finds himself besieged and reduced to a state of immobility. He impertinently invites his father to sit down; he orders a chair for the statue; to Elvire he says: "demeurez ici" and "Madame, vous me ferez plaisir de demeurer." But nobody will heed him except the stupid Monsieur Dimanche who accepts his offer of an armchair. Against the ceaseless motion around him, where even a marble monument, "une statue mouvante et parlante," easily catches up with him, he has recourse to hypocrisy (where outward tranquillity hides the agitation going on within) and, as a last resort, to a more intense form of immobility: he strives to make himself *inébranlable*. As he has made himself motionless and unmovable, he cannot avoid being crushed, for the essence of Don Juan consists in his mobility, in his changeability: he is a *coureur* both in the literal and figurative sense. In inaction lies his own negation. Conversely, he cannot resist the call to action, a tendency which goes far towards explaining his heroic and spontaneous decision to rush to the help of Don Carlos. We should add, however, that as Don Carlos, in facing a very real peril, does his utmost to defend himself, he is bound to enlist the help of Don Juan whose existence depends to a large degree on the actions of others. Similarly, the strong convictions of the Poor

---

[4] Movement is also a sign of affection, e.g., "la grosse Thomasse" is always pushing her friend Robin around, whereas Charlotte has no more life to her, according to Pierrot, than a log.

Man practically force Don Juan to give him the Louis d'or. The hero cannot help but render tribute to all those who demonstrate their worth. On the other hand, he shows no pity to those who give evidence of weakness. Thus he plays the part of tempter and devil on a purely secular level, testing everyone he encounters until his destruction by convention—by a convention which he had himself formally invited. And he cannot survive once he has switched from movement and action to immobility and hypocrisy.

WORDS

Words, which we may regard in many instances as a form of gesture, appear in all of Molière's comedies as the greatest enemies of action and the staunchest upholders of convention. As such, they fare scarcely better than reasoning. One of the axioms in these comedies is that no amount of *raisonnement* can ever persuade a person to change the impertinence of his conduct. These *raisonneurs* are frequently the most frustrated of characters who, though rarely ridiculous in themselves, provoke laughter by the inextricable situations in which they find themselves—and by the inevitability of their failure.

One of the key terms in *Dom Juan* is the unobtrusive word *dire,* with related expression such as *parler, parole, mot, discours, redites, expliquer*—in the sense of putting into words—*faire*— in the sense of *dire*—*bouche, entendre, ouïr, répondre, disputer.*
. . . The verb *dire* recurs nearly one hundred times in the course of the comedy. By adding the ten or so *faire,* the thirty-odd *parler,* and such related verbs as *réitérer, sarmonner, répondre, faire signe* . . . , we discover that the idea of communication intrudes some one hundred and fifty times. Moreover, the term *parole* appears no less than fifteen times. Usually, in Molière's comedies, a key word may reappear six or seven times: just enough to establish a theme, to drive home an idea, to clarify an issue; but this deluge of *dire* and *parler* must have a special function, for it does more than establish a theme. Indeed, it appears to express a way of life, a mode of existence. Whereas in previous

plays the author had created characters who tend to substitute words and concepts for action and existence, in *Dom Juan*, he makes speech itself a substitute for action.

Sganarelle does more talking than any other character in the play with the exception of his master. But he constantly acts at cross-purposes: his thoughts and his pronouncements contrast with his behavior. Sganarelle frequently attempts to convert his master by argumentation, in which endeavor he of course fails miserably. As M. Simon has pointed out, the servant represents a *reductio ad absurdum* of a character typical in Molière's previous comedies: the *raisonneur* who never convinces even though Molière sometimes rewards him, as in *L'Ecole des femmes*, with the last laugh. But in Sganarelle, Molière has created a *raisonneur* who cannot reason and who finally utters a veritable tidal wave of clichés in order to persuade his master of some deep religious truth. Not that we can accuse Sganarelle's arguments of being meaningless. As Professor Doolittle has shown, they do signify even though they sound very much like nonsense.

The conversations between Sganarelle and Don Juan often take the form of an argument or, as the valet calls it, a *dispute*. The servant, after his master's lengthy speech about the pleasures of seduction, praises him for talking just like a book. Unable to find an answer, he asserts that he will write down his *raisonnements* in order to convince Don Juan that he, Sganarelle, has truth on his side. Previously, the valet had compared a sequence of events in his master's existence to a chapter in a book. The omnipresence of *dire* and *parler,* together with the comparison between Don Juan and a literary work, that is with words in their most finished form, suggests that Molière, for reasons which we intend to discuss later, was gleefully trying to reduce existence to so many words—to its verbalizations. Indeed, in many of the speeches, we notice that characters recount not only actions and events but even conversations. For instance, Pierrot tells his reluctant fiancée not only about his rescue of Don Juan but repeats the dialogue between himself and Lucas which preceded it. Elvire's first speech to Don Juan reveals her inner dialogue or debate: "Mes justes soupçons chaque jour avoient beau me parler: j'en rejetois la voix qui vous rendoit criminel à mes yeux, et j'écoutois avec plaisir mille chimères ridicules qui vous peignoient innocent à mon cœur." If she has thus put herself *en campagne* to find Don Juan, it is merely to hear more words: "Je serai bien aise pourtant d'ouïr de votre bouche les raisons de votre départ. Parlez, Don Juan, je vous prie, et voyons de quel air vous saurez vous justifier." Her suffering consists mainly in hearing cruel words: "Il suffit. Je n'en veux pas ouïr davantage, et je m'accuse même d'en avoir trop entendu." She finally renounces, at least to a certain extent, the use of words, a domain where she has met with total defeat: "N'attends pas que j'éclate ici en reproches et en injures: non, non, je n'ai point un courroux à exhaler en paroles vaines" (I, 3).

It is thus mainly through words, those Trojan horses of temptation, that Don Juan gains access to the minds of his victims. In *Le Misanthrope,* words will represent a form of bargaining. But for Don Juan, traditionally a liar, they must serve as weapons with which he will conquer his intended victims. They help him to seek out some inveterate weakness in a human being. He thus derives his power mainly from words and appearances, from empty gestures which cannot prevail against a person like the Poor Man, who has strong convictions and who refuses to compromise. For that reason, words, in this and in many other of Molière's comedies, are frequently equated with money. Don Juan does not hesitate to use flattering words and gestures in order to avoid paying Monsieur Dimanche:

DON JUAN: Je suis votre serviteur et de plus votre débiteur.
DIMANCHE: Ah! Monsieur ...
DON JUAN: C'est une chose que je ne cache pas, et je le dis à
          tout le monde (IV, 3).

Thus, Don Juan clearly pays his debts in words. The Poor Man, on the contrary, receives real money in the name of humanity, not so much because Don Juan happens to take pity on him, but because, as Professor Doolittle has shown, he recognizes in this beggar a man worthy of the name. Characteristically, the seducer asks him to curse—to commit a sin in words. Sganarelle, who thinks nothing of blaspheming from here to tomorrow, encourages him to comply with his master's command. But if the Poor Man had obeyed, the tempter would probably have hypocritically refused to give him a farthing. Such, indeed, was his reaction to Elvire's demand of an excuse. His hypocritical answer, which as he well knows neither Elvire nor anyone else will take seriously, merely corresponds to his victim's own moral and religious anguish: "Il m'est venu des scrupules, Madame, et j'ai ouvert les yeux de l'âme sur ce que je faisois. J'ai fait réflexion que pour vous épouser, je vous ai dérobée à la clôture d'un couvent, que vous avez rompu des vœux qui vous engageoient autre part, et que le Ciel est fort jaloux de ces sortes de choses" (I, 3). Don Juan ironically and cruelly echoes the sort of reflections that must have passed through Elvire's tormented mind just before she decided to elope with her dashing young lover. In short, he leaves her with her sin and does not even bother to renew his false promises, for he really has no further use for her. Experience will be her sole reward. Still, her seduction may, from a religious standpoint, have served a worthy purpose. Her love for the unattainable tempter has perhaps enabled her to discover her true vocation: she will return to the convent out of choice after having sublimated her earthly passion into spiritual love. Needless to say, both her passion and the resulting vocation come from within her, and Don Juan has acted mainly as a catalyst. We cannot claim, however, on the basis of Elvire's self-discovery, that *Le Festin* is a religious as opposed to an irreligious play. Indeed, we can derive a secular meaning even from Elvire's conversion: each person must reward himself, in the sense that he has an obligation to seek out his own values and live in accordance with them. Sganarelle, who takes clichés for moral values, superstitions for religion, and who never practices what he preaches, will not even receive his wages at the end of the play. In trying to protect Pierrot, he receives a punch from his master for his pains: "Te voilà payé de ta charité" (II, 3). Thus, the absence of reward stands out as a major theme in this play. Every single character, including the Poor Man, meets, at one time or another, with frustration. The beggar does receive a reward in the form of a gold coin, but most of the time he lives in a state of misery and his prayers go unheeded, at least in this world. Ironically, the only time when he has a reward thrust upon him occurs upon his refusal to utter a word! In this respect, we can regard *Dom Juan* as a comedy of frustration and paradox, as a play about the absurdity of the human predicament. When Sganarelle asks his master what he thinks about the Commander's tomb, he receives an answer which reveals the absurdity of human values or rather of conventional values: "Qu'on ne peut voir aller plus loin l'ambition d'un homme mort; et ce que je trouve admirable, c'est qu'un homme qui s'est passé, durant sa vie, d'une assez simple demeure, en veuille avoir une si magnifique pour quand il n'en a plus que faire" (III, 5). Don Juan ironically stresses man's tendency to take gestures for values. And the Commander has truly attained the height of absurdity in this respect: "Parbleu! le voilà bon, avec son habit d'empereur romain!" It would seem that the worthy Commander has geared his entire existence to the perpetuation of a magnificent funeral, to the petrification of a commanding gesture. In a sense, the Commander has immortalized himself, or rather that public image of himself which very nearly coincides with status. When Don Juan invites this vain image to supper, Sganarelle raises a very sensible objection: "Ce seroit être fou que d'aller parler à une statue," thereby establishing a connection between the absurdity of words and this ridiculous marble monument which we may consider as absurdity in its most spectacular and most concrete form.

THE FALLACY OF MISPLACED CONCRETENESS

The idea of discernment plays an important part in practically every scene of the play. Like words, it maintains the closest connections with rewards and money. The most impressive scene from the standpoint of discernment is Pierrot's description of the rescue. Pierrot prides himself on his ability to see two men swimming in the sea, as opposed to the blindness of his friend Lucas who accuses him of double vision. Moreover, Pierrot has the wisdom to wager money on his splendid eyesight, and he thus reaps the rewards for his discernment. On the other side of the ledger, Pierrot does not exactly benefit from his rescue of the seducer, a fact which shows once again the discrepancy between service and reward. Indeed, Don Juan tries to seduce his fiancée and then beats him. And the unfortunate Pierrot exclaims: "... ce n'est pas là la récompense de v's avoir sauvé d'estre nayé" (II, 3).

Elvire's speech in Act I, Scene 3 reveals in a more subtle manner the struggle between discernment and imagination, which she defines as "mille chimères ridicules." And she admits: "J'ai été assez bonne ... ou plutôt assez sotte pour me vouloir tromper moi-même, et travailler à démentir mes yeux et mon jugement." The eyes appear to be less susceptible to illusion than the ears or the imagination. Actually, Elvire has deluded herself. Paradoxically, she has been Don Juan's chief accomplice in her own seduction.

The idea of discernment reappears in relationship with the marble statute. Don Juan tries at first to deny the testimony of his senses: ". . . nous pouvons avoir été trompés par un faux jour, ou surpris de quelque vapeur qui nous ait troublé la vue" (IV, 1). He thus finds himself in the same situation as Gros Lucas, who had been indulging in horseplay with his friend Pierrot. Sganarelle, like Pierrot, refuses to deny his senses: "Eh! Monsieur, ne cherchez point à démentir ce que nous avons vu des yeux que voilà." He thus establishes a further connection between discernment in the sense of physical perception, and proof or argumentation. Later in the scene, Don Juan, revolted by his servant's "sottes moralités," threatens to whip him with a bull's pizzle. The valet quickly changes his tone, because his master says things "avec une netteté admirable." Don Juan's "words," which like Hart Crane's gringo canons in "Imperator Victus," "No speakee well / But plain," appear even clearer to Sganarelle than the Commander's nod of acceptance.

What then can be the connection between discernment and proof, between argumentation and words, for these various themes intermingle in various ways throughout the play? Discernment inevitably leads to knowledge; in one instance, it leads, as we have seen, to a reward in the form of a fruitful wager. Pierrot, as a matter of fact, has bet on a sure thing; but Don Juan, who refuses to find any real significance in the signs and warnings which he perceives, will be chastized. Does this mean that we should take his destruction by a preposterous statue seriously? Of course not. But however we interpret this mysterious ending, we still would have to take into account the close connection that both words and perceptions maintain with reasoning.

From the beginning of the comedy until its theatrical *dénouement,* Molière creates a deliberately false air of philosophical discussion. The play opens with a pseudo-philosophical discourse on the virtues of tobacco. In his praise of tobacco, Sganarelle takes the apparently friendly gestures and generosity of smokers or takers of snuff for moral worth: the smoker, by virtue of his favorite drug, becomes an "honnête homme." And the play starts off ludicrously with a sweeping statement: "Quoi que puisse dire Aristote et toute la Philosophie, il n'est rien d'égal au tabac." We encounter in this opening sentence our key word: *dire,* as well as the idea of value: "il n'est rien d'égal." Professor Doolittle rightly interprets Sganarelle's speech about smoking as a criticism of gesture. We may also regard it as a *reductio ad absurdum* of reasoning, as a subtle way of connecting Aristotle with smoke and gestures, for tobacco smoke was used by seventeenth century writers as a symbol for meaningless ideas and dreams, or even lies and illusions, as in the current word: *fumisterie.* In fact, this opening gambit is reminiscent of Saint-Amant's well known sonnet: "La Pipe": "Car l'une n'est que fumée / Et l'autre n'est que vent," showing that the poet equates his dreams of success with the smoke spiralling upwards from his pipe.

Sganarelle's ludicrous equation between tobacco and human worth would imply that Molière never intended that his public take at face value the servant's subsequent pronouncements on religion. Rather, we should regard them as farcical variations on the opening statement. Moreover, Sganarelle exhibits here for the first but certainly not the last time his strange tendency to materialize thought. Referring to tobacco, he claims: "Non-seulement il réjouit et purge les cerveaux humains, mais encore il instruit les âmes à la vertu, et l'on apprend avec lui à devenir honnête homme." Absurdity, in this passage, results not only from the confusion between gesture and moral behavior, but from the still more fruitful identification of material objects such as tobacco or smoke with abstract thought and moral virtue. Later, while discussing with his master the proof of God's existence by proximate causes, he gets carried away by the movement of his own cogitations, much like La Fontaine's Perette, and he falls flat on his face. Don Juan comments, laconically: "Bon! voilà ton raisonnement qui a le nez cassé" (III, 1). The comic effect of this remark depends on the ludicrous confusion between the abstract and the concrete. Similar in nature was Sganarelle's previous statement about the doctor's robe he uses as a disguise: "... cet habit me donne de l'esprit." And the final argument with which the valet hopes to convince his master brings about a total confusion of verbal clichés and concrete examples, all under the guise of thought and reasoning.

An analogous mixture of abstract thought and spiritual values with concrete reality appears in the various signs that obsess the tempter towards the end of the play: the specter, which changes into the conventional symbol of Time the Reaper, and, of course, the marble statue. Previously, Don Juan had discoursed ironically about the discrepancy between spiritual values and material rewards, for instance in his conversation with the Poor Man, whose function in life consists precisely in praying Heaven every day for the prosperity "des gens de bien qui me donnent quelque chose" (III, 2). The beggar probably gave a spiritual meaning to "gens de bien" and even to "prospérité," but this does not prevent his words from suggesting rather subtly the ideas of wealth and material success. Don Juan, on the strength of this equivocation, can remark: "Il ne se peut donc pas que tu ne sois bien à ton aise?" Upon the beggar's negative reply, he exclaims in mock disbelief: "Tu te moques: un homme qui prie le Ciel tout le jour, ne peut pas manquer d'être bien dans ses

affaires," as though there must be a direct relationship between
material and spiritual values. Under these circumstances, and
granting the importance of the confusion between the abstract
and the concrete, we can expect that the Heaven which the
Poor Man invokes in his prayers should avenge itself on the im-
pious seducer by taking the most preposterously concrete form
imaginable: that of the marble statue of a general attired like
a Roman emperor. Spiritual values and the supernatural finally
materialize themselves in so crude a manner that it almost seems
as if poor Sganarelle had planned or imagined the whole spectacle
all by himself! Could this strange catastrophe imply that virtue
will be rewarded and evil punished when Hell freezes over?
Well then, the tempter's unlikely destruction would merely add
a final touch to the utter confusion of all values, intellectual as
well as moral, which so characterizes the play.

We have to admit, however, that Don Juan, who constantly
uses false values and plays the part of a counterfeiter in words,
is fully paid back in kind, defeated by an incredible illusion, by
a gesture, as empty as his own playful invitation to supper, or
his marriage promises, or his indebtedness to Monsieur Dimanche, or Sganarelle's hope of finally receiving his wages.
Thus, this creator of illusions is finally crushed by an illusion
and a convention. In fact, Don Juan not only creates illusions,
but he bases his success on a skilful manipulation of conventions to which he himself subscribes. When he sees Elvire "en
habit de campagne," he exclaims in shocked surprise: "Est-elle
folle, de n'avoir pas changé d'habit, et de venir en ce lieu-ci avec
son équipage de campagne?" (I, 2). According to the Don,
one should at least keep up appearances and wear appropriate
clothing in a palace. When he flees Done Elvire's brothers, he
wears country as opposed to courtly clothes, for he can be recognizable only when fashionably attired. Pierrot's minute description of Don Juan's clothes not only makes the peasant ridiculous
because of his ignorance of aristocratic dress, but transforms the
seducer himself into a figure of fun; and we suddenly have the
feeling that he owes his success with women partly to his costume, and partly to his rank, but precious little to his innate

charms. Thus our dangerous seducer, who frightens poor Sgana-relle into serving him against his will, has some of the silly faults of those *petits marquis* whom Molière will satirize in *Le Misanthrope.*

The confusion between abstractions and concrete reality per-vades also the realm of morality. Don Juan refuses to be tied down, and he regards the laws of the land as well as those of the Church as so many chains which he has so far succeeded in eluding. However, various other characters complain about these chains and obligations. Don Carlos, for instance, sees the aris-tocratic concept of honor as a form of enslavement. In a sense, the analogy of chains emerges here and there in the course of the comedy; and practically all of Sganarelle's arguments refer to a chain of causes which bind man morally and physically to his Creator. With the exception of Don Juan, everyone tends to sacrifice existence itself to these imprisoning moral bonds and conventions, everyone including of course the Commander whom the protagonist had killed, honorably, in a duel. His ornate tomb, complete with marble statue, represents the triumph of "moral" essence over life, freedom, and common sense. At the *dénouement,* all these immaterial obligations, all these social essences which man has created in his own image, but which he attributes to God, finally materialize in order to destroy Don Juan, who had done his utmost either to flout them or to turn them to his advantage. Everything in the play seems to lead up to this apocalyptic materialization.

STAGE PROPS

Although Molière consistently plays with ideas throughout *Dom Juan,* stressing such intellectual niceties as perception, dis-cernment, moral obligation, the efficacy of good, the goodness of knowledge, one must not attempt to transform the play into an ordered set of philosophical beliefs or moral tenets. That Molière should poke fun at various types of reasoning, both on the religious and the *libertin* side, does not necessarily mean that he has written a philosophical treatise or a thesis-play. Actually he has used philosophy as grist for his comic mill. And why should we be surprised that an author of the age of rationalism should have written an intellectual farce? In previous plays, Molière had made fun of intellectuals—of people who try to substitute a ready-made system for the vagaries of existence. But in *Dom Juan,* he has written a comedy not so much about would-be intellectuals as about man's intellectual and moral predicament to which he has given as absurd a solution as the most dogmatic irrationalist could wish. Still, all this intellectualism is no more than the subject matter and the pretext of the comedy. As such, it can tell us very little about Molière's artistic intent.

We might plausibly describe *Le Festin* as a play about words. Don Juan uses words to great advantage, even the liturgical words pronounced by a priest at a wedding. He also becomes the victim of the word he has given the Commander—the only word for which he will have to pay. But this theory concerning the comedy will not lead very far unless we explain why such a subject appealed to his theatrical talents in the first place. We know that the Italian comedians and other dramatic companies had performed various versions of *Dom Juan,* a "pièce à machines" that made the public flock to the theater. Indeed, *Le Festin de Pierre* has a most theatrical plot—so theatrical that even Molière's intellectual version offended many men of classical tastes. (The destruction of Don Juan by a moving statue might appeal to Spaniards.) But Molière may have seen in this strange subject with its tawdry and offensive *dénouement* the theater incarnate, the theater in all its marvelous absurdity as make-believe. And the shere scandal of this walking and talking statue crushing an aristocratic and mercurial seducer must have had an irresistible appeal for him. A dramatist, an actor, a theater director could not help seeing in this marble general a stage prop to end all stage props—a stage prop all dressed up in one of Molière's favorite costumes, that of a Roman emperor, that of Julius Cæsar! After all, he let Mignard paint him in such a garb. At the end of the play, we have a vision of the very essence of the theatrical crushing the protagonist. In fact, the play seems to put an end to itself by the shere impetus of its own movement, by the final materialization of all its words and concepts. The hero himself, according to Sganarelle, talks like a book and lives by chapters instead of years. Moreover, he needs servants to dress him for the part of seducer. In ordinary clothes, he behaves rather differently, just like Brecht's pope in *Galileo Galilei*. Finally, like the author himself, he spends much of his time in testing his fellow men, in bringing out their shabbiness or conversely in precipitating their worth. He is the active ingredient, the energumen of the comedy, who sets everything in motion, at least during the first-half of the work. In short, his function resembles that of Mascarille the intriguer, of Scapin, or of the evil Iago. Like them, he seems to create plots as he moves along. This does not mean that the resourceful Don Juan expresses any of Molière's ideas. One may even claim that he does not have any ideas whatever. Nonetheless, the author has entrusted his creative functions to him without forgetting a single artifice. And thus the destruction of this tester and catalyst of all values, of this inventor of stratagems, in short, of the Artist himself, by the strangest and unlikeliest of stage props is perhaps one of Molière's most original dramatic achievements. It strikes us as no less theatrical than the ballets which end *Le Bourgeois gentilhomme* and *Le Malade imaginaire*. We witness not so much the victory of absurdity as the triumph of the artistic imagination, which is the supreme and only valid illusion.

12

The Willing Dupes

IT APPEARS that Molière wrote *L'Amour médecin* in about five days, though nothing in its style or dramatic structure would indicate haste in composition. This ballet-comedy illustrates the truism, of which there exist numerous emblematic representations, that for the disease of love the only cure is love itself. Molière's originality consists in contrasting this type of remedy with the prescriptions of real physicians. And as love stands out as the most intense expression and attribute of life, physicians will appear, conversely, as death-dealing, self-seeking pedants.

Love must triumph in a world beset with egoism. Sganarelle, the father, loves his daughter, but in a selfish, possessive manner. He wishes to keep her (together with her dowry) for himself. Thus, whenever his daughter or her servant Lisette mentions matrimony, he simply refuses to listen: "Il est bon quelquefois de ne point faire semblant d'entendre les choses qu'on n'entend que trop bien; et j'ai fait sagement de parer la déclaration d'un désir que je ne suis pas résolu de contenter. A-t-on jamais rien vu de plus tyrannique que cette coutume où l'on veut assujettir les pères?" (I, 5). In refusing to lend an ear, Sganarelle is consciously acting in bad faith. His shamming gradually leads him to the belief that his daughter does not really want a husband, but rather, pretty clothes. This false assumption explains his strange consultations with his friends and relatives, who suggest solutions which may not help the girl but which will bring them handsome profits. The jeweler advises the purchase of a brooch; the decorator thinks that a new tapestry will turn the trick; Sganarelle's niece recommends a convent. And these patent forms of selfishness hardly differ, except by their lack of intensity and of sexual overtones, from Sganarelle's possessive

130

attitude. But the father's monologue expresses more than possessiveness. In alluding to marriage, he uses such terms as *coutume* and *usage*. By this characteristic twist he reduces matrimony to a social custom as far removed as possible from a vital
process. This transformation will allow Sganarelle to oppose
custom with custom, to subordinate his daughter's pressing desires to paternal authority. Moreover, he appears from the very
first scene as a pretentious old man addicted to clichés: "Ah!
l'étrange chose que la vie! et que je puis bien dire, avec ce grand
philosophe de l'antiquité, que qui terre a, guerre a, et qu'un
malheur ne vient jamais sans l'autre! Je n'avois qu'une seule
femme, qui est morte" (I, 1). His friend Monsieur Guillaume
underlines the apparent absurdity of his last statement: "Et
combien donc en voulez-vous avoir?" But underneath we can
detect his deepest preoccupations of the moment: I have lost my
wife and I shall have to struggle to keep my only daughter from
leaving me. He seems to confuse Lucinde with his defunct wife,
for, according to his lights, both of these women concerned him
as material possessions. He even admits that he really could not
stand this spouse: "Si elle étoit en vie, nous nous querellerions."
Nonetheless, he persists in mourning her, perhaps because she
belonged to him: "Elle est morte: je la pleure." His entire existence consists of a continual series of conforming gestures, so
much so that the reader can discern a discrepancy, in practically
all his undertakings, between his basic drive and the external
attitude he tries to assume. Paradoxically, he sees through the
egoism of his friends and relatives immediately and, more dimly,
through his own selfishness. This awareness does not prevent
him from shamming or from allowing the doctors to indulge in
their own particular brand of histrionics. He vaguely realizes
that his daughter cannot be suffering from a physical ailment
and that she too may have good reason to play a part. Ironically,
he insists on acting like a bountiful father. Indeed, he wants his
daughter to take the cue and behave as though she could scarcely
go on living without all sorts of expensive gifts. He will let her
pretend sickness as long as she refrains from demanding a husband. Lucinde and Sganarelle have therefore reached a stalemate.

The girl's malingering corresponds to her father's false generosity—a generosity which reaches the heights of absurdity when he convokes not one but several doctors to her bedside, and when he insists on paying them in advance to cure her imaginary disease.

It would seem as though every character in the play were trying at one moment or another to foist on the others a comedy of his own invention. Sganarelle's acquaintances feign concern for Lucinde's well-being; Sganarelle, as we have seen, plays throughout the part of a solicitous father; Lucinde makes believe that she is dangerously ill; the doctors, by such props as robes, mules, and Latin quotations, strive to impress the public with their competence, despite the fact that they do not know how to cure diseases; Lucinde's lover pretends to be a new type of physician, who cures through words. But beneath all this make-believe lurks self-interest—the mercenary attitudes of friends, relatives, and doctors; the possessiveness and stubbornness of Sganarelle; the wilfulness and determination of Lucinde and Lisette; the passion of Clitandre. In each instance, acting provides a means to an end; but in the final analysis, the type of shamming which is bolstered by the most powerful drive of all, love, will triumph and destroy the more conventional make-believe of the other characters. Molière has made good use of a device which had already served him well in *Tartuffe:* the play within the play, which eliminates histrionics and annihilates all rival performances.

To Sganarelle's shamming corresponds a willingness, on his part, to be deceived. He believes, at least to a certain extent, the rigmarole of the physicians, he sallies forth to buy Orviétan, a panacea sold by charlatans, and, finally, he swallows every word uttered by Clitandre. Through his own self-deception he has left himself open to the deceptions of others; and his false situation makes him vulnerable to any theatrical invention. Paradoxically, Clitandre fools Sganarelle by telling him nothing but the truth: "... et si vous voulez que je vous dise nettement les choses comme elles sont, cet habit n'est qu'un pur prétexte inventé, et je n'ai fait le médecin que pour m'approcher de vous, et obtenir ce que je souhaite" (III, 6). Naturally, Sganarelle thinks that this speech which the young man addresses to Lucinde is nothing but a fib. As love alone can cure Lucinde's affections, Clitandre can truthfully describe the notary to Sganarelle as "l'homme qui écrit les remèdes." In short, we may regard the concluding scene as little more than a protracted metaphor, which equates the antithetical ideas of love and remedy. The father, however, takes this metaphor at its face value and is therefore easily fooled by Clitandre. The comedy ends like Rotrou's *Le Véritable saint Genest* as Lisette tells Sganarelle: "Ma foi! Monsieur, la bécasse est bridée, et vous avez cru faire un jeu, qui demeure une vérité." [1] In this manner, Molière stresses for the last time the discrepancy between "jeu," or shamming, and the hard core of self-interest.

Sganarelle impresses us as one of the author's strangest creations, for his self-deception will go just so far and even his gullibility is strictly related to his own shamming. As we mentioned earlier, he is never deceived by his cronies, and yet his lucidity in this particular instance does not prevent him from believing all sorts of nonsense, including the image of the benevolent father which he himself has invented. Although he is literally addicted to clichés, although he behaves like a creature of habit, he purposely acts against custom, for instance in wanting to pay the doctors before their consultation. Moreover, he mourns his wife with genuine tears while publicly describing her as a shrew. This ambivalent, contradictory and ineffectual creature seems to live at times in a real world; more often he inhabits an imaginary universe as conventional as everyday existence, but where customs appear to change their direction, as though they had passed through Alice's looking-glass. Thus, he too lives in a world of make-believe, quite similar to the one that the spectators are watching in rapt attention. In a sense, poor Sganarelle behaves like a playwright, for he appears to stage a sort of play within himself for his own benefit or, conversely, for his own undoing.

We may also regard this entire ballet-comedy as a convenient pretext for writing a satire about doctors. Scholars have shown

[1] Cf. closing line: "D'une feinte en mourant faire une vérité."

that Molière portrayed or caricatured four well-known physicians of his day. He not only directs traditional barbs against them, for instance in Macroton's encouraging remark to Sganarelle: "vous. aurez. la con-so-la-tion, qu'el-le se-ra. mor-te. dans. les. for-mes" (II, 5), but he attacks particularly their reliance on authority, their professional solidarity, their lack of sincerity and authenticity. Bahys' maxim goes even further than Macroton's comment: "Il vaut mieux mourir selon les règles, que de réchapper contre les règles." On the surface, this statement may strike the reader as mere nonsense, but under the circumstances it suggests that the medical profession will always prefer its own advantages to the well-being of the patient. And these practitioners consider patients who survive despite their unfavorable prognosis as a threat to their entire corporation. From the selfish standpoint of the medical association, Bahys has a perfect right to say: "il vaut mieux ... ," for why should he accept the point of view of suffering humanity? Previously, Monsieur Tomès had expressed the same attitude as his colleague: "Un homme mort n'est qu'un homme mort, et ne fait point de conséquence; mais une formalité négligée porte un notable préjudice à tout le corps des médecins" (II, 3). Monsieur Filerin's speech to his quarrelsome colleagues contains all sorts of dangerous suggestions, because he tends to express himself more like a doctor of theology than like a doctor of medicine: "Ne voyez-vous pas bien quel tort ces sortes de querelles nous font parmi le monde? et n'est-ce pas assez que les savants voient les contrariétés et les dissensions qui sont entre nos auteurs et nos anciens maîtres, sans découvrir encore au peuple, par nos débats et nos querelles, la forfanterie de notre art?" (III, 1). Naturally, neither a physician nor a theologian would dare refer so blatantly to his art or profession as a fraud: it is the dramatist who puts this ugly word into his mouth. Nevertheless, theologians were no less prone than medics to warn against the dangers of internecine quarrels. Indeed, they invoked this peril in regard to the raging Jansenist-Jesuit controversy; and arguments such as those of Dr. Filerin eventually led to the so-called Paix de l'Eglise in 1668. Obviously, the good doctor's advice suits any organization that bases its prestige on a set of beliefs and procedures rather than on material accomplishments. Later on, Monsieur Filerin's words will become even more ambiguous: "Puisque le Ciel nous fait la grâce que, depuis tant de siècles, on demeure infatué de nous, ne désabusons point les hommes avec nos cabales extravagantes, et profitons de leur sottise le plus doucement que nous pourrons. Nous ne sommes pas les seuls, comme vous savez, qui tâchons à nous prévaloir de la foiblesse humaine" (III, 1). Shortly afterwards, Monsieur Filerin clears the air by mentioning such innocuous fakes as flatterers and alchemists, whom even the most orthodox would hardly attempt to defend. We cannot tell whether Molière wished to allude to an organization even more powerful and sacred than the "corps des médecins," for much would depend on just how the original Filerin in September 1665 played the part: was he unctuous or ironical, sanctimonious or angry, priestly or businesslike? The bare words do not suffice, for a comedy of this type oversteps at every moment the bounds of "pure" literature. Towards the end of his long speech, Filerin explains the financial success of the medical profession: "... le plus grand foible des hommes, c'est l'amour qu'ils ont pour la vie; et nous en profitons, nous autres, par notre pompeux galimatias, et savons prendre nos avantages de cette vénération que la peur de mourir leur donne pour notre métier." A "libertin" would use similar ideas and words in order to explain the success of religion. The presence of *vénération,* a term more suitable to priests than to doctors, might lead the reader or the spectator to make the most dangerous inferences.

In his last play, *Le Malade imaginaire,* Molière will again multiply these equivocations between theology and medicine. Such hints as these suggest that Molière was expressing a purely humanistic if not a libertine view concerning the Church. True, Filerin in his advice to his erring colleagues has practically repeated in dramatic form Montaigne's meditations on the medical profession.[2] But in literary matters, rewording can count as much and, in exceptional instances even more, than pure invention, if such a thing exists. Although some aspects of *L'Amour médecin*

[2] Cf. *Grands Ecrivains Ed.,* V, 337 ff.

might lead the reader to regard this play as a sort of first sketch of the more impressive *Malade imaginaire,* it actually has more in common with *Le Misanthrope* which deals primarily with self-deception.

13 *The Self-Deceivers*

$\mathcal{D}$RAMATICALLY, Alceste is so impressive a character that even those critics who regard him as a figure of fun rather than a hero can barely resist the temptation of putting him on a pedestal as though his sincere and apparently righteous behavior could have little in common with the frivolous futility of Célimène and her flock of admirers. Actually, the misanthrope shares with the society he so strongly condemns at least one serious fault: vanity, to which he adds the sin of self-deception.

BLINDNESS AND LUCIDITY

In previous plays, Molière had exploited the humor of psychological and intellectual blindness: e.g. Orgon's cecity to the obviousness of Tartuffe's hypocrisy; but until *Le Misanthrope* he had not attempted to combine systematically within a single character lucidity with blindness, unless we regard the hero of *L'Amour médecin* as lucid. Some two years before *Le Misanthrope*'s first performance, La Rochefoucauld had dramatized the ceaseless struggle of incompatible traits for the possession of man's will; but it is quite a different matter for a playwright to breathe life into a being capable of the sharpness and frankness of a Dorine as well as of the obtuseness of an Orgon.

Blindness to one's shortcomings often takes the form of complacency.[1] In this respect, Acaste's self-portrait stands out as a masterpiece—as a much more devastating piece of satire than Célimène's most withering sketches. Acaste, in damning himself with faint praise, prides himself only on externals; his noisy admiration for the latest literary craze; his sartorial elegance; his

[1] The words *complaisance* and *complaisant* reappear frequently in the course of the play.

winning smile. He boasts of a single *affaire,* thus demonstrating his physical courage if not his usefulness to the State. His friend and rival, Clitandre, voices his approval of this self-portrait, as though agreeing that Acaste has every right to be satisfied with his lot and with his accomplishments. Each marquis so little questions his own merits that he feels certain of obtaining Célimène's affection. The other suitors, Oronte and Alceste himself, express the same unwarranted confidence in the coquette's preference—a delusion which tends to put the high-minded misanthrope on the same footing as the *petits marquis* and the poetaster.

Against the pervasiveness of complacency, several of the characters stress the need for self-awareness. Clitandre, in concluding his remarks about Cléonte, asks rhetorically: "N'a-t-il point quelque ami qui pût, sur ses manières, / D'un charitable avis lui prêter les lumières?" (569–70). Clitandre and most of his acquaintances evidently lack this type of friend. Not that advice, whether charitable or cruel, would in any way modify their conduct: Acaste will interpret Célimène's strictures as proofs of her fickleness and lack of sincerity rather than as valid criticisms of his own behavior: "Et je vous ferai voir que les petits marquis / Ont, pour se consoler, des cœurs du plus haut prix" (1697–98). Previously, Célimène, in unmasking Arsinoé, had stated with obvious insincerity the usefulness of self-awareness: "... on doit se regarder soi-même un fort long temps, / Avant que de songer à condamner les gens" (951–52). And friendly frankness would be most beneficial, because: "On détruiroit par là, traitant de bonne foi, / Ce grand aveuglement où chacun est pour soi" (967–68). Now, one cannot accuse the sharp-eyed Célimène or the prying Arsinoé of blinding themselves to their own faults. Both deserve, of course, to be publicly exposed, but neither really requires self-revelation, for the hypocrite is consciously and consistently performing a part, while the coquette is breathlessly playing a perilous game for her own diversion. The young widow's barbed prediction that upon reaching Arsinoé's advanced stage in life, she too might consent to play the part of prude for want of a worthier pastime, shows unusual insight: the coquette of today can hardly avoid becoming the hypocrite of tomorrow. All in all, obtuseness, at least in *Le Misanthrope*, remains essentially a masculine prerogative. Awareness of the excruciating deficiencies of others would, however, be universal were it not for Eliante's constant efforts to see the sunny side of her various acquaintances: she esteems, and almost loves, Alceste for his frankness and sincerity, and she alone does not paint, or even enjoy, satirical portraits. At the conclusion of the comedy, she will marry Philinte: thus is tolerance rewarded.

Carping awareness of the imperfections of others most frequently takes the form of the satirical portrait: one after the other, the faults and vices of this milieu are made public. At the end, scarcely anyone has anything to hide, and the archpainter of them all, Célimène, is exposed, transformed into a reasonably definitive portrait. The *petits marquis* threaten: "Il suffit: nous allons l'un et l'autre en tous lieux / Montrer de votre cœur le portrait glorieux" (1693–94). The very first scene of the play had already contained a portrait, that of Alceste's hypocritical party: "Au travers de son masque on voit à plein le traître" (125). The victims of Célimène's etchings are by no means evil-doers, but merely *fâcheux:* pretentious bores whose presence she tries to avoid. M. Alfred Simon has pointed out the numerous analogies between *Les Fâcheux* and *Le Misanthrope,* whose plot consists of Alceste's repeated attempts to discover the true feelings of Célimène, attempts that are interrupted by various sorts of extraneous events: a lawsuit, a sonnet, Arsinoé, other suitors, and even Philinte.[2] And Alceste appears as a spectacular bore in the eyes of his rivals as well as in the letter of Célimène. As in *Les Fâcheux,* a person will become a nuisance, and arouse laughter, merely by making an appearance at an inauspicious moment. As these repeated interruptions are merely annoying and as the portraits themselves serve mainly to assess the nuisance value of a given character without ever delving into moral issues, the type of existence thus depicted appears as a mixture of idleness and futility. In this respect, the most striking portrait is that of the "grand flandrin de Vicomte" whom Célimène has watched "trois

---

[2] Alfred Simon, *Molière par lui-même* (Paris: Seuil, 1957), p. 119.

quarts d'heure durant, cracher dans un puits pour faire des ronds."
Molière here unmasks the spitten image of futility. These portraits tend to be revealing in three different ways, sometimes
simultaneously: as consciously depicting the faults of the "victim," as unwittingly pointing out the deficiencies of a given
social group and thereby exposing the painter. In this manner,
Le Misanthrope gives a complete picture of seventeenth-century
salon society while containing a thorough study of an "atrabi-
laire amoureux." But the character study itself provides an insight into the true nature of this corrupt society, condemned for
its futility, its idleness, and its general uselessness. These weaknesses will appear all the more ridiculous if we see them in the
perspective of Colbertism, which stressed practicality and efficiency—deeds rather than words.

As we have already suggested, the various characters uninten-
tionally reveal much more about themselves and their way of
life than they had anticipated, particularly when they attempt
to expose the deficiencies of their friends. Unmasking, as Arsinoé
and later on Célimène will discover to their sorrow, can work
both ways. As a comic device, it closely approximates the old
trick of the "voleur volé," with effects ever so much more subtle
and some times more devastating. But what about poor Alceste,
who objects to Célimène's *médisances* and who paints satirical
portraits only under emotional stress? True, he condemns the
entire race of man, but in the light of the highest and soundest
moral principles. As a result, critics, and particularly philosophers,
have been ashamed to laugh at him:

> Et enfin il faut bien l'avouer—quoiqu'il en coûte un peu de
> le dire—que nous ne rions pas seulement des defauts de
> nos semblables, mais aussi, quelquefois, de leurs qualités.

And in the next paragraph, Bergson adds:

> C'est donc la raideur d'Alceste qui nous fait rire, quoique
> cette raideur soit ici honnêteté. Quiconque s'isole s'expose au
> ridicule, parce que le comique est fait, en grande partie, de
> cet isolement même.[8]

[8] H. Bergson, *Le Rire* (Paris: P.U.F., 1947), pp. 105–106.

But must we let Alceste isolate himself from the rest of humanity, as though morality might perish with him? Will he not prove to be much more ridiculous if we can convict him of the same vices he condemns in others?

THE CASE AGAINST ALCESTE

Apart from Jean-Jacques Rousseau, few critics would deny that Alceste has serious faults. As Professor Jasinski and, more recently, Mr. Yarrow have pointed out, not only is he unreasonable, tactless and childish in his outbursts, but vain and egotistic to boot.[4] When Philinte admonishes him: "Mais on entend les gens, au moins, sans se fâcher" (4), he retorts, like a sullen boy: "Moi, je veux me fâcher, et ne veux point entendre." The absurd Argante, in *Les Fourberies,* will sound precisely the same note:

SCAPIN: Mon Dieu: je vous connois, vous etes bon naturellement.
ARGANTE: Je ne suis point bon, et je suis méchant quand je veux (I, 4).

Such petulance so early in the play should warn the audience not to regard Alceste as a sterling champion of moral principles in a corrupt world.

His vanity, which usually takes the form of egocentricity, appears everywhere. In the first scene, he exclaims:

Non, non, il n'est point d'âme un peu bien située
Qui veuille d'une estime ainsi prostituée;
Et la plus glorieuse a des régals peu chers,
Dès qu'on voit qu'on nous mêle avec tout l'univers: (53–56)

And a few lines later, he expresses still more clearly his sense of superiority: "Je veux qu'on me distingue" (63). Throughout the play, he exaggerates, if not his merits, at least the value of his opinions, of his feelings and of everything else that concerns

[4] R. Jasinski, *Molière et le misanthrope* (Paris: Colin, 1951), pp. 136 ff. P. J. Yarrow, "A Reconsideration of Alceste," *FS*, XIII, 4 (1959), 314–329.

him. His self-centeredness manifests itself only too clearly in his tactless proposal to Eliante, whose attitude towards humanity is diametrically opposed to his own. He actually believes that his personal revenge should matter so much to the world that Eliante will be overjoyed to marry him and subordinate her entire existence to his momentary spite. His tactlessness results no doubt from an overwhelming *dépit amoureux*.

He grossly exaggerates the importance of his trial, which he regards as a momentous battle in his war with the universe: "... je veux qu'il demeure à la postérité / Comme une marque insigne, un fameux témoignage / De la méchanceté des hommes de notre âge" (1544–46). His vanity thus transforms an ordinary legal matter, involving a goodly sum of money, into an historical event, comparable at the very least to the condemnation of a Montmorency or a Fouquet.

Célimène, in coldly adding Alceste to her list of bores, seems to question the authenticity of his misanthropy:

> Le sentiment d'autrui n'est jamais pour lui plaire;
> Il prend toujours en main l'opinion contraire,
> Et penseroit paroitre un homme du commun,
> Si l'on voyoit qu'il fût de l'avis de quelqu'un.
> L'honneur de contredire a pour lui tant de charmes,
> Qu'il prend contre lui-même assez souvent les armes;
> Et ses vrais sentiments sont combattus par lui,
> Aussitôt qu'il les voit dans la bouche d'autrui (673–80).

Alceste's attitude towards Arsinoé appears to confirm Célimène's judgment. When the prude accuses the court of having neglected a man of his tremendous merits, he immediately retorts:

> Moi, Madame! Et sur quoi pourrois-je en rien prétendre?
> Quel service à l'Etat est-ce qu'on m'a vu rendre?
> Qu'ai-je fait, s'il vous plaît, de si brillant de soi,
> Pour me plaindre à la cour qu'on ne fait rien pour moi?
> (1052–56).

This rejoinder reveals Alceste's eagerness to contradict even those people—and there are many of them, including at first Oronte—

who appreciate his merits. Paradoxically, he condescends to uphold the court—the only time in the entire course of the comedy when he rises to the defense of human behavior: "Elle auroit fort à faire, et ses soins seroient grands / D'avoir à déterrer le mérite des gens" (1063–64). Under normal circumstances, the mere idea of the court's callous indifference to merit would have aroused his wrath.

His retort to Arsinoé is important in still another respect. By admitting that he has not rendered any real services to the State, he puts himself in about the same position as the complacent Acaste. A few years later, Wycherley will create in the sea-captain Manly a misanthrope of more heroic dimensions than poor Alceste, who, in spite of his lofty language, is no more than a pillar of high society. He can spend the entire day in Célimène's cosy salon, idling away the hours, as indolently as Acaste, who exclaims: "Rien ne m'appelle ailleurs de toute la journée" (738), or Clitandre, who echoes: "Moi, pourvu que je puisse être au petit couché, / Je n'ai point d'autre affaire où je sois attaché" (739–40). The male characters, almost without exception, are domesticated oppressors leading a life of luxurious futility, while seeking means to gratify their egos: Acaste by his addiction to fashion; Oronte, by writing innocuous verse; Alceste, the noblest of the lot, through sterile misanthropy. They remind us of La Bruyère's Narcisse who, we are told, "se lève le matin pour se coucher le soir."

Because of his vanity and inaction, we cannot regard Alceste as an upholder of heroic virtue in a degenerate society any more than we could consider Sganarelle as a champion of religion against the atheistic Don Juan. Intent only on covering up the emptiness of his existence, he never suspects that he might accomplish something more useful than to stay in Paris courting a coquette or to retire in a huff to his country seat. His final exit confirms this barren attitude: he will seek "un endroit écarté / Où d'être homme d'honneur on ait la liberté." And perhaps Philinte will persuade him to stay, for in his *désert* he might not find any petty noblemen or hypocritical intriguers on whom

to vent his spleen. The evil world of Paris provides him with a
distraction, in the Pascalian sense of the term. By playing the
part of misanthrope, he can dissociate himself from the world he
condemns while continuing to partake in its activities.[5]

From the very first scene, Alceste opposes himself to the rest
of humanity: "... mon dessein / Est de rompre en visière à tout
le genre humain" (95–96). Philinte mockingly feigns concern
for the human race, after his friend's long tirade against mankind
and his hypocritical party: "... faisons un peu grâce à la nature
humaine" (146), as though the misanthrope's impotent and
hardly genuine hatred might consign man to eternal damnation. By setting himself up as a champion, as a knight errant
jousting against teeming millions, Alceste behaves in a manner
reminiscent of Corneille's more cowardly Matamore, who boasted
that with a single glance he could pulverize an entire army. But
Alceste's jousting remains purely moral, and he somehow finds
it more convenient to choose as opponent the human race in all
its vagueness than to join battle against a specific evil. Although
Molière nowhere suggests that his misanthrope is a coward, he
subtly indicates the hollowness of his heroism. Alceste's love for
Célimène, which he persists in regarding as the only chink in
his armor, in no way diminishes his sense of moral superiority.
Did not Samson yield to his passion for Delilah and Hercules
submit to the whims of Omphale?

In spite of the questionable nature of his misanthropy, Alceste,
who is potentially a hero, completely dominates the fops whose
life he shares, both by his dream of a more honest world and by
the intensity of his feelings. Moreover, he is potentially a tragic
figure, beset with trivialities instead of evils. Finally, he bases
his existence on a false premise: the identification of an insignificant fragment of humanity with the entire race of man. And
this false, unstated premise explains the strange dilemma which
imprisons him: the choice between Célimène's salon and isolation. In the glaring disproportion between so preposterous a

[5] W. G. Moore, *Molière: A New Criticism* (London: Oxford, 1949), p. 124:
Alceste "is ridiculous because he forgets that he is part of the picture."

premise and feelings so intense, Alceste resembles Arnolphe, who
strove to put himself above destiny itself in planning a perfect
marriage. He differs from him in the fact that his absurdity, far
from involving only himself, embraces the society of which he
is a reluctant member.

ALCESTE AND DON GARCIE DE NAVARRE

Alceste's absurdity will stand out more clearly if we compare
him to Don Garcie, with whom he shares two or three speeches.
Critics agree that Molière, in transferring these passages from
one play to another, was trying to salvage a few poetic gems from
an unsuccessful work. But critics have not explained why Don
Garcie's words do not seem out of character when spoken by the
misanthrope. The Prince, a pathologically jealous man of action
who lacks confidence in his merits, can have little in common
with the sedentary, self-deceiving Alceste who, until Arsinoé
arouses his suspicions, persists in trusting a notorious coquette.
Both Don Garcie and Alceste movingly express their despair and
indignation at the betrayal of the woman they love:

Voilà ce que marquoient les troubles de mon âme:
Ce n'étoit pas en vain que s'alarmoit ma flamme;
Par ces fréquents soupçons qu'on trouvoit odieux,
Je cherchois le malheur qu'ont rencontré mes yeux;
Et malgré tous vos soins et votre adresse à feindre,
Mon astre me disoit ce que j'avois à craindre.
Mais ne présumez pas que, sans être vengé,
Je souffre le dépit de me voir outragé.
Je sais que sur les vœux on n'a point de puissance,
Que l'amour veut partout naître sans dépendance,
Que jamais par la force on n'entra dans un cœur,
Et que toute âme est libre à nommer son vainqueur.
Aussi ne trouverois-je aucun sujet de plainte,
Si pour moi votre bouche avoit parlé sans feinte;
. . . .
Mon cœur n'auroit eu droit de s'en prendre qu'au sort.
Mais d'un aveu trompeur voir ma flamme applaudie,

C'est une trahison, c'est une perfidie,
Qui ne sauroit trouver de trop grands châtiments,
Et je puis tout permettre à mes ressentiments.

. . . .

Je ne suis plus à moi, je suis tout à la rage
        (*Le Misanthrope,* 1289–1310; *Don Garcie,* 1276–97).

The intensity of this reaction is not unexpected on the part of the Prince or the misanthrope. But even a cursory examination of the text shows that this speech does not quite fit Alceste's present predicament. He has no right to speak of the coquette's dependency upon him, or to mention his "astre," or even to refer to past or future violence—to "châtiments," whereas Don Garcie (granted his suspicions) is justifiably referring to the power he holds over Done Elvire. The point is that Molière wished to put in the mouth of his misanthrope the most intensely dramatic speech available, abounding in heroic and even tragic overtones. That the words did not quite fit the hero's situation probably suited the playwright's purpose, for the discrepancy between speech and action drives home the fact that Alceste is really living in an imaginary world, quite unrelated at times to his surroundings. Thus the chief value of his intensely dramatic speech stems from its irrelevance. It reveals Alceste in his true light as a mock-heroic character who vainly attempts to transform the banalities of Parisian salons into momentous, anachronistic adventures. His misguided efforts serve also a satirical purpose, for they show that the society in which he was born precludes all heroic values.[6]

    Alceste's lawsuit fulfils a purpose rather similar to Maurégat's usurpation in *Dom Garcie:* it provides the misanthrope with an ordeal; it ironically represents the triumph of injustice, of evil. And his fierce quarrel with Oronte over the sonnet, which nearly results in a duel, invites comparison with the rivalry between Don Garcie and Don Alphonse, who almost join in single combat.

---

   [6] Alceste is a burlesque hero in the same sense that Boileau's *Lutrin* is a burlesque poem. By his attitude and by his language, the misanthrope is trying to transform the trivial events which take place in a coquette's salon into heroic and even tragic happenings.

Obviously, both the trial and the quarrel represent a considerable come-down from the swashbuckling, if slightly comic, world of the jealous prince—a world in which Alceste, by temperament, really belongs. In facing his paltry obstacles, in courting a silly young widow, the misanthrope behaves as though the fate of kingdoms must hang in the balance. And throughout the comedy, this behavior is characterized by misplaced intensity, by the confusion between trivialities and absolutes. Oronte's sonnet suddenly becomes a matter of principle and must be judged according to absolute standards. Significantly, Oronte insists that it took him only fifteen minutes to write the poem, whereas Alceste retorts: "... le temps ne fait rien à l'affaire" (314), for the sonnet must be good or bad absolutely, and attenuating circumstances, such as time or poetic intent, simply do not count. He asserts, for the same reasons, that the result of his lawsuit must depend not on his own or on his friends' exertions on his behalf, but on "La raison, mon bon droit, l'équité" (187) or, in other words, on pure essences, as if human justice could deal only with absolutes, as if a judge could perceive, unassisted, the justice of a given cause, as though there never could be two sides to an issue.

Alceste is even more out of place in Célimène's salon, with his moral and esthetic absolutes, than a medieval knight-errant in the Spain of Philip III. Although he persists in dwelling in an imaginary realm, he does not, like Don Quixote or even Mascarille, recreate the world to suit his fancy, for he has nothing of the creator or of the poet in his make-up. Rather, he seeks to impose absolute standards where they do not belong. Instead of striving to modify the world and thereby increase his own merit, he perpetually interposes between outside reality and his inner being a scheme of values and a system of feelings that cannot possibly be relevant to a given situation. And he is continually suffering from the inevitable discrepancy between essences that cannot be realized and a reality for which he refuses to accept any responsibility whatever. Absolutes thus absolve Alceste from action or, rather, provide him with a seemingly valid excuse for inaction.

THE COUNTERFEITERS

If the foregoing interpretation of Alceste's motives and situation be correct, then *Le Misanthrope* should be regarded as a comedy of values, rather than as a mere character study or a play about manners. In opposing his principle-ridden misanthrope to a scheming but devitalized society, Molière is dramatizing, among other things, the divorce, inherent in every man, between so-called ethical laws and actual practice. As the old Latin saw puts it: *Video meliora proboque, deteriora sequor.* And Molière complicates the inevitable conflict between ethical absolutes and behavior by equating monetary with moral values, business with human emotions.[7]

Throughout the comedy, human relations are reduced to some form of commerce. Acaste's parting shot to Célimène humorously associates love with value: "Et je vous ferai voir que les petits marquis / Ont, pour se consoler, des cœurs du plus haut prix" (1697–98). Oronte concludes in a similar manner, when he says to Alceste: "Monsieur, je ne fais plus d'obstacle à votre flamme, / Et vous pouvez conclure affaire avec Madame" (1707–08). Alceste follows the general trend of this final scene in squelching Arsinoé: "Mon cœur a beau vous voir prendre ici sa querelle, / Il n'est point en état de payer ce grand zèle" (1719–20). And Arsinoé pays him back in kind: "Le rebut de Madame est une marchandise / Dont on auroit grand tort d'être si fort éprise" (1727–28). Already in the first scene, Philinte had excused in monetary terms his enthusiastic greeting of a nodding acquaintance:

> Lorsqu'un homme vous vient embrasser avec joie,
> Il faut bien le payer de la même monnoie,
> Répondre, comme on peut, à ses empressements,
> Et rendre offre pour offre, et serments pour serments (37–40).

[7] The ironical comparison between love and money completely dominates Corneille's *Menteur;* a similar comparison between friendship and money can be found everywhere in Shakespeare's tragedy about a misanthrope, *Timon of Athens.* It would seem that poets spontaneously reach the conclusion that lucre represents the most debased as well as the most superficial form of exchange known to man or to woman.

Human relations thus strike him as a system of barter and exchange, in which gestures and grimaces take the place of currency. Alceste, true to his nature, refuses to accept this type of tender, which he regards as counterfeit: "... on devroit châtier, sans pitié, / Ce commerce honteux de semblants d'amitiés" (67–68). The misanthrope would like to replace this "commerce honteux" of meaningless gestures by a total exchange in which both parties to a friendship would give themselves without any reservation. The petty commerce of commonplaces makes him furious, for he considers friendship and, of course, love, as absolutes, which the cursed superficiality of mankind puts beyond his reach. In his frustration he perpetually attacks the words and gestures of others; and he succeeds only in opposing them with words and gestures of his own making, which are no less futile and hardly more significant. At odds with humanity, he tends to use mercenary comparisons as a means of separating himself from the rest of the world. When Oronte showers him with compliments and protestations of friendship, Alceste warns him: "... nous pourrions avoir telles complexions, / Que tous deux du marché nous nous repentirions" (283–84).

It remains, however, for Acaste to bring out most clearly the relationship between love and money; more or less as a corollary to his complacent self-portrait:

> Mais les gens de mon air, Marquis, ne sont pas faits
> Pour aimer à crédit, et faire tous les frais.
> Quelque rare que soit le mérite des belles,
> Je pense, Dieu merci! qu'on vaut son prix comme elles,
> Que pour se faire honneur d'un cœur comme le mien,
> Ce n'est pas la raison qu'il ne leur coûte rien,
> Et qu'au moins, à tout mettre en de justes balances,
> Il faut qu'à frais communs se fassent les avances (815–22).

In other words: *donnant donnant* or *les affaires sont les affaires* in love as elsewhere. The device of Eros will no longer be the bow and arrow, but the scales of blind justice and the corner grocery. Acaste knows, or thinks he knows, his own value; but so do most of the other characters in the comedy. Esteem, the greatest single cause and sole justification of passion in seven-

teenth-century tragedy, becomes ridiculous as soon as it is metamorphosed into self-esteem by such people as Acaste, Oronte, or
even Alceste himself. No wonder Célimène enjoys cheating
them! The coquette and the prude bring to bear a veritable arsenal
of financial terms in their great battle of words. Célimène ham-
mers away at Arsinoé's hypocrisy: "Elle est à bien prier exacte
au dernier point; / Mais elle bat ses gens, et ne les paye point"
(939–40). Words, even in the form of orisons, are less costly
than cash. In a later retort, the prude describes Célimène's flirta-
tions in terms of a commercial enterprise. Referring to lovers, she
asserts: "Qu'on n'acquiert point leurs cœurs sans de grandes
avances, / Qu'aucun pour nos beaux yeux n'est notre soupirant,
/ Et qu'il faut acheter tous les soins qu'on nous rend" (1014–16).
The type of love she describes can have little to do with passion,
for on both sides of the ledger it is based on the coldest calculations.

Alceste's misanthropy is closely tied in with the idea of money:
"... je veux me tirer du commerce des hommes" (1486), particularly in regard to his lawsuit: "Ce sont vingt mille francs qu'il m'en
pourra coûter; / Mais, pour vingt mille francs, j'aurai droit de
pester / Contre l'iniquité de la nature humaine, / Et de nourrir
pour elle une immortelle haine" (1547–50). The laughable contrast between twenty thousand francs and immortal hatred sums
up the entire play. Alceste parts with real money as readily as
the other characters spend their counterfeit cash. It is as though
money could somehow give a solid valuation to the empty precepts which he takes for moral worth, to the withdrawal which he
substitutes for action.

His ultimatum to Célimène to choose between him and Paris
shows that he would like to end all his dealings with the world.
Ironically, the coquette responds by making her first genuine
offer: her hand; but she refuses to follow Alceste into his *désert*.
In short, she agrees to meet him half way: "Il faut qu'à frais
communs se fassent les avances," to quote, once again, Acaste.
Alceste, who sees human relations in terms of a total, unstinted
gift, without the least suggestion of compromise, must reject

her: "Puisque vous n'êtes point, en des liens si doux, / Pour trouver tout en moi, comme moi tout en vous, / Allez, je vous refuse, et ce sensible outrage / De vos indignes fers pour jamais me dégage" (1781–84). And the word *dégager* typifies Alceste's general attitudes towards the commerce of the world.

THE SONNET

In all his undertakings, Alceste confuses concepts with actions, words with reality, attitudes with heroism. By his imagined exclusion from the world, he plays the part of hero; and he wishes to take Célimène with him, not only because he loves her according to his fashion, but in order to become entirely self-sufficient in his private universe. He is so full of himself that he cannot judge the outside world (including Célimène) with any degree of objectivity. He criticizes Oronte's sonnet in the light of his own obsessions. Compared with similar *précieux* productions of the period, this poem is almost a masterpiece:

> L'espoir, il est vrai, nous soulage,
> Et nous berce un temps notre ennui;
> Mais, Philis, le triste avantage,
> Lorsque rien ne marche après lui!
>
> Vous eûtes de la complaisance;
> Mais vous en deviez moins avoir,
> Et ne vous pas mettre en dépense
> Pour ne me donner que l'espoir.
>
> S'il faut qu'une attente éternelle
> Pousse à bout l'ardeur de mon zèle,
> Le trépas sera mon recours.
>
> Vos soins ne m'en peuvent distraire:
> Belle Philis, on désespère,
> Alors qu'on espère toujours (315–32).

This sonnet fits perfectly into the plot and metaphorical structure of the play. Alceste has probably guessed that under the name of Philis Oronte is addressing Célimène. Moreover, he is expressing the wish of all the suitors, including Alceste: the young widow should reveal her true feelings and not make them wait any more. Finally, the poem contains key words: *complaisance,* which the misanthrope detests above all others, as well as the antithetical *donner* and *dépense.* In short, the sonnet refers to the commerce of love with its system of half-promises and empty exchanges. The famous *chute:* "Belle Philis, on désespère / Alors qu'on espère toujours" is not quite as trite as it sounds, for *désespère* does not really mean *despair,* but signifies merely that the suitor, namely Oronte, if forced to wait much longer, might possibly give up hope and try his luck elsewhere. The apparently conventional recourse to *trépas* contains a strong suspicion of irony. The sonnet can thus be interpreted as a witty statement of intention, quite devoid of passion. And the clever Oronte regards it perhaps as just another gambit in his playful pursuit of Célimène. As such, it cannot fail to arouse the wrath of Alceste, who refuses to see love as a parlor game:

> Si le Roi m'avoit donné
> Paris, sa grand'ville,
> Et qu'il me fallût quitter
> L'amour de ma mie,
> Je dirois au roi Henri:
> "Reprenez votre Paris:
> J'aime mieux ma mie, au gué!
> J'aime mieux ma mie" (393–400).

The misanthrope's archaic song foreshadows his ultimatum of the *dénouement.* It reveals his desire to escape to a century when men were men; and it expresses his refusal of the world—of the King's gift, namely Paris. The two poems, however, have an important concept in common: *donner.* In the sonnet, Philis gives nothing but promises, while in the lyric, in which the very idea of exchange is rejected, the hypothetical gift of Paris conveys the impression that the lover has already secured the affection of his *mie.*

Thus, the two rivals quarrel over words. The worldly superficiality of the sonneteer clashes with the wishful escapism of the misanthrope. Here as elsewhere in the comedy, Molière is amusing the audience with the interplay between antithetical forms of the unreal: Oronte's world lacks depth and substance, whereas Alceste's private universe lacks existence and being. In a society so devitalized, the only plausible attitude remains that of Eliante: you must recreate the outside world in the image of your more generous emotions and supply it with the values that it may lack. But here, Molière twisted Lucretius' satirical comments on man's blindness to suit his purpose. Moreover, he introduces a concept that was missing in the original Latin: that of naming. The true lover transforms the person he adores not directly, but by discovering nice words with which to describe her worst features: Lovers, according to Eliante, "comptent les defauts pour des perfections, / Et savent y donner de favorables noms" (715–16). For instance, "La malpropre sur soi, de peu d'attraits chargée, / Est mise sous le nom de beauté négligée" (721–22). Molière, or at least Eliante, has at last found a useful function for the imagination. Prompted by emotion, and with the help of names and words, it can attempt to conciliate the ideal with the real.

14

Beauty & the Beast

LE MÉDECIN MALGRÉ LUI

There is a prevailing elemental and even bestial quality about this farce which we cannot find in the rest of Molière's theater, even in so boisterous a comedy as *Monsieur de Pourceaugnac* or in so bitter a play as *George Dandin*. A cruelty reminiscent of Brueghel's genre paintings predominates throughout; and this cruelty by no means precludes gaiety. In other plays Molière tends rather to alloy suffering with wit. Naturally, both types of humor confirm Freud's theory that laughter depends for its intensity upon sex, aggression, or preferably an admixture of both. Indeed, *Le Médecin malgré lui* consists of nothing but aggression and sex! And the comedy definitely has a unity of tone: that of *goguenarderie,* a term that perfectly describes Sganarelle's boisterous, bullying, and jeering type of joviality. Characteristically, the play opens with a violent quarrel between the hero and his wife, Martine. The latter describes her husband as an improvident wife-beater; and Sganarelle retorts by administering quite a beating to Martine. Then both of them pounce on the interfering Monsieur Robert. Later in the play, Sganarelle himself will be clubbed into submission by Lucas and Valère. As a sort of compensation, he will then fall upon Géronte, the father of Lucinde, whose imaginary illness he is expected to cure. And at the end of the play, the woodcutter will find himself in imminent danger of being hanged for his part in the daughter's abduction.

The earthy humor which marks the opening quarrel provides a sort of tonal key to the entire comedy:

MARTINE: J'ai quatre pauvres petits enfants sur les bras.
SGANARELLE: Mets-les à terre.

MARTINE: Qui me demandent à toute heure du pain.
SGANARELLE: Donne-leur le fouet: quand j'ai bien bu et bien
mangé, je veux que tout le monde soit saoul
dans ma maison (I, 1).

And this same tone is maintained practically without interruption to the very end, for instance in Martine's ambiguously
consoling remarks to her husband:

MARTINE: Encore si tu avois achevé de couper notre bois,
je prendrois quelque consolation.
SGANARELLE: Retire-toi de là, tu me fends le cœur.
MARTINE: Non, je veux demeurer pour t'encourager à la
mort, et je ne te quitterai point que je ne t'aie
vu pendu (III, 9).

In short, Martine wants to make sure that her wife-beating
husband will not return to pester her. Moreover, the expression
fendre le cœur is marvelously appropriate to Sganarelle, who
earns his living, if not his family's keep, with his little hatchet.
Indeed, Molière chose to make his *vilain mire* a woodcutter
rather than a farmer, for his healthfully brutal occupation suits
to perfection the general tone of the play.

Actually, many theater directors suppress one of the most
characteristic scenes in the entire comedy as irrelevant to the plot
and detrimental to the action. In this strange scene, Sganarelle
prescribes a hunk of cheese for a dying woman. Her husband,
the peasant Thibault, gives the disguised woodcutter an amaz-
ingly realistic and lurid account of the syndrome of dropsy,
interspersing his description with suggestive mistakes such as
conversion for *convulsion,* and *hypocrisie* for *hydropisie.* While
listening to the peasant, Sganarelle holds out his hand in anticipation of a fee. His parting words are quite in keeping with the
rest: "Allez. Si elle meurt, ne manquez pas de la faire enterrer
du mieux que vous pourrez" (III, 2). Here at least, Molière
has equalled the Falstaffian humor of a Shakespeare or the
drollery of a Flemish kermesse. And in the very next scene,
Sganarelle, without any transition, will continue his erotic pur-

suit of the wet-nurse, Jacqueline, whose breasts would have tempted a Rubens.

Now, only a remarkable poet—in the broad sense of this term —could create a protagonist as consistently brutal and lewd as this somewhat pretentious woodcutter, described by his spouse as a "sac à vin," and maintain without a single false note a prevailing tone of brutal earthiness. Even when Léandre returns Lucinde to her father instead of eloping with her, he does so not for moral reasons, such as kindliness to the aged, but because he knows that the fortune he has just inherited from his uncle will appeal to the mercenary Géronte. That his unexpected return will incidentally save Sganarelle's neck has probably never occurred to Léandre or Lucinde. In fact, we scarcely realize that in the course of this farce we hear of two deaths: one of them impending (that of the old peasant woman), and the other a *fait accompli,* which conveniently brings the action to a close.

In spite or because of all this brutality, the comedy as a whole stands out as one of the gayest and liveliest in Molière's theater. In fact, we may regard it as an affirmation of life and love rather than a sardonic commentary on human existence. Sganarelle, in whom even the most painstaking disciple of Freud would have a hard time discerning even the faintest trace of a super-ego, behaves like an uninhibited force of nature, as an undiluted Id who simply revels in all the creature comforts. A healthy beast who works at a healthy job, he does not give a damn about the rest of humanity as long as he has enough to eat and drink, and a variety of women to go to bed with. In a way, he has attained a state of complete liberation from the sense of sin or, if we have to give this three-letter word a more modern sound, from inhibitions.

The author transforms this exuberant incarnation of health and animal vitality into a physician, a death-dealing pedant who strives to subordinate nature to a ready-made system which has no basis in reality. Sganarelle, masquerading in a doctor's habit, becomes a living contradiction. His true nature manifests itself in his outrageous flirtation with Lucas' wife and in his beating of Géronte. His dignified disguise merely brings out more dramatically his tremendous zest for life. And his praise of medicine as a lucrative profession not only provides Molière with an excellent pretext for satirizing doctors, but it is so outspoken and pronounced with so much buoyancy that the audience completely forgets the dire consequences of disease. In *Le Malade imaginaire,* Molière will take a much grimmer view of medicine.

From a technical viewpoint, *Le Médecin malgré lui* stands out as a remarkable achievement. Martine, merely by telling two servants that her husband is a medical genius who practices his art only under duress, starts him off on a tremendous if somewhat brief career as a physician. Before the final curtain, he has established so great a reputation that people come from afar in order to consult him. And the cause of all this activity was merely the usual beating that he had inflicted that very morning on his long-suffering wife. We notice the same kind of mechanical causality in Sganarelle's rapid cure of Lucinde who suddenly changes from a state of protracted muteness to a veritable verbal explosion which stuns her poor father: "Ah! quelle impétuosité de paroles! Il n'y a pas moyen d'y résister. Monsieur, je vous prie de la faire redevenir muette" (III, 6). The father objects all the more strenuously because Lucinde expresses and even shouts her desire to marry Léandre instead of Horace.

One of the most original scenes in the play occurs when Martine goes searching in her own imagination for a way to get even with her scoundrel of a husband, and literally bumps into Valère and Lucas, who happen to be looking for a doctor. And this physical contact brings both her search and theirs to a successful conclusion through the painful metamorphosis of Sganarelle into a doctor. Lucas and Valère firmly believe that Sganarelle is a mad doctor who plays the part of a woodcutter. Therefore, it would almost seem that Molière has written a farcical variation on the typical baroque uncertainty concerning identity.[1] Moreover, the author consistently makes fun of the idea of causality. Because Sganarelle has received a beating

[1] Cf. such plays as Rotrou's *Le Véritable saint Genest,* as well as Honoré d'Urfé's *L'Astrée.*

in his coercive initiation into the medical profession, he feels called upon to dish it out to the unfortunate Géronte before finally telling him: "Vous êtes médecin maintenant: je n'ai jamais eu d'autres licences" (II, 2).

LE SICILIEN OU L'AMOUR PEINTRE

After entertaining us with Falstaffian humor, Molière provides us with a close approximation of Shakespearian music. Since the *Menagiana* [2] critics have often commented on the unusual abundance of poetic lines in this prose comedy. We can find entire passages in rhymeless free verse where an occasional alexandrine stands out in bold relief.[3] Some critics have argued that Molière had intended to write it in verse but, lacking time, had left it in an unfinished state. We agree, however, with those critics who consider *Le Sicilien* as a finished work of art and as really a new departure in playwriting: Molière chose to write the ballet-comedy in what we may call incipient verse. Taking into account the general structure of the comedy, which we shall discuss later, we can claim that his incipient verse expresses a tendency towards the poetic and the artistic, towards the marriage of the various arts which coincides with Adraste's triumph in love. The *scènes de ballet* contain songs written in rhyming free verse: it would seem that as soon as actual verse takes the place of potential poetry the play must become lyrical in the strictest sense and culminate in a dance. Indeed, at the *dénouement,* the defeated Dom Pèdre cannot even obtain help from constituted authority, because the senator to whom he happens to appeal insists on watching a ballet!

Molière, from the very beginning of the comedy, subordinates everything, and even love itself, to poetic entertainment. Adraste attracts the attention of Dom Pèdre's freed slave Isidore by means of serenades; whereas the jealous Sicilian gives vent to his antagonism towards music. Finally, the young Frenchman reaches his goal, not by music alone, but by his talent as a painter

---

[2] Ménage, *Ménagiana* (3d ed.; Paris, 1715).
[3] Cf. *Grands Ecrivains Ed.*, VI, 213 ff.

of portraits. This alone gains him an access to his beloved Isidore. Molière insists on the fact that Adraste, unlike most of his aristocratic compatriots, knows how to use his hands and has become quite an accomplished artist. He can thus advance the cause of love in the very act of painting Isidore's portrait: hence the subtitle of the play, *L'Amour peintre.*

The idea of entertainment—particularly musical entertainment—provides a key to the poetic structure of this ballet-comedy. The action starts with the servant Hali's instructions to a troupe of musicians, in the course of which we find a most poetic and frequently quoted image: "le ciel s'est habillé ce soir en Scaramouche," which equates the blackness of a moonless night with the *commedia* clown Scaramouche. Molière, however, did not include this image merely for its immediate poetic value, but in order to identify nature itself with the world of the theater. In such an atmosphere, where the microcosm of art and the universe become practically indistinguishable, entertainment alone will prevail before finally merging into love.

Hali appears at first as the typical disgruntled slave: "Sotte condition que celle d'un esclave! de ne vivre jamais pour soi, et d'être tout entier aux passions d'un maître! de n'être réglé que par ses humeurs, et de se voir réduit à faire ses propres affaires de tous les soucis qu'il peut prendre! Le mien me fait ici épouser ses inquiétudes. ..." But this *topos,* which dates back to Greek and Roman theater, emphasizes the idea of subordination, and even the marriage of opposites. Hali's part is as instrumental here as that of the musicians; like them, he has no other function than to serve, and express, his master's passions. More important still, this *topos* enables Molière to establish a contrasting relationship between master and slave. In the second scene, this contrast becomes almost contrapuntal, because Adraste insists that the musicians play "quelque chose de tendre et de passionné," whereas Hali shows a marked preference for a type of melody he describes as *bécarre* (major) as opposed to *bémol* (minor). Adraste and Hali finally reach a satisfactory compromise: the musicians perform a miniature pastorale in which two unloved but faithful shepherds sing their sadness in *bémol* only to be interrupted by a gay philanderer who expresses his carefree attitude in a major key.[4] And the pastorale itself is in its turn harshly interrupted by Dom Pèdre's violent irruption, which disperses the music and the musicians. But the jealous Sicilian interferes not only with a melody; he also destroys a play within the play. Just before the performance, Hali had said: "Voici, tout juste, un lieu propre à servir de scène; et voilà deux flambeaux pour éclairer la comédie."

Dom Pèdre interrupts in a similar manner the second song-and-dance sequence, which, like the first, consists of strongly contrasting themes—of a *bémol* and a *bécarre,* of a love song addressed to Isidore followed by a grotesque lyric in *lingua franca* intended for Dom Pèdre. The Sicilian, who sees through Hali's musical manoeuvres, takes up the grotesque refrain and changes ever so slightly the *lingua franca* words while threatening to beat both musicians and dancers with a big stick.

In the climactic scene where Adraste paints Isidore's portrait and persuades her to elope, we find once again the contrapuntal contrasts of which *bémol* and *bécarre* provide the musical keys. While Adraste brings all the sweet persuasions he can muster, Hali, disguised as a Spanish grandee, asks the Sicilian's advice about an affair of honor: he has received a slap. But it so happens that this is the very slap that Dom Pèdre himself had given Adraste's servant when he so rudely interrupted the miniature pastorale! Finally, Adraste and Isidore turn the tables on the Sicilian by means of still another comedy where musical contrasts play a preponderant part. Adraste pretends to be even more jealous than Dom Pèdre himself! "Les françois excellent toujours dans toutes les choses qu'ils font; et quand nous nous mêlons d'être jaloux, nous le sommes vingt fois plus qu'un Sicilien" (Scene 15). Actually, the Frenchman has taken over Dom Pèdre's one and only theme in a sort of fortissimo, as though the entire orchestra had suddenly been entrusted with an air

---

[4] This relationship between slave and master also characterizes, but in reverse, sweet Isidore's enslavement to the harsh Dom Pèdre. It also appears in the *lingua franca* song, where the musicians try to sell their services to a generous master.

that so far had belonged exclusively to the wind instruments. And the violent, jarring Sicilian feels duty-bound to reconciliate Adraste with his supposed wife Climène, and he even advocates "une parfaite union" (Scene 17). Thus the play is brought to a musical conclusion by a switch in the original counter-point —by Adraste's clever theft of Dom Pèdre's discordance. And the quarrel between the forlorn Dom Pèdre and the good-time senator closes the play—a strong discordant note is followed by a ballet. And the audience knows that all the while Isidore, Adraste and Hali are making good their fugue. "O bords siciliens d'un calme marécage."

15

Three Conceptions
of Hercules

$\mathcal{A}$LTHOUGH WE are primarily concerned
with the manner in which Molière treated this traditional subject, we feel that the best way to show his originality consists
in comparing his work to its two models, Plautus' *Amphitruo*
and Rotrou's *Sosies*.

AMPHITRUO

Plautus dwells with obvious enjoyment on the paradoxical
sight of two gods, Jupiter and his son Mercury, taking part in
a play—an activity suitable only for slaves. In the prologue,
which Plautus probably did not write, Mercury makes an ironical distinction between his master, Jupiter, lord of the Roman
gods, and that other Jupiter—the author—who has put these
words into his mouth. In a sense then, Plautus has created a
double paradox, whereby the spectacle of gods indulging in a
lowly pursuit is mitigated by our awareness that the whole thing
is a mere fantasy dreamed up by a poor plebeian! Nonetheless,
the debased Jupiter remains all-powerful and, ably seconded by
Mercury, cruelly castigates mankind. Molière, who took as great
an interest as Plautus in the paradoxical situation of the artist,
will diminish the power of the gods by stressing the whimsy of
poets and dramatists.

Sosia, a slave, complains bitterly about his condition. Mercury,
however, describes him as a malicious bully who richly deserves
the beatings he will soon administer him. In fact, Sosia very
nearly punishes himself, for Mercury tells us: "Itaque me malum
esse oportet, callidum, astutum, admodum, / Atque hunc, telo
suo sibi, malitia, a foribus pellere" (268–69). "I must be / A ras-
cal, sly, astute; with his own arms / Of roguery I'll keep him

162

from the house." [1] Molière will carefully avoid this moral issue: his Mercury will beat Sosia merely for want of a more enticing pastime. Sosia may manifest serious faults and even criminal tendencies in all three plays, but in the Latin version Mercury certainly does not punish him for the sin of vanity—a character trait that both Rotrou and Molière will attribute to him. Indeed, Plautus' slave sees himself as others see him. He surprises Mercury by the frankness of his self-criticism: "Facit ille quod uolgo haud solent, ut quid se sit dignum sciat" (185). "Well, this fellow does / What is not common"; his deserts he knows." No doubt, Sosia's complaints about his lot conform to an ancient comic tradition; and what really matters is Mercury's reaction to these lamentations: "Satiust me queri illo modo seruitutem: / Hodie qui fuerim liber, / Eum nunc potuit pater seruitutis; / Hic qui uerna natust queritur" (176–79). "I have more reason to complain today; / For I was free, his father was a slave; / And yet this fellow, who was born a slave, thinks he may grumble." The god actually brings out the irony of man's condition. He has temporarily assumed the part of slave; and his loss of freedom appears as no more than make-believe. Plautus meant perhaps to develop the paradox of entrusting to a mere actor, to a slave, the part of Mercury—of Mercury who in his turn pretends to be a slave. This paradoxical situation puts into bold relief the cruel difference between Mercury's feigned loss of liberty and Sosia's life-long enslavement to Amphitryon.

Plautus cleverly and maliciously destroys theatrical illusion in order to produce comic effects. Mercury, upon hearing Sosia describe Amphitryon's recent victory, as a sort of rehearsal before entering the house (proloquar), remarks, as though he had just been listening to an actor reciting a speech: "Numquam etiam quicquam adhuc uerborum est prolocutus perperam" (248). "So far at least this man's said nothing wrong." Then fol-

[1] The English translation is by Sir Robert Allison, in *The Complete Roman Drama* (New York: Random House, 1942) Vol. I, with the exception of line 459, translated by Paul Nixon in the edition of Plautus' works published by G. P. Putnam's Sons, New York, 1921.

lows a sort of deafman's dialogue during which Mercury answers
each of Sosia's thoughts without, at first, letting the slave hear
him. Later, he allows his victim to overhear his thoughts in
order to frighten him; and finally, he answers the slave's silent
reflections. Only then can the real dialogue between them begin.
But throughout the entire scene, Plautus does not let the audience forget that here are two actors reciting their parts. The
paradoxical relationship between reality and representation which
results from this clever device will lead to the destruction of
Sosia's identity by Mercury's bullying make-believe. The god
insists on keeping his theatrical part all to himself: "Tu me
uiuus hodie facies quin sim Sosia" (398). "While you live / You
will not make me anyone today / But Sosia." In short, we
witness throughout a comic struggle between being and *persona*
—an underlying conflict which becomes still more explicit when
Sosia, almost convinced that he is no longer himself, asks: "Quis
ego sum saltem, si non sum Sosia? te interrogo" (438). "Then
if not Sosia, who the deuce am I?" His divine alter ego answers:
"Ubi ego Sosia nolim esse, tu esto sane Sosia / Nunc quando
ego sum, uapulabis, ni hinc abis, ignobilis" (439–40). "When
I'm not Sosia, you, of course, are he; / Now when I am, unless
you go, you wretch, / You will be beaten." At the end of this
scene, Plautus returns anew to the idea of playing a part and
therefore of wearing a mask. The unfortunate slave states ironically: "Viuo fit quod numquam quisquam mortuo faciet mihi"
(459). "Here I am alive and folks carry my image—more than
anyone will do when I am dead." Only great Romans enjoyed
the posthumous privilege of being represented by means of a
wax mast at their funeral. It would seem therefore that throughout the comedy the confusion concerning identity does not go
very far beyond the idea of mask or *persona*. Identity never
becomes a metaphysical or even a psychological problem as it
will in the seventeenth century, particularly in Rotrou's version.
Plautus is perfectly content to express the triumph of the theatrical over the real—a lead which Molière will follow with enthusiasm. In short, Plautus forces his slave to relinquish a part
rather than his individuality as such.

The *Amphitruo*, however, offers much more than a paradoxical interplay between *persona* and mask. Alcumena complains no less than Sosia about the vicissitudes of our human condition. She wonders why an overwhelming amount of frustration must always follow a short space of happiness. At the end of her monologue, she asserts: "Virtus omnia in sese habet, omnia adsunt bona quem penest uirtus" (653), "And he who valor has, has all things else," for indeed her husband possesses valor, manly dignity, excellence, which Romans regarded as the greatest of human values. This knowledge compensates for her unhappiness at being left alone. She takes pride in that highest of feminine virtues: *pudor,* which she doubts as little as her husband's *uirtus.* She probably feels that these two eminent qualities must transcend the vagaries of fortune. But it is precisely in the realm of human perfections, where the couple express so much self-confidence, that the gods launch their persecution. Amphitryon's undoubted *uirtus* will not help him to enter his own house, for he will be frustrated by his own valorous image —by Alcumena's love for that heroic image or *persona.* Thus the Theban leader, just like his slave Sosia, will have to submit to his own likeness. And Alcumena will become a victim of her chaste love for Amphitryon—of that very quality in which she takes the greatest pride. In a sense, Plautus in his tragicomedy concerns himself with a special form of hubris—a venial rather than a mortal sin in this instance, for neither Alcumena nor her husband is really guilty of arrogance, but only of their exaggerated faith in human virtue. After all, Amphitryon sees himself as a victorious general, favored by the gods, and his frustration will last only a short space of time, while Alcumena will not only recover her husband's trust, but will give birth to Hercules. Plautus rather than fate has persecuted them. He has made them, for a night, the victims of a superlative performance put on by two divine actors.

LES SOSIES

Rotrou has written an original play in spite of the fact that he has merely adapted the *Amphitruo.* Although his tragicomedy may lack some of the general effectiveness and deftness of Molière's *Amphitryon,* it may well have more real depth and dramatic power than any other comedy written about the birth of Hercules. This judgment will astonish only those readers who regard Jean Rotrou as a minor dramatist. Actually, in dealing with themes such as identity and metamorphosis, Rotrou must have felt perfectly at home, for nothing could have seemed more germane to his baroque world vision, where nothing is as it seems, where even the most solid objects suddenly become subject to change without notice, where the notion of self-identity is often if not usually an illusion, where mankind cannot distinguish between dreaming and waking.[2] And we can therefore expect that Rotrou will go way beyond the simple conflict which opposes the *persona* to the real self. Plautus never questions this so-called real self, or perhaps he merely took it for granted. Rotrou, on the contrary, by refusing to distinguish between reality and appearance, cannot take anything for granted, at least in his capacity as poet and dramatist. And he likes to play with metaphysical notions such as the identity and permanence of the self. In short, the old conflict between the *persona* and the self must now take place within the mind, where it will give rise to an entirely new set of paradoxes and tensions. Whereas Plautus used the stage as his point of departure, Rotrou starts out with a fundamental conflict between inner experience and the outside world, between warring aspects of the self.

This conflict begins quite early in the prologue, which consists of Juno's long monologue. Plautus refers to her only once: Mercury states ironically that if Jupiter's legitimate wife ever suspected the truth, the lord of the gods would willingly change places with Amphitryon for the rest of eternity. From this passing allusion to Juno's vindictive jealousy, Rotrou may have derived the fundamental dramatic idea of his play which we can regard as a prelude to the twelve labors of Hercules: the son of Jupiter and Alcumena will overcome all obstacles in spite of the powerful opposition of this goddess. In her monologue, Juno accuses her divine husband of turning the world upside

[2] We accept M. Jean Rousset's view of the baroque. Cf. *La Littérature de l'âge baroque en France* (Paris: Corti, 1954).

down—a typical baroque theme—of punishing virtue, of rewarding vice. All the mortal mistresses of Jupiter now have their shrine in the heavens, for instance Diana: "Elle occupe le ciel, et m'en voici dehors;" "L'honneur ne conduit plus en ces champs azurés; / Les vices aujourd'hui s'en sont fait les degrés." However, Juno's insane jealousy of Alcmène shows that the gods share many of the weaknesses of human beings. And she focuses her hatred on the still unborn son of Jupiter and Alcmène, Hercules, who, as she foresees, will overcome all his enemies with one exception: "D'autres armes manquant à ma fureur extrême, / Je n'opposerai plus que lui-même à lui-même; / Lui-même il se vaincra ... / Lui-même contre lui servira ma colère." In thus stating that the only invincible enemy Hercules will ever encounter will be himself, Juno obliquely proclaims the transcendent worth of mankind as well as the inevitability of internal conflict. Hercules, everywhere victorious, will have to pay dearly for every triumph: "Sa peine avec usure achètera sa gloire" and "son courage, égal à son malheur." In this manner, both Hercules and Juno, both virtue and courage, become somehow identified with suffering. To the bitter conflicts which continually tear the heavens asunder will correspond the inner conflicts of man. And these conflicts involve moral contradictions, for Juno claims that vice has succeeded in taking the place of virtue.

The idea of moral contradiction, so strong in the prologue, reappears in the first scene, where Mercury invokes Night: "Le rang des vicieux ôte la honte aux vices, / Et donne de beaux noms à de honteux offices." Although Mercury submits to the absolute power of his father, he seems to agree with Juno. He manages to persuade the virgin goddess of Night to advance more slowly: "Tiens le frein aux coureurs qui tirent la litière, / Cependant que mon père, enivré de plaisirs, / Au sein de ses amours le lâche à ses désirs." In this instance, Rotrou is playing on words: *lâcher le frein,* which means to indulge in license, contrasts ironically with chaste Night's control of her horses. Moreover, this pun establishes a relationship—a tension in the strictest sense of the word—between morality (or immorality) and space (or time). Indeed, Rotrou dramatizes much more than Plautus the idea of a suspension of time, which in its turn gives rise to the dissociation between two antagonistic aspects of the self. To Hercules' heroic struggle with the world and with himself will correspond, on the lowest human level, the beatings that Sosie must suffer at the hands of his alter ego, Mercury.

Rotrou, like Plautus, states that Sosie, in his beatings, receives the just retribution of his own faults: "Battons-le de ses traits," says Mercury. Under the circumstances, however, punishment matters much less to Rotrou than the uneven struggle between poor Sosie and his double. When the slave sees Mercury for the first time, he exclaims: "Dieux! quel homme voilà! quel port et quelle taille!" (I, 3). As the god has taken on the appearance of Sosie, the latter's fearful admiration adds a strong ironical note to the scene—a paradox which Rotrou did not find in Plautus. When Mercury approaches, Sosie expresses his growing terror in terms of a loss of identity: "J'ignore qui je suis / En l'état malheureux où mes jours sont réduits." In other words, Sosie expresses his confusion about his own being even before Mercury can launch his first attack against the slave's identity! Paradoxically, these attacks, when they do come, enable the servant to discover his true being or rather his true existence. After the first beating, Sosie does not really renounce his identity: he merely wishes he were someone else. When Mercury asks him: "Sosie?" he replies: "Et plût au Ciel ne le fussé-je pas?" And to the question: "Quel est ton maître?" he answers: "Tu m'as mis en état de ne me plus connaître." Surprising as this may seem, Sosie, after a second beating, asserts his now questionable being with renewed courage:

> Ta fourbe peut bien être un obstacle à mes pas;
> Mais toutes ces raisons ne me changeront pas.
> Je n'emprunte le nom ni la forme d'un autre;
> Je suis le vrai Sosie, et ce logis est nôtre (I, 3).

But his answer serves only to increase the irony of the situation, for Mercury has borrowed *his* name and *his* form.

After the beatings, Mercury attacks Sosie with intellectual weapons, proving that he knows every detail of events that the slave regards as personal secrets. In this, Rotrou follows Plautus quite closely, except in literary expression:

MERCURE: D'un flacon de vin pur ...
SOSIE: Il entre dans la voie.
MERCURE: Près d'un muid frais percé j'allai faire ma proie.
Hardi, je l'assaillis, et lui tirai du flanc
Cette douce liqueur qui tenait lieu de sang.

This warlike description of the act of stealing wine is not to be found in Plautus, but will reappear in Molière's version. Rotrou confuses war with tippling in order to give humorous expression, on the lowest and least dramatic level possible, to the idea of struggle. Sosie, beaten and, worse still, convinced by Mercury's irrefutable arguments, marvels at this miracle as a baroque character should: "En un autre aujourd'hui je me trouve moi-même" and "Moi-même je me fuis, moi-même je me chasse."

Throughout the *Amphitruo*, Sosia, in spite of his complaints, does not really express any feelings of revolt against his slavery. When insulted and threatened by his master to whom he has just recounted his strange encounter with this other Sosia, he says, touchingly: "Amphitruo, miserrima istaec miseria est seruo bono, / Apud erum qui uera loquitur, si id ui uerum uincitur" (590–91). "Amphitryon, the greatest trouble that befalls / An honest servant when he speaks the truth / Is, sure, to find the truth rammed down his throat / And disbelieved." His complaint does not involve his enslaved condition, but the fact that Amphitruo unjustly mistrusts a faithful servant. Rotrou in adapting these two lines completely changes the spirit of the play: "Malheur, Amphitryon, à ceux qui comme moi / Un sort abject et bas rend indignes de foi" (II, 1). Sosie's bitter comment sounds like the cry of the damned, for he has apparently taken it upon himself to speak in the name of the underprivileged, without reference to services rendered. He has gained a dangerous awareness of his condition—an awareness that involves much more than a knowledge of specific humiliations.

Previously, he had gone so far as to assert his debased condition: "Je ne me défendrai d'un traitement si rude / Qu'avecque la vertu qu'enjoint la servitude." He does not actually rebel, but his acceptance of the situation takes the form of a concession, as though to imply that under different circumstances he might call upon a somewhat different type of *vertu* (in a Cornelian sense) diametrically opposed to his present patience.

Sosie relishes the paradoxical situation in which he finds himself much more than Plautus' slave. He even identifies himself with this brutal alter ego who insists on beating him, and he takes pride in this painful achievement. Rotrou's slave definitely has a healthy sense of vanity and pride. He is a man:

> Il m'est pareil de nom, de visage, de port;
> Il m'est conforme en tout, il est grand, il est fort,
> Et m'a de sa valeur rendu des témoignages:
> Enfin je suis doublé; doublez aussi mes gages (II, 1).

This pride in himself transforms him from a Roman slave into a free servant who receives wages, and very nearly into a militant member of the working classes. Rotrou could not resist making this impudent witticism about wages, in flagrant contradiction with Sosie's previous wish, borrowed from Plautus:

> Retournons à mon mâitre.
> Et plût au Ciel aussi qu'il me pût méconnaître!
> De cet heureux malheur naîtrait ma liberté,
> Et ce serait me perdre avec utilité (I, 3).

Sosie, however, is not the only enchained character in the tragi-comedy. In transforming Alcumena's monologue into a dialogue between Alcmène and her confidante Céphalie, Rotrou ascribes the preponderance of pain over pleasure in human existence to a "loi suprême." Alcmène who wonders: "Quel important besoin, quelle nécessité / Enchaîne ainsi la peine à la prospérité?" (II, 3) complains that "ici bas un plaisir s'achète avec usure." In short, Alcmène replaces by a perilous question Alcumena's resignation to the will of the gods: "Ita diuis est placitum." But Plautus' beautifully expressed *lieu commun* has given rise to an important theme in *Les Sosies:* Alcmène, who has to pay so dearly for every advantage, particularly for the happiness of having a famous husband, finds herself in the same predicament as Hercules who will have to pay for his triumphs with blood, sweat, and tears: *travaux,* in both senses of the word—labors and torments. Such is the only ineluctable law of existence: "C'est la première loi des lois de la nature." All other laws, such as those of marriage and, in some respects, the principle of identity, are subject to change and vulnerable to illusion.

Before the intervention of the gods, everything had followed its normal if precarious course and had remained in its accustomed place. Alcmène can therefore refer quite simply to the "loi d'hymen, immuable et sacrée" which entitles her to her place in bed beside her husband. But it so happens that Jupiter has already usurped the place of her spouse; indeed, nobody and nothing can persist in the usual manner either on earth or in the heavens. Like Sosie, Amphitryon, who has just restored law and order in the kingdom, will sink into a state of utter confusion: "Je ne me connais plus; moi-même je m'ignore" and "J'ignore qui je suis, et ne connais personne." Sosie gives a baroque explanation of everything that has happened: "Quelque savant démon, en la magie expert, / Fait qu'ainsi tout se change, et se double et se perd" (II, 3). Moreover, Sosie describes Amphitryon's cuckolding by his own double in terms of a battle: "Ailleurs que dans le camp il s'est porté des coups; / Combattant pour autrui, l'on combattait pour vous." This cruel remark reminds us of an earlier comparison between Sosie's theft of wine and the spilling of blood in mortal combat. Indeed, the entire comedy consists, as we have already suggested, of a series of struggles on the lowest as well as the highest levels, all of them serving as preludes to the great adventures of Hercules. And it so happens that the amorous struggle between Jupiter and Alcmène will soon lead to the miraculous birth of that hero.

The ludicrous doubling of Sosie and his master necessarily corresponds to a separation, a severance. Amphitryon asks for a divorce: "Consens-tu ... à rompre le lien qui joint nos libertés?"

This divorce would probably put Alcmène in a situation similar to that of Juno, who describes herself as: "Sœur du plus grand des dieux (car ce nom seul me reste)"—as the widow of an immortal and eternal husband. Rotrou frequently emphasizes the similarities between the predicament of gods and the situation of mankind, and he shows the repercussions of one realm on the other. We realize that both men and gods are enchained. Mercury submits to Jupiter in much the same way that Sosie obeys Amphitryon. Moreover, these two masters have themselves forsaken their freedom, mastered in their turn by that supreme power, Eros. Jupiter admits as much in the beautiful monologue which opens the third act. He states that it is the god of love who has forced him to undergo all his strange metamorphoses, for instance, "... sous la forme d'or ton pouvoir souverain / M'a fait trouver passage en des portes d'airain." He regards his courting of Alcmène as an "abaissement." Prompted by love, he even consents to play the part of a baroque magician, or of a Circe: "Je suis ce suborneur, ce faux Amphitryon / Qui remplis tout d'erreur et de confusion." But Jupiter himself must undergo a transformation, almost to the point of losing his divine identity, for which he substitutes his temporary identity as a submissive lover. He says to Alcmène:

> Pour moi, si, souverain des dieux et des mortels,
> Je voyais cet objet au pied de mes autels,
> M'en laissant adorer, je croirais faire un crime;
> Je voudrais de son dieu devenir sa victime,
> Et je croirais du prix de la terre et des cieux
> N'acheter pas assez un regard de ses yeux (III, 2).

Because of love, all values human and divine as well as all hierarchies are turned upside down. As though to take advantage of this confusion, Jupiter does not hesitate to reveal in veiled terms his divinity:

> Juge combien l'espoir d'obtenir davantage
> Mettrait donc d'artifice et de soins en usage;
> Et si ni ton époux, ni ta fidélité
> Aux vœux d'un tel rival soustrairait ta beauté (III, 2).

And when the astonished Almène remarks: "Un pareil compliment ne vous est pas commun," Jupiter replies, somewhat ambiguously: "Je ne l'achève pas puisqu'il t'est importun: / Il témoigne en effet un peu de jalousie." How can the audience tell whether Jupiter has just referred with cruel irony to Amphitryon's inevitable jealousy, or whether he has himself become jealous of the real husband. Quite probably, each one must be jealous of the other.

Jupiter and Amphitryon are not, however, completely identical even in their physical appearance. Alcmène senses a difference in Jupiter:

> Si je vous l'ose dire, et si j'en crois mes yeux,
> Le temps qui détruit tout vous est officieux:
> Il semble que ce corps tienne des destinées
> L'heur de ne vieillir pas avecque les années,
> Et ce teint, que les soins ne sauraient altérer,
> Jette un éclat nouveau qui vous fait révérer (III, 3).

The lord of the gods has thus transformed himself into an idealized or an archetypal Amphitryon. In the midst of the general confusion of levels, Rotrou somehow stops short of a complete identification between the human and the divine, between the temporal and the eternal.

A good example of this wilful confusion of levels appears in the coincidence of the drunken revels in heaven with the more stately banquet offered by Jupiter to Amphitryon's officers. Mars himself gets drunk and completely loses his grasp of reality:

> Mars voit, pris comme il est, des troupes d'Encelades
> Qui dans le ciel encor dressent des escalades,
> Et, de son coutelas son ombre poursuivant,
> Au grand plaisir de tous se bat contre du vent (III, 5).

Mars, struggling with his own shadow, finds himself in a situation analogous to that of Sosie, Amphitryon and Hercules. Juno alone refuses to drink because of her jealousy. Mercury tries to explain her attitude: "Ainsi la jalousie a jusque dans le ciel / Dégorgé son poison et répandu son fiel." Drunken revels and jealousy thus bring the gods down to the level of humanity.

This entire description of a divine orgy somehow anticipates the burlesque technique of a Saint-Amant and may even have its source in Ronsard's imaginative account of revelry on Mount Olympus.[3] Mercury will eat and drink his fill at both tables. On earth, he becomes, even in character, exactly like Sosie: "... lorsqu'il s'agit d'un excellent repas, / Mille secrets d'état ne m'arrêteraient pas" (III, 6).

The ethics of heaven, so similar to the morality or immorality of mankind, will finally corrupt even the righteous Amphitryon's sense of values. When, at the end of the play, he learns that Jupiter has condescended to become his rival, his anger quickly subsides:

Ma couche est partagée, Alcmène est infidèle:
Mais l'affront en est doux, et la honte en est belle;
L'outrage est obligeant; le rang du suborneur
Avecque mon injure accorde mon honneur (V, 5).

Amphitryon echoes an earlier statement by Mercury expressed in more cynical terms: "Le rang des vicieux ôte la honte aux vices, / Et donne de beaux noms à de honteux offices" (I, 1). And thus from top to bottom everyone, with the exception of the lowly Sosie, adopts the same submissive or hierarchical attitude, tantamount to the negation of all moral values. But it is a paradoxical negation, at least in the way Amphitryon expresses it: "Alcmène, par un sort à toute autre contraire, / Peut entre ses honneurs conter un adultère; / Son crime la relève, il accroît son renom, / Et d'un objet mortel fait une autre Junon" (V, 6). This paradox very nearly makes the celestial Juno jealous of herself and transforms Jupiter's escapade into a legitimate affair. In short, the earth scarcely differs from heaven, and Rotrou can direct his irony in both directions at the same time. Sosie alone refuses to conform: "On appelle cela lui sucrer le breuvage." He refuses to regard his master's freshly-planted horns as an honor and a privilege. In fact, he considers both the victorious general and himself as victims: "Si le bois nous manquait, les

[3] Pierre de Ronsard, "Hynne de l'hyver," in *Œuvres complètes*, (Paris: Pléiade, 1958), II, 250 ff.

dieux en ont eu soin; / Ils nous en ont chargés, et plus que de besoin." However, he had rather be beaten with a stick than adorn his brow with horns—*bois* in a derivative sense. In this manner, the comedy ends with the devaluation of both hierarchies, that of human leaders and of gods, all of whom find it convenient to act in accordance with status and prestige. They manage to put righteousness on their side even when it happens to dishonor them.

Where, according to Rotrou, can true morality lie if not in hierarchy? How can a man become a hero if he must subordinate honor to rank? On one side, the author shows us the tremendous struggles of Hercules; on the other, the corruption that prevails on earth and in the heavens. Amphitryon partakes of this so-called honor, which frequently is a euphemism for corruption, and of the struggle, wherein lies the very essence of heroism. First Jupiter, then Mercury, and then Jupiter again place him in the same situation as Sosie. Like his servant, he expresses his confusion in baroque terms, particularly in the monologue which opens the fourth act: "Je trouve tout changé, tout ici est confus; / On s'y perd, on s'y double, on ne s'y connaît plus." The world, which previously he had taken for granted, has become the prey of disorder and the image of chaos. Amphitryon has lost his identity: "Dessille-nous les yeux, dissipe ce nuage; / Et rends-moi pour le moins mon nom et mon visage" (IV, 2). And finally our triumphant general will anticipate, if only for a few hours, Hercules' struggle with himself:

> Une guerre où pour vaincre il faut que je succombe,
> Où pour me soutenir le sort veut que je tombe,
> Un prodige, un désordre, une confusion
> Où contre Amphitryon combat Amphitryon;
> Mais plutôt un duel que l'enfer me déclare.
> En deux Amphitryon son pouvoir me sépare (IV, 4).

The hidden divorce in the recesses of his own being which the presence of another Amphitryon externalizes may well provide a clue to the moral meaning of this great comedy. The doubling of the Theban general and of his servant points to a discrepancy in human nature—a discrepancy which appears most clearly in the conflict between hierarchy and honor. Rotrou seems to imply that man himself is a chaos, torn between heroic ideals and expediency. The realm of essence, where Jupiter reigns supreme, is itself slippery, ambiguous, and uncertain, no better perhaps, but only more permanent, than the world we live in. True morality, on the contrary, pertains to action and takes the form of a struggle: it is the awareness that arises from existence and which almost defies conceptual formulations. Amphitryon may esteem himself as a great leader and a good husband, but he is too much the prisoner of his status in the world and of conventional order to attain to this riskier type of morality. True heroism must belong to Hercules and, strange as this may seem, to the lowly Sosie who, at the end of the play, will accede to a more authentic sort of wisdom.

The fifth act opens with the miserable Sosie absorbing another beating at the hands of Mercury: "Je suis mort! au secours! épargnez-moi de grâce. / Sosie! hélas! ta main sur toi-même se lasse! / Tu frappes sur Sosie! Arrête, épargne-toi." And the cruel god's reply serves only to increase the paradox: "Ce passe-temps me plaît; j'aime à frapper sur moi." For the moment at least, the malicious Mercury hardly bothers to deny Sosie's identity. The slave, however, can no longer recognize himself:

> Trêve, au nom de Mercure, à ta valeur extrême!
> Je renonce à mon nom, je renonce à moi-même.
> S'il est vrai que Sosie aime à s'outrager,
> Je ne suis plus Sosie, épargne un étranger (V, 1).

Later in this same scene, when the god asks him whether he still lays claim to the name of Sosie, he replies:

> ... non,
> Battu, froissé, meurtri, ces titres sont mon nom,
> Puisque je n'ai tendons, muscles, veines, artères,
> Où ce nom ne se lise en sanglants caractères;
> Mon nom, nom maudit, dont ton bras est parrain.

Sosie may have renounced his name, but he has discovered himself as a suffering being; he has been newly christened, not with the name of a god or a saint or a sprinkling of holy water, but with heavy fists. Upon Mercury's departure, Sosie flies into a towering rage and, on the basis of his suffering, reaffirms his identity: "Reviens, oui, je soutiens que Sosie est mon nom. / Ah! de quelle fureur est mon âme saisie! / Oui, je suis une, deux, trois, quatre fois Sosie." Then follows a metaphysical struggle with himself which leads to a discovery of his own being, his own existence. We quote this impressive speech almost in its entirety:

> Et je commence enfin, non sans quelque raison,
> A douter qui je suis, d'où, de quelle maison:
> Car pour quel intérêt voudrait m'ôter mon être
> Ce Sosie inconnu qui me fait méconnaître?
> M'envîrai-il un sort dont les fruits les plus doux
> Sont des veilles, des soins, des jeûnes et des coups?
> Non, mon cerveau, troublé de quelque frénésie
> S'est à tort imprimé ce faux nom de Sosie,
> Ce nom qui, malheureux entre tout autre nom,
> Comme l'ambre la paille, attire le bâton.
> Mais quoi! qui suis-je donc? Ah! cette ressemblance
> Tient à tort si longtemps mon esprit en balance:
> Convainquons l'imposture, et conservons mon nom;
> Soyons double Sosie au double Amphitryon.
> Malheureux que je suis, par une loi commune,
> Cherchons le malheureux et suivons sa fortune;
> Compagnon de son sort, partageons son souci;
> S'il périt, périssons; s'il vit, vivons aussi.

His torment, his struggle with his alter ego, his new awareness of his situation in the world have given him insight. And this discovery, based both on experience and on close reasoning, leads him to choose, as though for the first time in his life, his identity—his only possession. And he proposes, as though he were a free man, to remain faithful to the suffering Amphitryon by an act of human solidarity. In so doing, he suddenly becomes a much greater man than the complacent Theban leader who will soon derive prestige as well as material advantages from the divine horns which Jove has already planted on his fertile brow. Sosie, for that very reason, has a right to comment, just before the final curtain: "Cet honneur, ce me semble, est un triste avantage; / On appelle cela lui sucrer le breuvage." Sosie, the former slave, has become a more authentic moralist than his masters, human or even divine. And we can compare his protracted struggle with Mercury to Jacob's struggle with the angel.

AMPHITRYON

The plot of Molière's *Amphitryon* differs from the comedies of Plautus and Rotrou mainly because of the introduction of a new character: Cléanthis, wife of Sosie. This addition allows Molière to use one of his favorite tricks: parallel scenes between masters and servants. The invention of a new character will matter, however, in still another respect, for Molière will emphasize throughout his play the idea of marriage. *Amphitryon* is essentially a play about matrimony—about young and middle-aged couples, about husbands, wives, and lovers. The attitude which predominates is cynical, urbane, and witty; so much so that the reader sometimes has the impression, increased by the author's skilful use of *vers libres* that La Fontaine may have influenced Molière in this particular work.

Unlike Rotrou, Molière has by no means written a "metaphysical" comedy. As usual, he has concerned himself much more with human relations than with man's fate. Molière's Sosie, just like Rotrou's servant, returns to his master after having received, in his own kitchen, a final beating at the hands of Mercury; but instead of returning as an equal, if not in rank at least in manhood, he immediately humiliates himself:

> Je viens, Monsieur, subir à vos genoux,
> Le juste châtiment d'une audace maudite.
> Frappez, battez, chargez, accablez-moi de coups,
>   Tuez-moi dans votre courroux:
>   Vous ferez bien, je le mérite,
> Et je n'en dirai pas un seul mot contre vous (1846–51).

Even in his humiliation he shows cleverness, for he adopts precisely the attitude and chooses exactly the tone of voice that will mollify his master. Mercury's big stick has by no means changed him, for he continues to act like a slave. If anything, he has become more servile, as though the gods had punished him for shirking his duties as a faithful footman. He has not, however, lost his impudence:

> La rigueur d'un pareil destin,
> Monsieur, aujourd'hui nous talonne;
> Et l'on me des-Sosie enfin
> Comme on vous dés-Amphitryonne (1858-61).

His play on words implies only that destiny operates on different levels. Their fate may have certain similarities, but their relationship will always remain that of servant and master, and their common humanity cannot, as in Rotrou's comedy, constitute a bond between them.

Molière's characters remain the eternal prisoners of their status, of their *état civil,* of their past, of their instincts or habits, whether they be gods like Mercury, or slaves, like Sosie. But the power that imprisons them, and which they apparently cannot elude, has no real validity or meaning. From the very beginning of the comedy, the author makes fun of these so-called ineluctable laws, of these great authorities which force men as well as gods to act against their desires. Already in the prologue we see that Mercury willy-nilly must submit to various forms of constraint. He obeys his master Jupiter to the point of exhaustion, as he humorously complains to Night:

> Ma foi! me trouvant las, pour ne pouvoir fournir
> Aux différents emplois où Jupiter m'engage,
> Je me suis doucement assis sur ce nuage,
>   Pour vous attendre venir (7-10).

Mercury talks like an underling. Even before his metamorphosis he resembles Sosie, who also acts as a messenger and general factotum. Night, shocked by Mercury's words, reminds him of another type of constraint: *bienséances:* "Sied-il bien à des

Dieux de dire qu'ils sont las?" (12). When Mercury retorts:
"Les Dieux sont-ils de fer?" the goddess admonishes him: "Non;
mais il faut sans cesse / Garder le *décorum* de la divinité." The
dramatist alludes very cleverly not only to literary *bienséances,*
which prevent gods and kings from using, in a self-respecting
play, so base a term as *las,* but also to the social status of aristocrats, who, whatever else they do, should at least keep up appearances.

Mercury is a prisoner of still another convention, that of
poetry. He complains to Night:

> Et je ne puis vouloir, dans mon destin fatal,
> > Aux poëtes assez de mal
> > De leur impertinence extrême,
> > D'avoir, par une injuste loi,
> > Dont on veut maintenir l'usage,
> > A chaque Dieu, dans son emploi,
> > Donné quelque allure en partage,
> > Et de me laisser à pied, moi,
> > Comme un messager de village,
> Moi, qui suis, comme on sait, en terre et dans les cieux,
> Le fameux messager du souverain des Dieux (24–34).

He mixes, in his ludicrous complaint, the burlesque with the
mock-heroic style. The humor of these lines stems not only from
the mingling of literary genres, but from still another kind of
hybrid; for Mercury appears, in his own words, as a mere
figment of the poetic imagination and at the same time as a
being capable of criticizing poets for their lack of pertinence.
We see him, in the final analysis, as the creature of two creators
—of the writer and of the sovereign of the gods. And obviously,
neither of his masters allows him much freedom to do what
he wants. Poets, however, ironically enjoy a measure of freedom
or at least license. Night comments: "Les poëtes font à leur
guise: / Ce n'est pas la seule sottise / Qu'on voit faire à ces
Messieurs-là" (40–42). In a sense, Mercury has become a prisoner of his own imaginary identity, imposed on him by all
those purposeful poets and their trite conventions.

Molière makes even Jupiter a prisoner of his rank and of his identity; and this constraint explains why the master of the gods does his best to escape now and then to earth. As Mercury gaily remarks, Jupiter "aime à s'humaniser pour des beautés mortelles" (56). The divine messenger easily justifies his master's propensities:

> Il n'est point, à mon gré, de plus sotte méthode
> Que d'être emprisonné toujours dans sa grandeur;
> Et surtout aux transports de l'amoureuse ardeur
> La haute qualité devient fort incommode.
> Jupiter, qui sans doute en plaisirs se connaît,
> Sait descendre du haut de sa grandeur suprême;
> Et pour entrer dans tout ce qu'il lui plaît
> Il sort tout à fait de lui-même,
> Et ce n'est plus alors Jupiter qui paraît (84–92).

If Jupiter so enjoys metamorphoses and, paradoxically, condescends to transform himself into a husband, it is merely to escape his own tiresome identity with its eternal *decorum*. But these escapades rarely last very long; and both Olympus and the Earth can count on Jupiter's prompt return to his "real" identity and, no doubt, to his usual boredom. Identity and rank have a repulsive air of permanence if not of impenetrability, as any self-respecting prison should.

When prudish Night accuses Mercury, in veiled terms, of pimping for Jupiter, he retorts, cynically:

> Pour une jeune déesse,
> Vous êtes bien du bon temps!
> Un tel emploi n'est bassesse
> Que chez les petites gens.
> Lorsque dans un haut rang on a l'heur de paroître,
> Tout ce qu'on fait est toujours bel et bon;
> Et suivant ce qu'on peut être,
> Les choses changent de nom (124–31).

It scarcely matters whether or not the actual names of these activities change anything morally; for these names depend upon rank and status, which we may regard, at least in the present context, as equivalent to being. Thus Molière, for satirical purposes, has subordinated everything to social importance, to hierarchy. In this manner, morality as such must depend, for its very existence, on social identity and position. Absolute standards have long since become an archaic nuisance, good for the "bon temps" which misanthropes like Alceste can admire from a distance. Later in the play, Sosie will confirm this moral trend by proclaiming rank as the supreme standard or criterion:

> Tous les discours sont des sottises,
> Partant d'un homme sans éclat;
> Ce seroit paroles exquises
> Si c'étoit un grand qui parlât (839–42).

Rank must therefore prevail over all other values—over morality, which many of Molière's contemporaries regarded as an absolute; over reason and truth, for the status of the speaker matters ever so much more than what he has to say or what he chooses to do. At the *dénouement,* the supremacy of Jupiter will excuse adultery in the eyes of everyone concerned—everyone except Sosie who obviously belongs to that innocuous category known as "petites gens," or small fry: "Le Seigneur Jupiter sait dorer la pilule." Thus hierarchy possesses, at least on the level of the gods, who are at times its victims, the value of an absolute; it tends to debase morality as well as reason and to enchain or petrify all human relations. The ambiguity of this situation lies in the attitude of the public or, for that matter, in the attitude of the author himself. On the one hand, we view with mixed emotions the subordination of values to the accidents of social prestige; on the other, we grudgingly admit that hierarchy ensures a measure of moral freedom or at least license by allowing indulgence in pleasures—including of course Molière's own comedies which required the court's approval or the King's enjoyment in order to be performed at all, and that in the teeth of ecclesiastical resistance.

Morality itself can constitute an hermetic type of prison, particularly for Cléanthis, the most inhibited character in the play. This Cléanthis is the very embodiment of a prudish, henpecking wife. And when Mercury, impersonating her miserable husband, Sosie, comments: "J'aime mieux un vice commode / Qu'une fatigante vertu" (681–82), Cléanthis, in her impotence, can only exclaim: "J'enrage d'être honnête femme!" (688). In the presence of her real husband, she expresses more explicitly the same frustrating sentiment: "Si je puis une fois pourtant / Sur mon esprit gagner la chose ..." (1194–95). On the classical stage, it usually takes resolution to do one's duty and abide by the dictates of higher morality; but in the present play, it requires even more resolution to rush in the opposite direction and abandon oneself to license, at least when one belongs, like Cléanthis, to those "petites gens," enslaved to their good habits. We hardly can consider Sosie, who obviously belongs to the small fry, as a prisoner of his good habits; but we may regard him as a slave of his own essence which, unlike his namesake in Rotrou's comedy, he cannot change. This essence is cowardice. Beaten by Mercury, he retorts: "Tu triomphes de l'avantage / Que te donne sur moi mon manque de courage" (370–71). Later in the scene, he will express a similar attitude: "Que son bonheur est extrême / De ce que je suis poltron!" (402–03). Cowardice happens to be the law of his nature against which, do what he may, he cannot react. And nature or perhaps destiny has made this essence an integral and recognizable part of his identity. His humiliation before Amphitryon shows that he will never escape his inferiority, which usually takes the form of cowardice. Probably the bitterest and most ludicrous expression of his identity appears in his answer to Mercury's question: "Hé bien! es-tu Sosie à présent? qu'en dis-tu?" (379): "Tes coups n'ont point en moi fait de métamorphose; / Et tout le changement que je trouve à la chose, / C'est d'être Sosie battu" (380–82). Unfortunately for Sosie, identity had something very solid and permanent about it in Molière's day, as opposed to its instability during the previous period. Sosie will ask his tormentor: "Etre ce que je suis est-il en ta puissance? / Et puis-je cesser d'être moi?" (426–27).

As a result of this state of permanence, which tends to make the individual a perpetual slave of his own nature, Sosie remains even more distinct from his persecutor than his namesakes in

Plautus or Rotrou. This distinctness manifests itself even in the scene where Sosie shows inordinate pride and vanity at the prowess of his other self. He boasts to Amphitryon:

> Le moi que j'ai trouvé tantôt
> Sur le moi qui vous parle a de grands avantages:
> Il a le bras fort, le cœur haut;
> J'en ai reçu des témoignages ... (801–04).

In order to describe this other self he merely emphasizes its differences with his own cowardly being: "ce moi plus robuste que moi" and, especially, "ce moi vaillant, dont le courroux / Au moi poltron s'est fait connoître" (811; 815–16). Rotrou had avoided such absolute distinctions. His Sosie had boasted: "Il m'est conforme en tout, il est grand, il est fort, / Et m'a de sa valeur rendu des témoignages" (II, 1). Rotrou's Sosie may have acted at one time or another in a cowardly manner, but his so-called cowardice was no more than an accident or a temporary reaction to a given situation, but never an indelible aspect of his being. As such, his cowardice under certain circumstances does not preclude courage in another situation. Molière's servant, on the contrary, can in no way escape his *poltronnerie* or really identify himself with this superior being who has repeatedly beaten him.

The various characters in *Amphitryon* stay prisoners not only of their own nature, but of human institutions or, in other words, of their social essence or public image. Marriage for obvious reasons is frequently equated, as an institution, with incarceration, even by those people who regard it with favor. The happily-married Alcmène refers to matrimony as "les nœuds d'un hyménée / Qui me tient à vous enchaînée" (1043–44), in spite of the fact that throughout the play she refuses to distinguish in Jupiter-Amphitryon between the husband and the lover. Cléanthis refers to marriage as an obligation. She reproaches her husband with his refusal "de prendre au lit la place / Que les lois de l'hymen t'obligent d'occuper" (1134–35). Quite understandably, Jupiter, unlike Alcmène, insists on distinguishing between the husband and the lover. It was the husband alone who accused her of adultery: "A son dur procédé l'époux s'est

fait connoître, / Et par le droit d'hymen il s'est cru tout permis"
(1315–16). We must agree that, in this particular instance,
Jupiter has told her nothing but the truth.

In the prologue, Mercury had expressed some astonishment
at the nature of his master's impersonation:

> Mais, près de maint objet chéri,
> Pareil déguisement seroit pour ne rien faire,
> Et ce n'est pas partout un bon moyen de plaire
> Que la figure d'un mari (72–75).

Jupiter's strange disguise has some justification, at least in
Molière's version, where war has rudely interrupted Alcmène's
honeymoon with an apparently youthful conqueror. He might
have chosen a likelier travesty in the *Amphitruo*, for Plautus
refers to the Theban general as "senex," or even in *Les Sosies,*
where Alcmène suddenly notices that her spouse looks younger
than usual. This chronological change saves the day for Molière,
who requires above all the incompatibility between pleasure and
institutions: "L'état des mariés à ses feux est propice: / L'hymen
ne les a joints que depuis quelques jours" (66–67). Sosie and
Cléanthis, on the contrary, have been married some fifteen years.

Jupiter, however, regrets that, in order to obtain the good
graces of the beautiful Alcmène, he must play the part of husband and thus institutionalize his pleasures as though he had not
left heaven. He therefore tries to persuade Alcmène to look upon
him as a lover and forget the husband.

> Mais l'amant seul me touche, à parler franchement,
> Et je sens, près de vous, que le mari le gêne.
> Cet amant, de vos yeux jaloux au dernier point,
> Souhaite qu'à lui seul votre cœur s'abandonne,
> Et sa passion ne veut point
> De ce que le mari lui donne.
> Il veut de pure source obtenir vos ardeurs,
> Et ne veut rien tenir des nœuds de l'hyménée,
> Rien d'un fâcheux devoir qui fait agir les cœurs (591–99).

He wishes only that "l'amant ait tout l'amour et toute la tendresse"
(607). Poor Amphitryon, by a sort of dramatic compensation,
is cast throughout in the unenviable part of husband. Even in

his first words to Alcmène, he by no means plays the part of lover: "Fasse le Ciel qu'Amphitryon vainqueur / Avec plaisir soit revu de sa femme" (851–52). This statement is psychologically out of place, for why should he give expression at this triumphant moment to the possibility that his wife might not rejoice at his return? Dramatically, however, his strange wish fits the situation perfectly, for Amphitryon must never behave in the same manner as Jupiter the great seducer. Moreover, Molière has packed a lot of irony into the words: "Fasse le Ciel," for the sovereign of the gods has just accomplished the opposite of what poor Amphitryon has a right to expect. It would seem that Alcmène alone fails or refuses to differentiate between husbands and lovers. She refers to Jupiter's need to distinguish between these two categories as a "nouveau scrupule" (579), a comic term in this particular instance for it introduces the idea of ethics where morality definitely does not belong. Moreover, the god and the general appear to move in opposite directions, because the former's ambition to owe as little as possible to "hyménée" coincides with the latter's obligation to play to the hilt the part of the injured husband so early in his marriage. Both attitudes reveal in quite different ways a thematic opposition to duties and to institutions that by their very nature take all the pleasure out of existence. Indeed, the sight of Amphitryon's injured dignity as opposed to Jupiter's lyrical expressions of love—borrowed in part from Don Garcie de Navarre's impassioned speeches in *Le Prince jaloux*—shows the artistic superiority of illicit love-making over the legitimate variety.

Amphitryon does not differ from Rotrou's *Les Sosies* only in the meaning of identity and in the stress placed upon imprisonment (as opposed to the emphasis on self-knowledge), but also in the importance attributed to art and the theater. Molière remains faithful to Plautus in this respect, for his comedy starts out with a discussion of the habits of poets and of the *bienséances* of literary language. Mercury, Jupiter, and all the mortals involved in the legend are no more than figments of the poetic imagination. Sosie's last speech, which parallels Mercury's prologue, becomes a sort of epilogue; as such, it does not really pertain to the action of the comedy:

> Mais enfin coupons aux discours,
> Et que chacun chez soi doucement se retire.
> Sur telles affaires, toujours
> Le meilleur est de ne rien dire (1940–43).

Sosie gives this bit of advice to Naucratès and the other partici-
pants in the divine cuckolding of his master; but at the same
time he addresses himself to the audience, which we may regard
as the knowing accomplice of both Jupiter and the author. The
sophisticated Sosie implies that although we may not openly criticize what has just taken place and although we cannot change
the world or even ourselves, we may at least appreciate and perhaps enjoy the situation without becoming anyone's dupes. Understanding leads at best to amusement for the public, but for
Molière, it leads to authorship and performance. Jupiter and his
crowned representatives on earth may dispose of more effective
means in their pursuit of happiness or, at least, of diversion: "pour
entrer dans tout ce qu'il lui plait / Il sort tout à fait de lui-même"
(90–91), but fundamentally they behave in the same manner
as the dramatist and the humblest audience.

Molière's downtrodden Sosie will seek compensation in playing a part and even in writing a play, for he transforms into a
dramatic dialogue events in which he had not exactly distin-
guished himself by his valor. Plautus' and even Rotrou's Sosie
rehearse the story of the battle before attempting to enter the
house as messengers. Molière's hero does much more than that,
for he dramatizes the whole thing, puts Alcmène into the show
(as audience), and behaves at the same time like an appreciative
public by enjoying the recounting of his own accomplishments.
Through drama, he has transformed the world and his own experience; he need not, therefore, change himself or even rebel
inwardly at his own fate. The pride of Rotrou's servant is thus
reduced to auctorial vanity by Molière. The new Sosie emerges
as a complete man of the theater. And one of his first actions in
the play consists in setting the stage:

> Pour jouer mon rôle sans peine,
> Je le veux un peu repasser.
> Voici la chambre où j'entre en courrier que l'on mène,

Et cette lanterne est Alcmène,
A qui je me dois adresser (200–04).

When the imaginary Alcmène asks him what her husband has accomplished, she receives this answer: "Il dit moins qu'il ne fait, Madame, / Et fait trembler les ennemis." Surprised at his own heroic cliché, Sosie remarks: "(Peste! où prend mon esprit toutes ces gentillesses?)" (226). At that point, the slave becomes a self-complacent man of letters, revelling in his own genius, as later on he will marvel at the valiant behavior of the other Sosie. His dramatization leads him to suggest that he has played a heroic part in the battle. His imaginary prowess satisfies him completely, for he can identify himself with a heroic being without really losing touch with his own identity. Such is the vicarious enjoyment of literary creation that he will take pleasure in recounting his own persecution at the hands of Mercury, for this more robust and more courageous alter ego behaves precisely like the Sosie he might himself have invented in a daydream. And he suffers much less from his beatings than Rotrou's slave; in fact, he can joke about his *bastonnade:* "Ah! qu'est-ceci? grands Dieux! il frappe un ton plus fort, / Et mon dos, pour un mois, en doit être malade" (522–23). The tonal quality attributed to the intensity of Mercury's blows takes the spectator's attention away from the idea of suffering. Moreover, Sosie himself cannot have suffered too much, for, at least in this remark, he behaves like a spectator, whose involvement in the procedings falls short of completeness. Throughout the comedy, we see him simultaneously as a participant and as a witness. For instance, when Amphitryon, who refuses to credit his strange tale, grumbles: "Le moyen d'en rien croire, à moins qu'être insensé?" (777), he agrees: "Je ne l'ai pas cru, moi, sans une peine extrême: / Je me suis d'être deux senti l'esprit blessé." This remarkable alexandrine reveals that Sosie has become the unwilling but appreciative spectator of his own doubling.

In conclusion, and with the help of hindsight, we can say that *Amphitryon* is precisely the sort of comedy that a skeptical genius would write about identity in a period when social positions had become momentarily crystallized. In order to play their parts, the courtiers and even the King himself unavoidably required a minimum of complacency, or suspension of disbelief, on the part of their far-flung and teeming audiences. Obviously, *Amphitryon* did not by any means contribute to this state of complacency. In its own special way, it is almost as subversive as *Les Sosies*.

16

The Legalistic Mind

*A*FTER HIS VERSE PLAY about matrimony, Molière wrote besides *L'Avare* two *comédies-ballets* in prose, the former dealing with misalliance, the latter with a marriage which, fortunately, fails to take place. In *George Dandin,* only the title character participates both in the play and in the ballet. Rather, the dancers carry him away as a somewhat recalcitrant spectator. The title character in *Monsieur de Pourceaugnac* not only must let himself be carried away by dancers, but he must continually suffer their persecutions, particularly in the scene where dancing apothecaries pursue him with their clysters. Moreover, the plebeian Dandin and the noble Pourceaugnac have one thing in common: innocuousness combined with a legalistic mind.

GEORGE DANDIN: LUCIDITY

Unlike the Sganarelle of *L'Ecole des maris,* or Orgon, Dandin refuses to blind himself to reality or to assert, like Arnolphe, a fanciful system of his own making. Reduced by his isolation to confide in an unsympathetic audience, he behaves like a fairly intelligent, normally-constituted member of the Tiers Etat. He is never guilty of the slightest aberration, and we may regard him as the most "average" person among Molière's entire repertory of clownish victims. Poor Dandin has lost all his illusions about his marriage long before the play opens. He realizes that he has made the worst possible mistake by marrying into a family of impoverished gentry. He has no one but himself to blame for this abysmal failure. In this respect, we might possibly regard his self-criticism as obsessive, for he frequently repeats to himself such statements as "Vous l'avez voulu, vous l'avez voulu, George Dandin, vous l'avez voulu ..." (I, 7).

As the victim has nothing more to learn about marriage, his various tribulations in the course of the play will merely confirm his awareness of defeat. From the very beginning, he actually expects the worst to happen. His very lucidity makes him a figure of fun by transforming him into a futile and impotent spectator of his own misfortunes. At the *dénouement*, Molière will save him from despair by forcing him to watch, as a reluctant participant, a more enjoyable spectacle: a ballet which replaces reality by illusion.

George Dandin, like Arnolphe, discovers each new misfortune practically at the moment it occurs. He owes this ironical advantage to a blunderer who confides in him. As a result, he possesses more than enough evidence to confound his wife. Unfortunately, he must contend with the blindness of his wife's parents who refuse to see the obvious. Unlike the hero of *L'Ecole des femmes,* he never attempts to prevent the inevitable from happening, but tries to convince two wilfully stupid people of his shame. And George Dandin is isolated from the other characters, not only because of his misalliance, but also by reason of his incapacity to make another person share his knowledge and take his side. This isolation explains in part his efforts to enlist the sympathy of the audience.

Lubin, the oaf who reveals to Dandin the latest conspiracy against him, is in the pay of the lover, Clitandre. He makes the unhappy husband see himself in a most unfavorable light as a repulsive *jaloux*. Lubin shares the blindness of the Sotenvilles, but for different reasons. It never enters his thick head that this bystander to whom he has told the story of Dandin's impending horns might turn out to be Dandin himself. In their second meeting, Lubin, none the wiser, accuses the victim of having betrayed his confidence by blurting out the whole story to the husband. At the very instant when he refuses to confide in him, he lets the cat out of the bag: "Point d'affaire. Vous voudriez que je vous disse que Monsieur le Vicomte vient de donner de l'argent à Claudine, et qu'elle l'a mené chez sa maîtresse. Mais je ne suis pas si bête" (II, 5). Horace had at least the excuse of Arnolphe's double identity; but the bumpkin has only himself to blame.

He participates in the action, but he appears to derive so much enjoyment from Dandin's cuckolding, that we must consider him not only as an accessory but as an enthusiastic spectator who, in order to increase his pleasure, needs other people to share it: "Testiguiéne! cela sera drôle; car le mari ne se doutera pas de la manigance, voilà ce qui est de bon; et il aura un pied de nez avec sa jalousie: est-ce pas?" (I, 2). The stupid Lubin has some justification in regarding Dandin as a bystander, for the latter has become so estranged from his own household and from his marital rights that nobody would take him for Angélique's husband. The yokel's blindness thus suggests an important truth concerning Dandin's situation, or lack of situation.

The protagonist frequently insists on his lucidity, not only in his monologues, where he has the benefit or rather the disadvantage of hindsight, but in his quarrels with Angélique, e.g., in the second scene of Act II: "J'ai de meilleurs yeux qu'on ne pense, et votre galimatias ne m'a point tantôt ébloui ... Au travers de toutes vos grimaces, j'ai vu la vérité de ce que l'on m'a dit .... Mon Dieu! nous voyons clair." Moreover, he boasts that he can read Angélique's mind: "Je sais votre pensée, et connois ..." But during most of this scene the lucid cuckold fails to see Clitandre and he therefore misunderstands Angélique's frantic gestures. This temporary blindness serves perhaps as an ironical commentary on his painfully-acquired lucidity—a lucidity which can no longer help him.

Dandin does his utmost to transform the Sotenvilles into witnesses. At a critical moment, he tells them, breathlessly and almost jubilantly: "... j'ai en main de quoi vous faire voir comme elle m'accomode, et, Dieu Merci! mon déshonneur est si clair maintenant, que vous n'en pourrez plus douter" (II, 7). When these promising appearances finally turn against him, he exclaims: "O Ciel, seconde mes desseins, et m'accorde la grâce de faire voir aux gens que l'on me déshonore" (II, 8). Thus, he prays for the clear-sightedness of others when most cuckolds would sell their souls in order to ensure the blindness of the rest of humanity. Obviously, Dandin does not behave like a gentleman.

Molière dramatizes the theme of blindness by staging the final act in almost total darkness. Even then, Dandin maintains his lucidity; and he moves with a fair degree of ease among the benighted characters who do not even suspect his presence. When Lubin remarks to Clitandre: "Morgué! voilà une sotte nuit, d'être si noire que cela" (III, 1), the lover shows too much optimism in his reply: "Elle a tort assurément; mais si d'un côté elle nous empêche de voir, elle empêche de l'autre que nous ne soyons vus." Indeed, Dandin did not exaggerate when he boasted of his good eyesight. True, he bumps into his servant Colin; but we cannot really blame the hero, for Colin happens to be walking in his sleep. Dandin's lucidity is, of course, limited or perhaps specialized: although he does not see his servant or, in a previous scene, Clitandre, he does manage to perceive and overhear more than enough to confirm his clear appraisal of the situation. For instance, he does not miss any of Angélique's or Clitandre's disparaging remarks about himself. In his asides, instead of expressing his own private emotions, he universalizes his predicament as well as the behavior of wives: "Voilà nos carognes de femmes" and "Pauvres maris! voilà comme on vous traite." We might expect such remarks from an audience, sympathetic to Dandin's misfortune, but certainly not from the victim himself. But these asides have further implications, which we shall discuss in the second part of the chapter: Dandin is actually giving a *lesson* to the audience.

When Dandin feels that he has at last cornered his wife, he uses terms such as *éclaircir, éclater, éblouir, voir, convaincre*, in referring to her parents; and he adds *confusion* and especially *confondu*, a word which appears in the subtitle. Now, *confondu* does not only mean that Angélique has fooled Dandin, but that she has refuted him, as though she had gotten the upper hand in an argument or in a philosophical discussion. Although Dandin has the truth on his side, his wife will succeed in turning the tables on him by a trick—by pretending suicide. In a sense, the hero is hoisted by his own lucidity. Believing his wife capable of any crime, he half suspects that she has done herself in out of revenge: "Ouais! seroit-elle bien si malicieuse que de s'être tuée pour me faire pendre? Prenons un bout de chandelle pour aller voir" (III, 6). The symbol of the lighted candle heightens the irony of the situation. By this action, Dandin somehow over-reaches himself, for Angélique has prepared a much simpler and more childish trick: that of enticing him out of the house in order to take his place. In the following scene, the Sotenvilles' cecity will attain synesthesic heights: they will actually believe Angélique's accusations that their sober son-in-law has been out drinking all night: "Fi! ne m'approchez pas: votre haleine est empestée" (III, 7).

Angélique has so much trust in her parents' blindness that she does not even attempt to hide the truth—a truth that her lover, her servant and, of course, her husband understand perfectly. When Clitandre asks her: "Est-ce donc vous, Madame, qui avez dit à votre mari que je suis amoureux de vous?" she blurts out: "Vous n'avez qu'à y venir, je vous promets que vous serez reçu comme il faut" (I, 6). She of course realizes that her answer will sound like a complete rejection of Clitandre's welcome advances. Dandin, whom she has openly defied, can only watch and protest helplessly.

GEORGE DANDIN: THE LESSON

Traditionally, critics have tried to discern in almost every comedy of Molière some sort of moral lesson. Molière has only himself to blame in this respect, for he did not hesitate to invoke in self-defense the old *utile dulci* principle. The controversy concerning the didactic intentions of *George Dandin* has been particularly acute. Some readers have frowned on the author for having dared to stage an (impending) adultery; others have praised him for his realism, without which he could not have revealed the dire results of misalliance. But must we accuse Molière of immorality or, worse still, of didacticism? After all, the perils of misalliance are an accepted cliché, particularly in a century that believed so strongly in social hierarchy. Moreover, Molière has somewhat weakened the import of his so-called lesson by choosing so bourgeois a character as Dandin as a caution to social climbers, for the latter usually ape the aristocracy before they decide to marry into it. It therefore seems more likely that the author has purposely used a moral commonplace so that the misadventures of his hero would *appear* as a demonstration, thus killing any inclination on the part of the audience to sympathize with him as a human being. Indeed, you cannot expect a sophisticated audience to identify itself with a case history.

The shrewd Dandin would never have married into the Sotenville family. Unlike Monsieur Jourdain, he has no aristocratic pretensions worth mentioning. Indeed, Molière describes him as a rich peasant rather than as a bourgeois. Moreover, he appears to possess that quality which La Rochefoucauld praised so highly: he knows "le prix des choses." Throughout the play, the author stresses to the point of caricature the social differences between the rich countryman and the impoverished squires. In Dandin, he has created the least noble character imaginable, both from the standpoint of language and behavior—in short, the perfect foil for the Sotenvilles, who are completely obsessed with their blue blood. Scholars have noted Dandin's use of homey proverbs as well as terms of commerce, e.g., "Marchand qui perd ne peut rire" (II, 7), as opposed to the Sotenvilles' preference for expressions borrowed from heraldry and feudal customs: "Jour de Dieu! je l'étranglerois de mes propres mains, s'il falloit qu'elle forlignât de l'honnêteté de sa mère" (I, 4). Obviously, the Dandins and the Sotenvilles cannot possibly have anything in common, Angélique notwithstanding.

Dandin complains that his marriage, so profitable to the Sotenvilles, has never brought him anything but misery and the stretching of his name to La Dandinnière. He dares not even call his wife "ma femme" or his mother-in-law "belle mère," for his social inferiority will not allow him to use terms indicative of equality in addressing people of noble birth, even though he "belongs" to their family. His wife complains that nobody asked her consent to this marriage, adding: "... ce sont eux proprement qui vous ont épousé, et c'est pourquoi vous ferez bien de vous plaindre toujours à eux des torts que l'on pourra vous faire" (II, 2). Angélique insists on considering her marriage merely a transaction between Dandin and her parents. As she had no choice in the matter, she refuses to assume her matrimonial responsibilities. Her interpretation of the proceedings appears all the more ludicrous because everything, with the exception of a legal document, separates the plebeian Dandin from her aristocratic parents. They have legally contracted a non-marriage, that has served only to separate poor Dandin from his own class while estranging him still further from the aristocracy. When he pleads with his wife, it is not to obtain her affection, but only to persuade her to live up to the contract—to those "engagements de la foi que vous m'avez donnée publiquement" (II, 2). He does not expect anything for himself—for his own human merits. Although his plight may or may not serve as a warning to social climbers, it does seem to arise from a false identification between human values and legal contracts: a substitution which has frequently tempted the middle-classes. Dandin's legalistic obscuration of his humanity runs afoul of a quite different type of inhumanity on the part of the Sotenvilles: their pedantic obsession with aristocratic codes. In short, two legalistic or essentialistic approaches to existence meet head on; and we can hardly blame Angélique for seeking compensations elsewhere. Dandin wishes to obtain a legal separation from Angélique that would be to his advantage; but Angélique requires only a *de facto* separation which gives her complete freedom without endangering her reputation or jeopardizing the material benefits which she and her family have derived from her misalliance.

If *George Dandin* does contain a lesson, it is perhaps the proof by the absurd of the superiority of human values over words and documents. The play contains, however, a lesson in quite a different sense—a sense that anticipates Ionesco's use of the word in the title of one of his comedies. In the idea of giving a lesson or, conversely, of receiving one, we have one of the preponderant themes of the work. With the exception of terms referring to lucidity, blindness, and money, words such as *leçon* and *apprendre* appear to be the most obtrusive. In the opening monologue, Dandin describes his marriage as a "leçon bien parlante" for peasants who seek to marry aristocrats. He fancies himself a living demonstration or a living emblem of this truth. In this manner, he combines within himself the functions of chief participant, principal spectator, and object lesson, e.g., "Pauvres maris! Voilà comme on vous traite." The term *voilà*, here and elsewhere in the play, could hardly carry more demonstrative weight.

Dandin not only sees himself in the unenviable role of object lesson, but he repeatedly receives lessons of a different sort from the pedantic Sotenvilles. They insist on teaching their son-in-law how to behave. They treat the middle-class and probably middle-aged Dandin like a child who has to be scolded whenever his manners fail to conform to the behavior they expect from an inferior who has married into their family. In giving Dandin, early in the play, his first lesson in etiquette, Monsieur de Sotenville twice uses the word *apprenez*. Later, he advises his son-in-law to accept his guidance and take his orders. Worse still, he forces him to ask Clitandre's pardon, ordering him to repeat verbatim his words: "Répétez après moi ..." (I, 6), as though he were giving orders to a naughty boy. At the *dénouement,* he will make Dandin kneel down before Angélique and repeat: "Madame, je vous prie de me pardonner ... l'extravagance que j'ai faite ..." and Dandin will add, in an aside: "de vous épouser," which is precisely the sort of remark that a bad boy, punished for some misdeed, might utter under his breath. The implications of this lesson or dictation are not entirely didactic, for we witness the complete humiliation of the hero. His social inferiority, by way of a lesson, leads to the negation of his manhood. In the presence of the aristocratic Sotenvilles, this adult member of the Third Estate, this wealthy landowner, this successful businessman, becomes a mere child, despite the fact that he has rescued them from poverty.

Dandin is not the only character who receives a lesson and acts like a child. In the second scene, when Lubin blurts out the truth to Dandin, he acts as though he were reciting a lesson learned by heart: "Elle m'a dit de lui dire ... attendez, je ne sais si je me souviendrai bien de tout cela ... qu'elle lui est tout à fait obligée de l'affection qu'il a pour elle ..." In short, Dandin receives the necessary information from a childish person who tries rather lamely to recite what a superior has told him. Lubin, by this childish behavior, becomes a mocking echo of Dandin. He even tells Clitandre about the things he has just learned or that he understands without having had to learn them. And he asks his master: "Je voudrois bien savoir, Monsieur, vous qui êtes savant, pourquoi il ne fait point jour la nuit" (III, 1). Then follow other absurd remarks, all of them referring to study and to lessons. He uses the word *apprendre* twice. Lubin wants to marry the clever Claudine, who will certainly make him wear horns as conspicuous as those of the wealthier and better-educated Dandin. Molière might well have entitled this play: *L'Ecole des Cocus*. Indeed, the subtitle of this comedy: *Le Mari confondu* suggests adultery and even the idea of a lesson.

MONSIEUR DE POURCEAUGNAC

In this particular play, Molière reverts to the slapstick techniques of his early farces and comes as close as possible to "pure entertainment." In any case, moral and psychological preoccupations are reduced to a minimum. The author, to the horror of many of his admirers, has chosen as victim a person as harmless as the peasant Dandin—an unoffending nobleman from Limoges. He does not really deserve the preposterous fate which befalls him on his arrival in Paris. It would seem that in this work even more than in the preceding play Molière required the presence of a guiltless stooge. On the other hand, two of his chief tormentors, Nérine and Sbrigani, would, out of sheer exuberance, commit any crime in the book. The compliments which they exchange at the beginning of the comedy and which reveal the pair of them as consummate rogues, inordinately proud of their evil doing, leave the audience in a state of uneasy expectancy. Eraste, who wants to marry Oronte's daughter Julie, has hired them, as well as several other scoundrels, to prevent Pourceaugnac from seeking her hand. Julie herself does everything to avoid this match arranged by her father: in order to frighten away her provincial suitor, she plays the part of a libidinous coquette in urgent need of a man. Considering the fearful array of determined characters whom the disarmed Pourceaugnac must face on the very hour of his arrival in a strange city, we must conclude that Molière has reversed the usual procedures of comedy. Mascarille in *L'Etourdi,* Scapin in *Les Fourberies,* or even such heroines as Agnès and Léonor triumph against fairly heavy odds—against opponents who hold most of the trump cards. We may wonder why Molière chose to reverse this traditional situation and show a multitude of shady and resourceful characters dedicated to the persecution of a victim quite incapable of defending himself or even of understanding what is happening to him. Pourceaugnac's parting words prove that he will return to his province none the wiser. He tells his chief tormentor, Sbrigani: "Adieu. Voilà le seul honnête homme que j'ai trouvé en cette ville" (III, 5). Unlike his fellow dupes in Molière's repertory, the Limousin gentleman never wakes up, no doubt because knowledge and discovery in this play do not matter in the least.

What makes Monsieur de Pourceaugnac so intensely ludicrous is precisely this disproportion between the aggressive forces arrayed against him and his incapacity to resist them. Merely by substituting destiny or some tyrannical power for Eraste's multifarious hirelings, and an embattled prince for the ridiculous Limousin, we could easily obtain a tragedy or at least a tragicomedy typical of the period. We may therefore claim that Molière has again reduced a potentially tragic or dangerous situation to the purest kind of farce. Whereas the audience can follow with perfect clarity the various plots which Eraste and Sbrigani invent to foil their victim, the Limousin, like so many heroes of tragedy, has no comprehension of the apparently irrational forces which, for no conceivable reason, have decided to hound him— forces which he dimly identifies with the Evils of Paris, with a cliché.

His persecutors play on his ignorance and on his imagination. They stage a series of more or less disconnected comedies and ballets, highly entertaining to the audience, but which Pourceaugnac considers only too real. He and his prospective father-in-law, Orgon, become the victims of a set of theatrical sketches

—victims of the theater, which has suddenly become virulently aggressive, as in a play by Jean Genet. And Pourceaugnac, throughout the entire comedy, willy-nilly plays a leading part in the various skits of which he is at the same time the object and the chief spectator. Indeed, everything that happens on stage throughout the three acts is really for his "benefit." Moreover, the gentleman from Limoges must, from the standpoint of the audience, appear as the star performer, as the chief spectacle. Molière makes him an object of laughter at his very first appearance on stage: "Hé bien, quoi? qu'est-ce? qu'y a-t-il? Au diantre soit la sotte ville, et les sottes gens qui y sont! ne pouvoir faire un pas sans trouver des nigauds qui vous regardent, et se mettent à rire!" (I, 3). He immediately gives one the impression that he is a reluctant performer, mocked simultaneously by the spectators on stage and by the general public. In all likelihood, Eraste, who has not left a single detail to chance, has hired these idle onlookers to make fun of the Limousin and thus give Sbrigani a good chance to intervene and take charge of his victim. As a result, Pourceaugnac's pathetic tribulations coincide throughout with the idea of theatrical success—the success of Eraste's and Sbrigani's theatrical plots against him.[1]

In the midst of all this play acting, the two doctors and the apothecary behave in their usual manner and take their assignments seriously. All Eraste need do is to put the stupid Limousin in the presence of two doctors no more intelligent than their patient for everything to follow a predictable, if highly dramatic, course. Perhaps Molière wished to imply that medical practitioners will give a better performance, merely by doing what comes natural, than actors who require a minimum of direction. At the same time the author seems to suggest that doctors are, by their very profession, frauds and mountebanks who fool the public by means of their dramatic techniques and even delude themselves into believing in their own grimaces. In short, Mo-

---

[1] Throughout the comedy, Molière alludes to the theater; e.g., when Sbrigani advises Eraste: "Songez de votre part à achever la comédie ..." (III, 1). We never forget that the persecution of Pourceaugnac is continually being directed by a team of stage managers and writers.

lière has gone very far in his satire of medicine, even though we
do not sense the bitterness which will characterize his attacks
on doctors in *Le Malade imaginaire*.

The physicians do not really speak the same language in
Monsieur de Pourceaugnac as in Molière's last comedy. In both
plays, to be sure, he makes them sound pedantic and archaic in
their sententiousness and choice of words. But whereas Purgon
speaks like a theologian, Pourceaugnac's two physicians express
themselves like lawyers and administrators—in fact, they talk
like the Limousin gentleman himself: Witness the following
speech, by the apothecary: "... j'aimerois mieux mourir de ses
remèdes que de guérir de ceux d'un autre; car, quoi qui puisse
arriver, on est assuré que les choses sont toujours dans l'ordre; et
quand on meurt sous sa conduite, vos héritiers n'ont rien à vous
reprocher" (I, 5). In his next speech, he praises one of the (absent) doctors in the following terms: "... c'est un homme expéditif, expéditif, qui aime à dépêcher ses malades; et quand on
a à mourir, cela se fait avec lui le plus vite du monde." Molière,
by playing on the word *dépêcher,* which means both to kill and
to do business efficiently and rapidly, establishes a relationship
between administration, in particular the administration of justice, and medicine. In the third act, Sbrigani will make his victim
believe that Parisian justice acts too swiftly, much too swiftly:
"... ils commencent ici par faire pendre un homme, et puis ils
lui font son procès" (III, 2). In justice and in medicine, you cannot be more expeditious than that!

Although legal language is less marked in the wonderfully
pedantic consultation of the two physicians than in the First
Doctor's subsequent quarrel with his patient, we simply must
quote the definition of Pourceaugnac's melancholy as the disease
of which "il est manifestement atteint et convaincu" (I, 8), as
though contracting an illness meant the same thing as being con-
victed of a crime. In this diagnosis, he mixes a medical with a
legal terminology. He claims that Pourceaugnac suffers from
hypochondriac melancholy: "laquelle maladie, par laps de temps
naturalisée, envieillie, habituée, et ayant pris droit de bourgeoisie
chez lui, pourroit bien dégénérer ou en manie, ou en phthisie,

ou en apoplexie, ou même en fine frénésie et fureur." When
Pourceaugnac manages to escape with his life from their tender
ministrations, one of the physicians becomes so furious that he
continuously blends the language of medicine with that of the
law: "Il est lié et engagé à mes remèdes, et je veux le faire saisir
où je le trouverai, comme déserteur de la médecine, et infracteur
de mes ordonnances" (II, 1). According to this particular physician, *ordonnances* not only means medical prescriptions, but it
possesses the power of legal writ. Moreover, Pourceaugnac, at the
end of the play, will flee Paris for fear of being condemned and
executed for the crime of *desertion,* which shows that Molière
has connected, on the level of the plot, the medical and the legal
aspects of the play. The same doctor complains to Sbrigani: "Il
est hypothéqué à mes consultations," a remark so purely legalistic that Despois and Mesnard were moved to remark that
this doctor "a une prédilection marquée pour la langue de la
pratique." [2]
      The First Doctor maintains his legalistic attitude in the pres-
ence of Oronte: "... je vous défends, de la part de la médecine, de
procéder au mariage que vous avez conclu," and "sa maladie ...
est un meuble qui m'appartient" (II, 2). The physician will
not let Pourceaugnac get married before he has "satisfait à la
médecine, et subi les remèdes," as though the Limousin had committed a crime against medicine. And he even threatens Orgon
himself, who receives a direct order not to go through with the
wedding "sur peine d'encourir la disgrâce de la Faculté, et d'être
accablés de toutes les maladies qu'il nous plaira." As for the guilty
Pourceaugnac, a terrible fate awaits him: "Il a beau fuir, je le
ferai condamner par arrêt à se faire guérir par moi." Molière, for
comic and satirical purposes, has thus combined two incompatible forms of systematic thought and destroyed one by means
of the other. The entire comedy marks the triumph of make-
believe over all types of systematic behavior. Pourceaugnac may
be innocent and even innocuous, but, in spite of his pride in his
blue blood, he acts like a lawyer and tries to substitute legal forms
for life itself. He comes to Paris to sign a marriage contract; he

[2] *Grands Ecrivains Ed.,* VII, 286, note iv.

is therefore induced to flee because of a fabricated but highly expeditious justice. We can regard the Limousin's presence in the capital as an encroachment of systematic behavior in its most lifeless form. Pourceaugnac flees Paris, less because of his fear of death than to avoid an injury to his prerogatives as an aristocrat: "Ce n'est pas tant la peur de la mort qui me fait fuir, que de ce qu'il est fâcheux à un gentilhomme d'être pendu, et qu'une preuve comme celle-là feroit tort à nos titres de noblesse" (III, 2). In this respect he reminds us not only of the Sotenvilles, but of the apothecary who had described the First Doctor as a person "qui, quand on devroit crever, ne démordroit point d'un *iota* des règles des anciens" (I, 5). In the final analysis, the prerogatives of the nobility become as illusory not to say fraudulent as the doctrines of the Faculté de Médecine. Thus Pourceaugnac, hounded by doctors and apothecaries, persecuted by scoundrels impersonating justice, receives a punishment which may not quite fit his crime, but which certainly suits his illusions and which is proportioned to his false and lifeless values—the essential values of a lawyer and of a provincial nobleman.

17

The Inhumanity of Harpagon

$\mathcal{A}$LTHOUGH *L'Avare* is by no means lacking in originality, borrowings from literary sources are particularly heavy. Nearly every important scene, from the farcical intrigues of Frosine to Harpagon's famous monologue, has been traced back to Plautus, Ariosto, Larivey, Boisrobert or even to the *commedia dell'arte*. Moreover, Molière remains faithful to one of the oldest traditions in comedy: the eternal triumph of youth over age.

The chief source of *L'Avare* is of course the *Aulularia*. However, in spite of several scenes practically translated from the Latin, the French comedy differs from its Roman counterpart both in intention and in structure. In the *Aulularia*, Plautus stresses the various relationships between hidden gold and marriage, giving free play to sexual connotations. Dionysiac and phallic elements appear everywhere. Compared with *L'Avare*, the *Aulularia* is an astonishingly brutal and elemental comedy in expression as well as in subject matter: rape; beatings of surly slaves; the noisy preparations for a feast; the cries of childbirth. . . . In addition, religious attitudes and beliefs play a not unimportant part, for Plautus dramatizes a conversion from frugality or sterility to abundance, from poverty to fertility and wealth. Throughout this transformation, the characters remain fatalistically resigned to the will of the gods. Even the rape of Euclio's daughter was not premeditated.

The portrait of Euclio can by no means be regarded as a character study, and Plautus does not even attempt to show the dire effects of avarice. Euclio's meanness merely reflects the temporary sterility of nature. Traditional, and frequently vulgar, comparisons are used to define the protagonist's avarice, e.g., "Etiamne obturat inferiorem gutturem, / ne quid animae forte amittat dormiens?" "Oh yes! And he puts a stopper on his lower windpipe, doesn't he, so as not to chance losing any breath while he's asleep?" (II, 4). This remark would be unthinkable in *L'Avare,* not only because of the seventeenth-century *biensé-ances,* but also because Molière systematically rejects the "oneiric" earthiness of Plautus, who apparently was aware of the scatological associations of money and avarice, so frequent in folklore: "pecunia olet." [1]

MAMMON AND EROS

Molière replaces the rape of Phaedria by Valère's respectful love for Elise; and Euclio's hidden pot of gold, in becoming Harpagon's *cassette,* loses most of its erotic connotations.[2] This sublimation or *épuration* is apparent in the very first scene, where Molière establishes the essential themes of the play. Valère and Elise are discussing their secret troth. And it so happens that their conversation abounds in expressions better suited to Harpagon's financial transactions than to the *confidences* of young lovers. An important word in this scene—and, for that matter, in the entire play—is *engagement,* which appears in the very first speech.[3] Nothing could be more foreign and more antithetical to this meaning of *engagement* than its financial derivative, with which Harpagon is familiar. But *engagement,* in love or in usury, always entails a certain amount of risk, prudence, and even suspicion. Elise, her trust in Valère notwithstanding, has, like her father, many fears. She is very much afraid that her fiancé might cease to love her. And in expressing this suspicion, she makes use of a financial term: "... cette froideur criminelle dont ceux de votre sexe payent le plus souvent les témoignages trop ardents d'une innocente amour." And Valère answers her in kind: "Soup-çonnez-moi de tout, Elise, plutot que de manquer à ce que je

---

[1] For the sources of *L'Avare,* see *Grands Ecrivains Ed.,* VII, 3–208. English translation from the *Aulularia* is by Paul Nixon, *Plautus* (New York: G. P. Putnam's Sons, 1921), I, 267.

[2] There is a hint of eroticism in Harpagon's question to Valère regarding the *cassette:* "Hé! dis-moi donc un peu: tu n'y as point touché?" (V, 3).

[3] *Engagement,* or *engager,* appears some seven times in the play.

vous dois." Elise, like Harpagon, but for quite different reasons, puts herself into a state of *soupçon* and *inquiétude*. She requires tangible proof of Valère's sincerity, even though he had already provided the requisite guaranty by saving her life at the risk of his own. Harpagon's daughter recognizes this fact in a speech where key words (italicized) are by no means lacking: "Mon cœur, pour sa défense, a *tout votre mérite*, appuyé du secours d'une *reconnaissance* où le Ciel *m'engage* envers vous. Je me représente à toute heure ce péril étonnant qui commença de nous *offrir* aux regards l'un de l'autre; cette *générosité* surprenante qui vous fit *risquer* votre vie, pour *dérober* la mienne à la fureur des ondes. ..." The key words create the impression that Elise's love for Valère stems from her indebtedness to him. Of course, both her affection and his risk were entirely spontaneous and thus radically exclude any idea of consciously and coldly repaying a debt. Love is an immediate result of *générosité*—in the Cornelian as well as in the ordinary sense—without any thought of gain. In this manner, the opening scene forms a contrasting background for Harpagon's calculated risks as a usurer and for his almost pathological distrust.

At the end of *L'Avare,* we learn that Valère himself, his sister Mariane, and both their parents had, like Elise, been rescued from drowning. In spite of this painstakingly-planned relation between the opening and closing scenes of the comedy, the *dénouement* is hardly convincing, nor is it meant to be. Indeed, Molière makes Anselme exclaim at the very moment when his true identity stands revealed: "Oui, ma fille, oui, mon fils, je suis Dom Thomas d'Alburcy, que le Ciel *garantit* des ondes avec tout *l'argent* qu'il portoit ..." (V, 5). By placing suitable emphasis on *garantit* and *argent,* an actor can make even so contrived a recognition yield its share of laughter.

Already in the second scene Molière had established a strong opposition between generosity and happiness on the one hand, avarice on the other. Mariane is characterized by her "bonté toute engageante," by her tenderness towards her old and sickly mother. Cléante would be perfectly happy if he could only help these two women, but, as he bitterly complains to his sister:

"... concevez quel déplaisir ce m'est de voir que, par l'avarice d'un père, je sois dans l'impuissance de goûter cette joie, et de faire éclater à cette belle aucun témoignage de mon amour." And throughout the play happiness, no less than love, is invariably connected with generosity. Harpagon, on the contrary, is frequently characterized by his *dureté* or *sécheresse*.

The old man's hardness reduces Cléante to a most unpleasant type of *engagement:* "... il faut que maintenant je m'engage de tous côtés. ..." And thus his love for a poor girl and his natural generosity—qualities that appeal to most audiences—aggravate his enslavement to the sordid world of avarice and usury. This strange world, where his father is the dominant figure, precludes normal human feelings and thrives on aggression, hatred and betrayal. Harpagon lives in a constant state of siege: "Je ne veux point avoir sans cesse devant moi un espion de mes affaires, un traître, dont les yeux maudits assiégent toutes mes actions, dévorent ce que je possède, et furettent de tous côtés pour voir s'il n'y a rien à voler" (I, 3). It is by this very suspiciousness that Harpagon, like Euclio before him, betrays himself; and La Flèche, to whom these insulting accusations are addressed, will eventually discover the *cassette*. The miser considers both Elise and Cléante not as children but as enemies: "Cela est étrange, que mes propres enfants me trahissent et deviennent mes ennemis!" (I, 4). The hostility which he attributes to Cléante and Elise shows that he is totally incapable of establishing natural relationships with the outside world. Moreover, Harpagon's anti-social vices, avarice and aggressiveness, somehow transcend his physical presence and tend to invade his entire environment; and although Molière makes him ridiculous throughout, he frequently appears as a force of evil capable of blighting life itself. He behaves as though possessed by some evil genius and he alienates himself to such an extent that, upon discovering the theft of his treasure, he clutches himself by the arm and exclaims: "Rends-moi mon argent, coquin!" Although this aberration on the part of the miser is undoubtedly a source of laughter, it nonetheless provides a fitting climax to Harpagon's all-encompassing suspiciousness.

Not only does Moliere make frequent use of financial terms in expressing the affection of Valère, Cléante, and Elise, but he selects words from the vocabulary of love in order to show Harpagon's addiction to money, thus achieving a strong contrapuntal effect: "Hélas! mon pauvre argent, mon pauvre argent, mon cher ami! on m'a privé de toi; et puisque tu m'es enlevé, j'ai perdu mon support, ma consolation, ma joie; tout est fini pour moi, et je n'ai plus que faire au monde: sans toi, il m'est impossible de vivre. C'en est fait, je n'en puis plus; je me meurs, je suis mort, je suis enterré" (IV, 7). Harpagon's passionate addiction to gold has nothing to do with love or friendship, and his endearments to his stolen *cassette* accentuate his rejection of more tender emotions. Molière adds the crowning touch in the very last sentence of the comedy, when Harpagon replies: "Et moi voir ma chère cassette," to Ansèlme's invitation to his children: "Allons vite faire part de notre joie à votre mère." Such a response reveals that happiness has as its corollary the definitive exclusion of all false values.

The verbal dovetailing of the incompatible worlds of love and avarice often becomes a source of laughter, notably when Harpagon accuses Valère of stealing the *cassette*. This scene, adapted from the *Aulularia,* is based on a perfect *quiproquo,* in which Harpagon is obsessed with his lost treasure and Valère can think only of his love for Elise. The comic effect of this total misunderstanding is greatly increased by the perplexity of the scribbling *commissaire* combined with complete awareness on the part of the audience. Throughout the scene, Molière repeatedly plays on such words as *trésor, bien, sang, enlever, toucher,* and even *engager.* Obviously, each of these terms can have but one meaning—which completely excludes the other—to the two characters involved.

An exclusion of a somewhat similar nature determines Harpagon's attitude towards Mariane. Clearly, the old miser does not really fall in love with this kindhearted girl: his every act confirms his total lack of affection; and, after all, tender feelings are foreign to his nature, almost by definition. This strange infatuation is usually regarded as a clever means of stressing Harpagon's stinginess in a situation where even a miser might be expected to become a spendthrift for a day. That marriage is nothing more to him than a business transaction, the more profitable the better, is brought out in the famous *sans dot* scene and in his own insistence on a dowry from poor Mariane: "Mais, Frosine, as-tu entretenu la mère touchant le bien qu'elle peut donner à sa fille? Lui as-tu dit qu'il fallait qu'elle s'aidât un peu, qu'elle fît quelque effort, qu'elle se saignât pour une occasion comme celle-ci? Car encore n'épouse-t-on point une fille, sans qu'elle apporte quelque chose" (II, 5). The term *occasion* appears all the more ironical in this context because Harpagon insists that Mariane's impoverished mother must bleed herself for his benefit.[4] Frosine replies that Mariane, being used to thrift, will save him money: she thus reduces the girl's "moral" qualities to the false "reality" of gold: "N'est-ce pas quelque chose de *réel,* que de vous apporter en mariage une grande sobriété, l'héritage d'un grand amour de simplicité de parure, et l'acquisition d'un grand fonds de haine pour le jeu?" But such specious arguments will never convince Harpagon, who requires more tangible goods. The humorous contrast between such intangibles as *sobriété, simplicité, haine, amour,* and such fugitives from law and finance as *héritage, acquisition, fonds,* is just another instance of the frequent verbal interweaving of incompatible attitudes.

Frosine herself is a sort of marriage broker and, if need be, an *entremetteuse.* Although she does not lack human feelings and shows a willingness to help lovers in distress, she combines, on the lowest level, love affairs and business, e.g.:

LA FLÈCHE: As-tu quelque négoce avec le patron du logis?
FROSINE: Oui, je traite pour lui quelque petite affaire, dont
j'espère une récompense (II, 4).

Far from being an amusing episodic character, relevant though not indispensable to the plot, Frosine by her dubious activities provides just one more example of the clash between opposite values, whose irreconcilability is momentarily disguised. She

---

[4] This is not the only time that Harpagon equates blood with money: in Act V, Scene 3, he refers to his stolen treasure as *sang.*

even brags that she could marry the *Grand Turc* to the Republic of Venice, a feat undoubtedly less difficult than the transformation of Harpagon into a lover, or of his grasping avarice into natural human affection. Indeed, she excels in twisting values and in turning the world upside down, to the extent of making Harpagon believe that young Mariane insists on a husband at least sixty years old: "Trouver la jeunesse aimable! est-ce avoir le sens commun?"

Taking into account the various relationships which have been established between love and money, it would appear that the entire comedy consists in artificially forcing together two series of mutually exclusive concepts and attitudes, only to have them break apart with increasing violence until Harpagon's final banishment from the world of happiness.[5]

APPEARANCE AND REALITY

Pierre Brisson sees in *L'Avare:* "... une réplique pauvre de *Tartuffe.*" [6] And he adds: "Ce n'est pas le portrait de l'avare qui détermine l'intrigue, mais l'intrigue qui détermine les façons de vivre d'Harpagon." Although Brisson makes these comments in order to prove the manifest inferiority of the play as compared with the true masterpieces of Molière—an opinion which we do not share—his suggestions that *L'Avare* cannot be reduced to a mere character study and that it is a replica of *Tartuffe* are certainly worth discussing.

From a realistic or psychological point of view, Molière's portrait of a miser is not entirely satisfactory. Compared with Grandet's sensuous dedication to gold, Harpagon's fumbling affection for his *cassette* is little more than a caricature. Balzac's hero keeps but one old servant, whereas Harpagon must have a

---

[5] Thus Bergson's concept of "interférence des séries" rather than of "raideur" provides the best means of explaining laughter in *L'Avare:* cf. H. Bergson, *Le Rire* (Paris: P.U.F., 1947), pp. 74 ff., 108. In this connection, cf. also the penetrating remarks of W. G. Moore, in his *Molière: A New Criticism* (London: Oxford, 1949), pp. 108 ff. Structurally, most of Molière's comedies are based on the clash of mutually exclusive attitudes: e.g., the blindness of Orgon as opposed to the blatancy and obviousness of Tartuffe.

[6] P. Brisson, *Molière, sa vie dans ses œuvres* (Paris: N.R.F., 1942), p. 211.

household of domestics, a stable full of horses—to which he expects to add an expensive young wife! This obvious contradiction, far from constituting a weakness, can be regarded as an intentional dramatic device, comparable in importance to the mutual exclusion of love and money. For Harpagon is not merely a miser: he wishes to cut a decent, if not dashing, figure among his equals. His vanity ceaselessly attempts to get the better of his avarice. In the very first scene, Valère dwells on Harpagon's susceptibility to the most obvious flattery. Later, the miser takes Frosine's mercenary compliments at their face value, even though he does not untie his purse strings for her. And when Maître Jacques gives him a true report of what his neighbors are saying, Harpagon immediately flies into a rage.

Harpagon's vanity appears not only in his susceptibility to false adulation, but occasionally in the pretentiousness with which he addresses his many servants. To *Dame* Claude, Harpagon says: "Je vous commets au soin de nettoyer partout ... Outre cela, je vous constitue, pendant le souper, au gouvernement des bouteilles ..." (III, 1). No less affected are his orders to the two butlers: "Vous, Brindavoine, et vous, la Merluche, je vous établis dans la charge de rincer les verres, et de donner à boire ..." This language—which appears to justify his startling title of "Seigneur Harpagon"—contrasts with the admonitions he showers on his help to refrain from polishing the furniture with undue vigor for fear of wearing it out, to pour wine only upon request, as well as with the devices to which his butlers must resort in order to hide the shameful state of their livery. Obviously, Harpagon intends to live up to his position in the world without for one moment departing from the most stringent stinginess. The contradiction lies in the discrepancy between the public image of himself which he so ludicrously strives to impose on others, and the reality of his sordid avarice and usury. No doubt, he is the only person taken in by this false image of his own creation, for he somehow combines within himself the amazing credulity of Orgon with the deception of Tartuffe.[7]

[7] In a sense, Harpagon's pursuit of Mariane could have been included in this section, for although the miser respects the outward appearance of a normal courtship, he remains in total ignorance of the real attributes of love and marriage.

Apart from his avarice, Harpagon's entire existence appears as a series of empty roles which he plays in the most miserable manner possible: the man of high rank; the devoted father; the would-be suitor. His neighbors, far from being impressed— for no one ever fails to see him in his true character of miser— accuse him of stealing his horses' fodder. Whatever the validity of this accusation, it cannot be denied that the beasts are starving: "Vos chevaux, Monsieur? Ma foi, ils ne sont point du tout en état de marcher. Je ne vous dirai point qu'ils sont sur la litière, les pauvres bêtes n'en ont point, et ce serait fort mal parler; mais vous leur faites observer des jeûnes si austères, que ce ne sont plus rien que des idées ou des fantômes, des façons de chevaux" (III, 1). Harpagon retorts: "Les voilà bien malades: ils ne font rien." In other words, his horses are deprived of their very being: they neither eat nor work, but are confined to their bare manger for reasons of status. Symbolically, these unhappy nags represent the lamentable state to which Harpagon would reduce all living creatures, his own children included, who happen to fall within his clutches. Carried away by his desire to give symbolic utterance to the miser's destructiveness, Molière does not hesitate to put in the mouth of a servant words that are quite out of character: "... ce ne sont plus rien que des idées ou des fantômes, des façons de chevaux." Maître Jacques' subsequent speech becomes him better: "Et pour ne rien faire, Monsieur, est-ce qu'il ne faut rien manger? Il leur vaudroit bien mieux, les pauvres animaux, de travailler beaucoup, de manger de même. Cela me fend le cœur, de les voir ainsi exténués; car enfin j'ai une tendresse pour mes chevaux, qu'il me semble que c'est moi-même quand je les vois pâtir; je m'ôte tous les jours pour eux les choses de la bouche; et c'est être, Monsieur, d'un naturel trop dur, que de n'avoir nulle pitié de son prochain." [8] Although the coachman's strictly un-Cartesian tenderness towards his charges, with whom he identifies himself, is meant to provoke laughter, his words should be regarded not only as an affirmation of humaneness, but of life itself, as opposed to the *dureté,* the *sécheresse,* and the con-

---

[8] Maître Jacques would undoubtedly side with Mme de Sévigné and La Fontaine in their opposition to "l'automatisme des bêtes."

stantly devitalizing influence of Harpagon. Molière's miser who, through usury and niggardliness, transforms life into useless buried gold, appears as a seventeenth-century version of King Midas, who wilfully blights everything he touches: he is a magician in reverse, who substitutes his illusory, death-dealing values for the normal processes of Nature. Only a successor of the baroque dramatists could have created such a character as Harpagon—a master of empty metamorphoses, a Circle among misers.

No less characteristic of Harpagon's true nature than his treatment of the horses is the weird collection of useless objects which he tries to foist on Cléante instead of cash, the list of which reads like the inventory of a junk shop. Among the most ironically suggestive items in the long *mémoire* are an over-stuffed, dangling lizard and especially a tapestry: "Plus, une tenture de tapisserie des amours de Gombaut et de Macée" (II, 1)—a thread-bare representation of pastoral love that had probably passed out of fashion during Harpagon's childhood. It is by such means that the miser smothers the impulses of the young or at least makes them pay dearly for their advantages. Usury becomes in this manner more than a means to increase as rapidly as possible his wealth: it is the best way of getting even with the next generation. That the userer discovered by La Flèche should turn out to be none other than Harpagon is much more than a mere coincidence, for this chance encounter drives home the fact that the miser behaves less like a father to Cléante and Elise and more like a bloodsucker and an extortioner.

DUALITY, IDENTITY, AND COINCIDENCE

Coincidences of one sort or another occur with such frequency in *L'Avare* that they appear to form a creative theme and pattern within the comedy. Symbolically as well as dramatically, the coincidental meanings of *engagement*—a term applied with equal felicity to usury and betrothal—are not unrelated to the strange coincidences which bring Cléante face to face with his father, first as money-lender and borrower, then as rival. And it is by still another series of far-fetched coincidences that Molière contrives a happy but incredible ending.

That coincidence can become a source of high as well as of low comedy, Molière had already demonstrated in such plays as *L'Ecole des femmes* and *Sganarelle*. But in *L'Avare*, this time-honored trick seems to have a special purpose, for it involves in a new and peculiar manner the interplay of identity and duality. At the *dénouement*, Valère and Elise, Cléante and Mariane, Anselme and his (absent) wife, all appear, through a change of identity, to fuse together into one happy family, while Harpagon leaves the scene in order to dote on his cold coins, beyond the pale of humanity.[9] On his clear-cut exclusion depends the uniting of the other important characters, who lose their separateness in joyful recognition. The final scenes are perhaps comparable to a non-religious Last Judgment, with a sort of heaven on one side, and illusory, soulless values, equivalent to damnation, on the other.[10]

Harpagon's multiplicity of functions: as father, rival and money-lender to Cléante; as miser, suitor and aristocrat—to which may be added his momentary confusion as to his identity when he discovers the theft of his treasure—is echoed by most of the other characters, who assume a dual identity. And we refer less to the double identity of Anselme and his family than to the willful duplicity of Valère and the hilarious separation of functions for which Maître Jacques is justly famous.

Maître Jacques carries the theme of duality to the height of absurdity, or rather, down to the level of farce and slapstick. In spite of the fact that he does not receive sufficient food to demonstrate his competence as a chef and that his ghostlike horses are too weak to drag a carriage, he prides himself on being

---

[9] Harpagon's exclusion is somehow more complete than that of any other character in Molière's comedies—including Arnolphe, the Sganarelle of *L'Ecole des maris*, Alceste, Tartuffe, and even, so to speak, Don Juan—because his avarice separates him not only from a given society, but from the rest of humanity, be it militant or damned.

[10] The prominence of the word "sauver" at the beginning and especially at the end of the comedy, where it appears no fewer than five times, suggested this comparison.

both cook and coachman, and goes through the pretense of changing his jacket according to whichever of his two exalted functions is involved. His antics surprise Harpagon, who exclaims: "Quelle diantre de cérémonie est-ce là?" (III, 1). By this absurdity, perhaps borrowed from the *commedia dell'arte,* Molière humorously points out the patent falsity of the cook-and-coachman's situation as well as the sham and pretense of the miser's way of life.

Maître Jacques' duality is not limited to his two functions in the usurer's household. At first he tries to be perfectly frank, and Harpagon furiously beats him with a stick for his pains. He then resolves to tell nothing but fibs, yet fares no better. Moreover, Maître Jacques' mechanical duality has a contagious effect on others, e.g., the false reconciliation between Cléante and Harpagon, and the protracted *quiproquo* concerning Elise and the *cassette.*

In Maître Jacques we can see a *reductio ad absurdum* of practically all the themes in the play: identity, coincidence, duality, exclusion, incompatibility, tenderness, generosity, and vanity. By taking such stupid pride in his dual capacity within the miser's miserably pretentious world he becomes a willing accomplice of Harpagon; by his humane attitude towards the horses, he puts himself on the side of Elise, Mariane, and even of his enemy Valère: hence his paradoxical situation, which gets him into trouble with everyone. But why should poor Jacques be victimized throughout, punished first for his sincerity and then for his impostures? One might answer quite plausibly that the play must have its clown whose misfortunes do not count.[11] Still, the coachman richly deserves his fate, for in spite of his kindheartedness he so often behaves in an absurdly systematic manner. Moreover, his vanity—a capital sin which he shares

[11] In this respect, Maître Jacques' tribulations scarcely differ from the indignities suffered by the Sganarelle of *Le Médecin malgré lui,* by Sosie, or by Géronte. They constitute a traditional and probably eternal element in comic literature, running the gamut from the beatings given and received in Punch and Judy shows to the murder of Amédée Fleurissoire in Gide's *Les Caves du Vatican.* The multiplicity of functions and the duality which characterize Maître Jacques and Harpagon are akin to the medleys that we noticed in Orgon and Tartuffe.

with Harpagon and with as little justification—makes him the perfect target of beatings and humiliations. Indeed, vanity, pretense, and pride are opposed, practically by definition, to all forms of spontaneity: they are, nearly to the same degree as avarice, the causes of separateness and exclusion. Would it be exaggerated to claim that in Maître Jacques Molière has caricatured our suffering humanity, continually shuttling back and forth between sentimentality and pretense, remaining untrue both to itself and to Nature?

Humanity's only means of escaping these two pitfalls would appear to lie in spontaneity, generosity, and affection. But in all probability Molière considers even this escape as no more than an illusion, for the happiness of Anselme's family is based after all on an incredible coincidence. The very artificiality of the *dénouement,* far from revealing a structural weakness in the play or lack of imagination on the part of the author, expresses a fundamentally ironic attitude. Most human relationships in Molière's comedies are founded on some form of misunderstanding or mental isolation. Seekers of unambiguous human values, such as Arnolphe and Alceste, are doomed to failure. And in *Dom Garcie de Navarre,* Molière develops the crying incompatibility of Don Garcie and Elvire.

From this standpoint, the very artificiality of the *dénouement* in *L'Avare* appears unavoidable. Mechanically contrived though it may be, it is in no way more mechanical than the rigidity we find in all of Harpagon's actions, or the separation between love and money, between status and avarice, between sincerity and imposture, between cook and coachman. In short, the ending brings to a climax the various artificialities in character and plot. When the curtain falls, Harpagon, like the proverbial scapegoat, has taken unto himself all the meanness, all the meaningless vanity, all the unfeeling harshness that could possibly exist in a single family, leaving all the life-giving qualities and all the generous emotions to his and Anselme's children, whose love will be miraculously immune to the usual human foibles. The *dénouement* thus resembles a fairy tale: when the witch is exiled, the prince and princess live happily ever after in a timeless world. It is unashamedly a fantasy, similar in spirit to the joyful ballets that conclude *Le Bourgeois gentilhomme* and *Le Malade imaginaire*. As such, it represents a mock evasion of the drab ending inevitable in a drama dealing with such inveterate evils as usury and vanity.

18

A Lesson for a Maecenas

Le Bourgeois gentilhomme is undoubtedly excellent theater, with its farcical scenes, its music, its dancing. But just for this reason, it would seem to lend itself less readily to stylistic analysis than more strictly literary works such as *Le Misanthrope*. Moreover, it hardly seems to provide critics with suitable material for deep psychological analysis or moral pronouncements. They may regard Jourdain as a madman, but unfortunately for moralists his madness does not obliterate his good nature. Actually, his aberrations seem to move in the right direction, for they contribute to the well-being of society and to the prosperity of artists. As Rameau's nephew would say, Jourdain *restitue,* and in the least vicious manner possible, for he becomes, in spite of his ignorance and his atrocious bad taste, a patron of all the arts and of all forms of entertainment, and thus of Molière himself. In Monsieur Jourdain, the author has created one of his rare ridiculous characters whose behavior is almost entirely beneficial. In spite of his admiration for the aristocracy or at least for aristocratic titles and mannerisms, we cannot even accuse him of that horrendous intellectual sin: *esprit de système,* to which so many of Molière's characters must plead guilty. He can even afford to blind himself to certain truths. On the whole, old Jourdain, by the very exaggeration of his behavior, which becomes unbelievable in the Turkish ceremony, reminds us of a character from one of Scarron's comedies, such as Don Japhet d'Arménie. It would seem that Molière has at last succumbed to the temptation of creating a fancy character, dramatically impressive by dint of his very strangeness. But the fantastic element in Monsieur Jourdain happens to suit the play, not only because of the numerous weird ballets it contains, but because of the masquerade which terminates it, and in which

218

the protagonist plays a preponderant part. Throughout the comedy, Jourdain's aberration consists in wanting to play a part in high society. In order to live with aristocrats, he feels that he must learn an entirely new role, which necessitates music, dancing, as well as various physical and linguistic gestures. He therefore transforms his entire existence into a vast apprenticeship and initiation. At one point, he expresses his desire to return to school, even at the expense of being whipped as a fair exchange for the privilege of acquiring knowledge or rather polish. Consequently, the performers in the Turkish ceremony do not forget to beat him with a stick. Throughout the comedy, his acquisition of a few aristocratic mannerisms with which he tries to replace his bourgeois habits takes the form of a masquerade, particularly in the scene where the tailor and his assistants dress him in his new, aristocratic clothing. Quite appropriately, this scene is danced, and the central image which emerges is that of Carême-prenant, of Mardi-gras, as Madame Jourdain so frequently repeats.

Compared to *Le Misanthrope*, *Le Bourgeois gentilhomme* seems loosely constructed and, at times, almost thrown together. This rather superficial impression by no means signifies that Molière composed the play hastily or that he failed, from an esthetic point of view. Rather, it may imply a subordination of dramatic, if not of metaphorical, structure to the idea of spectacle. In this connection, the critic may wonder why the author had to add a spectacular lovers' quarrel to a plot that does not seem to call for that type of scene. In *Tartuffe*, the quarrel between Mariane and Valère had provided just another variation on the themes of blindness and play-acting. In the present work, where the quarrel involves not only Cléonte and Lucile, but their servants Covielle and Nicole, it provides among other things an absurd example of class differences. The discrepancy between Cléonte's aristocratic love-making and Covielle's preoccupations with life in the kitchen would by itself justify the inclusion of this scene in a play entitled *Le Bourgeois gentilhomme*. Let us then assume that the air of slapdash improvisation which marks this comedy from beginning to end was intended by the author.

The lovers' quarrel can even provide us with the unifying theme of this play. The scene begins with a double discord: the underlying discord between servants and masters; the clashes between Cléonte and Lucile on the one hand, and between Covielle and Nicole on the other. But this double discord will lead to a reconciliation, to a final, precarious harmony. The various tensions or discords in the play will lead, in a similar manner, to a total spectacle combining masquerade, ballet, drama, painting. And this triumph of the theatrical and the artificial will conciliate, temporarily and perhaps ironically, the insuperable differences between two classes. In a sense, Molière transforms social hierarchy into a sort of musical scale. Quite fittingly, the comedy ends with a double marriage and the conferring on Monsieur Jourdain of a theatrical title consonant with his admiration for values that do not correspond to his upbringing and his actual status in society.

For the sake of contrast or discord, Molière has created Madame Jourdain, a sensible woman who appears to revert more quickly to her popular, as opposed to bourgeois, origins, than her husband can move in the opposite direction. Her very language puts her in a social group much lower than that of her daughter or Cléonte. She seems to belong to the hearty race of Parisian *commères,* of which Nicole is a sterling example. One of the cleverest tricks in the play is the rapid pace with which Jourdain tries to step from one class to another by means of education. In the course of a morning he takes lessons in music, dancing, fencing, "philosophy," and tries on his first thoroughly aristocratic suit of clothes. And these breathtaking developments take place almost simultaneously, as though he had suddenly decided to become a nobleman! Still, we may assume that he has entertained this silly ambition for some time now, for his friendship with Dorante must have started a long time ago, if we can take as an indication the large sums of money the dashing marquis already owes him. Poor Jourdain obviously behaves like a mere beginner in each of his attempts to graduate into a new social class. For instance, we actually witness his first lesson in "philosophy." And his deportment in other fields shows that his teachers cannot have given him many hours of their attention. By this strange telescoping of what would normally constitute a long and tedious process, Molière subtly conveys the impression that Jourdain is starting to rehearse for a play, and that there remains only a short span of time for further practice. Indeed, the beautiful marquise, in whose honor Monsieur Jourdain has undertaken most of his activities, will arrive a short time later, and our hero will then have to apply his newly-acquired manners to a "real life" situation. The various ballets which intersperse the action increase our impression that we are watching a rehearsal—a rehearsal for the grand finale, the Turkish ceremony, where Jourdain will perform in earnest a part that he has been rehearsing all along. In this manner, Molière manages to conciliate, if only for a moment, the crass mercantile world to which Jourdain really belongs and his own special universe: the realm of art and of make-believe.

THE THEMES

Thus, the old relationship between money and reality will play a part in *Le Bourgeois gentilhomme*. It could hardly have been otherwise, for Jourdain tries to transform his wealth into social status. As he has climbed financially above nearly every subject of His Majesty, Louis XIV, he perhaps feels that these golden heights should also lift him up socially. He attempts to buy his way into the inner sanctum, not directly perhaps, but by "lending" money to Dorante, by spending vast sums for the entertainment of the beautiful Marquise, by paying at their highest price for lessons in the various arts. He even pays for flattery, in a manner so obvious that the satire loses all bitterness and becomes purely farcical, as though Jourdain himself wished to make fun of his ambition to transform himself into an aristocrat. When the *garçon tailleur* addresses him as *"Mon gentilhomme,"* he gleefully answers: *"Mon gentilhomme!* Voilà ce que c'est de se mettre en personne de qualité. Allez-vous-en demeurer toujours habillé en bourgeois, on ne vous dira point: *Mon gentilhomme.* Tenez, voilà pour *Mon gentilhomme."* The tailor boy, elated at receiving a handsome tip, then calls him *Monseigneur;* in exchange, Jourdain increases the tip. Finally, when he hears himself addressed as "Votre grandeur," he even adds to the sum, after saying to himself: "Ma foi, s'il va jusqu'à l'Altesse, il aura toute la bourse" (II, 5). The humor of the scene results from the complete identification between status on the one hand, and words and clothing on the other. Jourdain believes, or rather he makes believe, that he has actually become what these flatterers call him and that his new suit has really metamorphosed his very being. Jourdain behaves like an actor who, merely by donning the costume of a king, immediately acts and even feels like a ruler.

The scene where Dorante borrows a further sum of money from Jourdain brings to a climax the relationship, or lack of relationship, between friendship and money. Anticipating René Clair's comic insistence on exact figures, Molière provides, to the last farthing, a memorandum of the numerous sums that Dorante owes Jourdain. But the very precision of these figures somehow dulls the satirical edge of this scene and makes the relationship between friendship and lucre a fit subject for farce. Thus, Dorante, after Madame Jourdain's bitter intervention, cleverly equates loans with friendliness: "J'ai force gens qui m'en prêteroient avec joie; mais comme vous êtes mon meilleur ami, j'ai cru que je vous ferois tort si j'en demandois à quelque autre" (III, 4). Jourdain, in order to placate his wife, asks her: "Que faire? voulez-vous que je refuse un homme de cette condition-là, qui a parlé de moi ce matin dans la chambre du Roi?" Jourdain thus consents to pay good money for the words which Dorante may or may not have spoken about him at court and in the presence of the king. And what if these words of Dorante had been spoken in mockery of poor Monsieur Jordain?

WORDS AND CONCEPTS

As in *Dom Juan,* terms such as *dire, parler, parole* abound, particularly in certain scenes. Usually, they express one form or another of futility. Unlike the Sganarelle of *Dom Juan,* Monsieur Jourdain does not try to substitute words and arguments for action; nor does he, like Don Juan himself, attempt to get the better of another person. Rather, he finds himself in the same situation as Monsieur Dimanche, with Dorante playing, albeit in a less flamboyant manner, the part of the Don. Dimanche, however, had no other concern than to get his money back; and Molière never suggests that he may have had social ambitions. As a result, Monsieur Dimanche obtains only a commodity for which he has absolutely no use: words, and leaves the scene empty-handed. Monsieur Jourdain, on the contrary, readily agrees to buy words that flatter him, such as the titles given him by the tailor-boy and the imaginary dignity of Mamamouchi. As he refuses to distinguish between concepts and objects, he finds it perfectly natural to pay high prices for words. The status he acquires in this strange manner may appear empty to the audience; but that happens to be the type of merchandise he really values, and he therefore obtains exactly what he wants. However, words in *Le Bourgeois gentilhomme* do more than reveal the exorbitant price Jourdain is prepared to pay for an illusion of status. To rise in the world, our hero must acquire not only new clothing, but new gestures, and a brand new vocabulary. And, for this reason, he hires, in addition to a dancing master, a "maître de philosophie." He has to learn how to bow and how to scrape and how to speak to aristocratic widows. From the standpoint of verbal gesture, the play reaches a climax in the scene where Jourdain first addresses the radiant Dorimène: "Madame, ce m'est une gloire bien grande de me voir assez fortuné pour être si heureux que d'avoir le bonheur que vous ayez eu la bonté de m'accorder la grâce ..." (III, 16). The almost tongue-tied Jourdain haltingly repeats various "formules de politesse" that have no meaning, after having unsuccessfully attempted a series of curtseys. Jourdain, a competent businessman, behaves like an idiot in acquiring new manners, linguistic or otherwise. Moreover, he uses these gestures not as conventions that may have currency in a given milieu, but as cantraps which must possess the power of magically transforming him into a gentleman.

Throughout the play, Molière exploits the absurdity of mistaking words, divested of their meaning, for concrete reality, e.g. Monsieur Jourdain's desire to metamorphose, by dint of some mysterious flourish, his "Belle marquise, vos beaux yeux me font mourir d'amour" (II, 4) into a purely aristocratic compliment; and his momentous discovery that all his life he has unwittingly been speaking and writing prose. From this standpoint, we can regard the lesson he receives from his "maître de philosophie" as much more than a brilliant fantasy, somewhat extraneous to the action. As language, in this play, is gesture and performance divorced from usefulness, Monsieur Jourdain learns about the pronunciation of letters as though he had never uttered a syllable in his life. Rather, the "maître de philosophie" transforms meaninglessness into a ludicrous science by reducing speech to its component gestures. And this famous scene fits into the general scheme and structure of the comedy precisely because it equates, on the most pedantic level possible, syllables or phonemes with gestures.

The dancing and music masters had already proposed fairly analagous equations: "Si tous les hommes apprenoient la musique, ne seroit-ce pas le moyen d'accorder ensemble, et de voir dans le monde la paix universelle," and "Lorsqu'un homme a commis un manquement dans sa conduite, soit aux affaires de sa famille, ou au gouvernement d'un Etat, ou au commandement d'une armée, ne dit-on pas toujours: *Un tel a fait un mauvais pas dans une telle affaire?*" (I, 2). Through these two puns, which confuse concepts with facts or actions, both masters try to prove the practical importance of their art. Their statements represent a victory of words over sense. The greatest triumph of this type will occur in the Turkish ceremony, where Jourdain will receive the glorious but meaningless title of Mamamouchi.

Molière makes reasoning, though to a lesser degree than words, the butt of his satire, particularly in the scene where the Maître d'Armes tells his awkward pupil: "Je vous l'ai déjà dit, tout le secret des armes ne consiste qu'en deux choses, à donner, et à ne point recevoir; et comme je vous fis voir l'autre jour par raison démonstrative, il est impossible que vous receviez, si vous savez

détourner l'épée de votre ennemi de la ligne de votre corps"
(II, 2). Jourdain reduces this idea to absurdity merely by describing his fencing master as a person "qui sait tuer un homme
par raison démonstrative." The gentle art of fencing, which consists, just like dancing, of a series of movements, becomes a sort
of concept. Earlier, Monsieur Jourdain had implied that this
type of logic could replace human qualities: as a result of this
raison démonstrative, "un homme, sans avoir du cœur, est sûr
de tuer son homme, et de n'être point tué." He thus tries to substitute an art made up of gestures for physical courage, a virtue
regarded by Molière's contemporaries as a prerogative of the
aristocracy.

Jourdain does not know how to distinguish between theory,
words, and concepts on the one hand, and objective reality on
the other; and he tends to confuse the various levels of abstrac-
tion, a tendency which explains his reluctance to study ethics
and physics. To his question: "Qu'est-ce qu'elle dit cette morale?" the "maître de philosophie" replies: "Elle traite de la
félicité, enseigne aux hommes à modérer leurs passions, et. ..."
Jourdain, who will have none of this, interrupts: "Non, laissons
cela. Je suis bilieux comme tous les diables; et il n'y a morale
qui tienne, je me veux mettre en colère tout mon soûl, quand
il m'en prend envie" (II, 4). The literal Jourdain just cannot
conceive that ethics, as a branch of philosophy, is theoretical
and speculative in nature. Instead, he regards it as a concrete
obstacle, as a sort of policeman, capable of reducing his freedom
of action and of moderating, against his will, his passions. When
his teacher tells him that physical science, among other advantages, reveals the causes of "tous les météores, l'arc-en-ciel, les
feux volants, les comètes, les éclairs, le tonnerre, la foudre, la
pluie, la neige, la grêle, les vents et les tourbillons," Jourdain
protests violently: "Il y a trop de tintamare là-dedans, trop de
brouillamini," as though the mere study of such phenomena
might set off all the noisy and stormy aspects of nature. Moreover, he tends to react esthetically, as though his teacher had
offered him a spectacle or a performance that did not appeal to
him. He had reacted in a similar fashion to an earlier suggestion

that he study logic—syllogistic forms such as "Barbara, Celarent, Darii, Ferio, Baralipton, etc."—"Voilà des mots qui sont trop rébarbatifs. Cette logique-là ne me revient point. Apprenons autre chose qui soit plus joli." Thus, Jourdain feels that knowledge should, at the very least, be entertaining.

HARMONY

It is certainly not by accident that the play begins with a conversation between a musician and a dancer—between the two chief exponents of gracefulness. Their puns on *accord* and *pas* —a triumph of verbalism—reveal nonetheless an attempt to impose a form of harmony or accord on human endeavor. Consequently, even though each one regards his own art as supreme, they never quarrel. Indeed, these two complementary arts must support each other, particularly in such hybrid forms as the ballet. The series of quarrels which will oppose them, first to the fencing master and then to the most aggressive of the lot, the philosopher, a person who, by virtue of his profession, should be more peaceful than anyone else, contrasts sharply with their harmonious agreement. The affirmation of harmony, followed by violent disagreement, or of accord followed by discord, produces, perhaps intentionally, a contrapuntal effect. This contrast carries over into the vocabulary, not only through the aforementioned puns, but also in the philosopher's efforts to reestablish harmony between the fencing master and the two other teachers: "... la raison ne doit-elle pas être maîtresse de tous nos mouvements?" (II, 3) where the word *mouvement*, which means passion, may also refer, in the fashion of a subdued pun, to the various motions involved in fencing, dancing, or making music.

Counterpoint plays a much more important part in the lovers' quarrel, where Molière manages to produce two quite different types of contrapuntal effect: the contrast between Cléonte and Covielle, who tends to echo his master's words on a lower social register; the discord between the two men and the two girls. The former happen to share the same attitude, in spite of the differences in tone; and as the causes of discord are superficial and even accidental, the dissonance can only enhance a fundamental harmony. This scene contains several comic analogies and plays on words, which we have underlined:

> CLÉONTE: Après tant de sacrifices ardents, de soupirs, et de vœux que j'ai faits à ses charmes!
>
> COVIELLE: Après tant d'assidus hommages, de soins et de *services* que je lui ai rendus dans sa cuisine!
>
> CLÉONTE: Tant de larmes que j'ai versées à ses genoux!
>
> COVIELLE: Tant de seaux d'eau que j'ai tirés du puits pour elle!
>
> CLÉONTE: Tant d'*ardeur* que j'ai fait paroître à la chérir plus que moi-même!
>
> COVIELLE: Tant de *chaleur* que j'ai soufferte à tourner la broche à sa place! (III, 9).

Cléonte and Covielle echo each other's feelings in different registers: the précieux and the materialistic.

The end of the scene contains still more interesting contrapuntal effects. Covielle has been told by his master to disparage Lucile's beauty and personality; but the latter, just like Éliante in *Le Misanthrope,* immediately transforms these derogatory remarks into positive qualities. The scene reaches a crescendo, with Cléonte affirming Lucile's hated perfections: "C'est en quoi ma vengeance sera plus éclatante, en quoi je veux faire mieux voir la force de mon cœur: à la haïr, à la quitter, toute belle, toute pleine d'attraits, toute aimable que je la trouve. La voici."

The comedy ends with a triple marriage and a ballet, in other words with a final affirmation of harmony, however precarious this accord may prove to be. Earlier, Dorimène had expressed her fear of discord: "Mon Dieu! Dorante, il faut des deux parts bien des qualités pour vivre heureusement ensemble; et les deux plus raisonnables personnes du monde ont souvent peine à composer une union dont ils soient satisfaits" (III, 15). Her vocabulary echoes that of the music master: "La guerre ne vient-elle pas d'un manque d'union entre les hommes?" (I, 2). Harmony, in the form of a ballet, will prevail, if not in politics at least in marriage, despite the tremendous discord which marks the relationship between Monsieur and Madame Jourdain.

The Turkish ceremony represents a successful attempt to reach a satisfactory accord which will harmonize with Jourdain's delusions of grandeur. Covielle tells Madame Jourdain: "Ne voyez-vous pas bien que tout ceci n'est fait que pour nous ajuster aux visions de votre mari ..." (V, 6). Early in the play, the musician had used the term *ajuster* in a somewhat different sense: "Lorsque la danse sera mêlée avec la musique, cela fera plus d'effet encore, et vous verrez quelque chose de galant dans le petit ballet que nous avons ajusté pour vous" (II, 1). As an artistic creation, the Turkish ceremony resembles no doubt the *petit ballet* which the music master has prepared, in so far as both of these works attempt to blend the various arts of the theater.

Molière, however, pokes fun at this mingling of the arts in Dorante's description of the banquet which he has arranged, at Jourdain's expense, for his beloved Dorimène:

> ... vous n'avez pas ici un repas fort savant, et vous y trouverez des incongruités de bonne chère, et des barbarismes de bon goût. Si Damis s'en étoit mêlé, tout seroit dans les règles; il y auroit partout de l'élégance et de l'érudition, et il ne manqueroit pas de vous exagérer lui-même toutes les pièces du repas qu'il vous donneroit, et de vous faire tomber d'accord de sa haute capacité dans la science des bons morceaux, de vous parler d'un pain de rive, à biseau doré ... (IV, 1).

Molière subtly equates gastronomy with the art of writing a book, or rather the preparation of food with the selection of words. Dorante the esthete describes the main course in such a fashion that, through the use of puns, it becomes an unheard of mixture of music, marriage, and heraldry: "... et pour son opéra, d'une soupe à bouillon perlé, soutenue d'un jeune gros dindon cantonné de pigeonneaux, et couronnée d'oignons blancs, mariés avec la chicorée." Four of the terms that Dorante brings to bear pertain to the science of heraldry: *perlé, soutenu, cantonné, couronné.* A dinner *ordonné* by this Damis would defi-

nitely appeal to the palate of an aristocrat; in addition, it would
be literary and musical, and it would contain all the assorted
themes of *Le Bourgeois gentilhomme*.

The greatest clash or discord of them all appears, of course,
in the title itself: *Le Bourgeois gentilhomme*. Monsieur Jourdain
does his best, and spends enormous sums of money, to acquire
the behavior or deportment of an aristocrat; but at the same time
he remains faithful to all the attitudes and habits peculiar to petty
merchants. He is not always a dupe. He realizes, for instance,
as a *marchand drapier* should, that his tailor has made him pay
not only for the material that went into his own suit, but into
the clothes that this worthy artisan is now wearing. True to
his mercantile upbringing, he keeps within easy reach the receipts
of the various sums that Dorante has so far borrowed. The
contrast and discord between Monsieur Jourdain's inveterate
nature or bourgeois essence and the lofty status he would like
to acquire could scarcely be greater: only the most skillful composer and choreographer will ever succeed in harmonizing them
and in transforming them into esthetically pleasing counterpoint.
How could Molière have writen about a would-be gentleman
anything but a comedy ballet, with music and dancing interrupting or sustaining at every moment action and words?

THE THEATER

Le Bourgeois gentilhomme not only dramatizes a somewhat
ironical victory of harmony over discord, but, like *Dom Juan,*
it constitutes a sort of Te Deum of the theatrical. As already
stated, each one of Monsieur Jourdain's lessons constitutes a
rehearsal. His awkwardness in all his movements, his blindness,
his stupidity seem inevitably to lead to the Turkish ceremony,
which combines practically all forms of entertainment. And
when the time comes, Jourdain will come prepared: "... il est
homme à y jouer son rôle à merveille" (III, 13). Later on, Covielle
will express the same idea even more explicitly: "Quelle dupe!
quand il auroit appris son rôle par cœur, il ne pourroit pas le mieux
jouer" (IV, 5). During the ceremony itself, Jourdain plays his

part with such consummate mastery that one tends to forget his stupidity and consider him as an accomplice in his own undoing. Everything becomes spectacular at the end. But Jourdain, throughout the play, had wanted to make a spectacle of himself. He had asked his dancing and music masters to watch him fence after having staged a one-man fashion show in their honor. To be sure, his various teachers, including even the philosopher, either try to make Jourdain perform or else they transform him into a somewhat reluctant spectator of their own performances. Thus, two different but complementary considerations dominate the comedy: rehearsal and performance, and discord and harmony, both of them leading to an apotheosis of entertainment and to a general reconciliation of all the characters concerned. Even in this respect, everything that precedes the ceremony can be interpreted as a preparation and a rehearsal.[1]

There is, however, still another aspect of the play which involves the idea of the theater: the situation of the artist, of the entertainer in the world. In the conversation which opens the play and serves as a sort of prologue to the action, the music master discusses with his friend and ally the dancing master the knotty problem of reward in art. An artist cannot wish for a greater reward than the applause of connoisseurs, but how can he possibly live on it? Ignorant plutocrats such as Jourdain can justify their existence by supplying artists with the solid values in life or, as the music master puts it: "Il est vrai qu'il les connoît mal, mais il les paye bien; et c'est de quoi maintenant nos arts ont plus besoin que de toute autre chose." The dancer, on the contrary, insists on the importance of reasoned approval by the best people: there alone will the artist find true rewards and a worthy if not valuable payment for his pains: "... ce sont des douceurs exquises que des louanges éclairées." They finally reach an harmonious conclusion, expressed by the musician: "Mais, en tout cas, il nous donne moyen de nous faire connoître dans le monde; et il payera pour les autres ce que les autres loueront pour lui." By this convenient solution, they somehow

---

[1] The idea of rehearsal or preparation might explain the abnormal frequency of the verb *attendre* and of other terms indicating expectancy.

eliminate the discrepancy between *louanges éclairées* and Jourdain's lucre. The "nouveau riche" has, after all, his little niche in the paradise of art. Artists can use him as a means to attain their ends—ends that will prove beneficial, they hope, not only to them but to the happy few. This solution may even justify the conduct of Dorante who, through the generosity or the gullibility of Jourdain, manages to live in the style to which he is accustomed and, in addition, win the hand of the young widow he loves. Dorante, like a true artist, had been staging, through the expenditures of his friend the merchant, his courtship. His conduct hardly differs from that of the music or dancing master who must use Jourdain's money to win an audience of "honnêtes gens." In short, Monsieur Jourdain is a most praiseworthy dupe, the kind of dupe that entertainers and artists like Molière pray for. And it scarcely matters whether they be tradesmen or sun-kings as long as they pay for services rendered. Monsieur Jourdain, who justifies his existence only by the money he spends so lavishly on artists of various types—artists in music, or dancing, or just existence, is finally transfigured, during the final masquerade, into a Mamamouchi; and his empty but spectacular attainment of status coincides with the triumph of art, the only harmony.

19

A Man of the Theater

TODAY, critics and even scholars can enjoy a farce without becoming indignant because of so-called infringements of theatrical *bienséances*. For this reason, *Les Fourberies de Scapin* has greater appeal for contemporary critics, interested in Molière as a man of the theater, than for such pundits as Boileau and Voltaire, who could not condone, among other things, the farcical scene of the sack. But does *Les Fourberies* have literary merit in addition to stageworthiness? It definitely abounds in literary sources: Cyrano de Bergerac's *Pédant joué*, Plautus' *Phormio*, Rotrou's *La Sœur*.[1] Like *L'Avare* and *Amphitryon* before it, it is a patchwork masterpiece, but highly original in spite of all the borrowings.

Scapin resembles the Mascarille of *L'Etourdi*, the *furbum imperator*, the lyrical master of intrigue. But Scapin need not oppose an invincible obstacle akin to destiny itself: the blundering interference of a master. Instead, he really has everything his way, and, like the slaves of Roman comedy, can rely on destiny as his chief ally. We can detect, however, one major difference between Molière's Scapin and his ancient models: it so happens that all the energy he expends and all his wondrous intrigues must go for naught, for the end would have been the same whether or not he had intervened. As Silvestre puts it: "... le hasard a fait ce que la prudence des pères avoit délibéré" (III, 8). It thus transpires that all the characters concerned: Scapin, the two couples, and the parents were all along moving in the same direction, that of a happy ending contrived by destiny or, rather, prearranged by the author. In this respect, *Les Fourberies* has a plot structure somewhat similar to that of *L'Ecole des femmes* or even of *L'Avare*, where an artificial and quite incredible denouement saves the situation by cancelling

[1] Cf. *Grands Ecrivains Ed.*, VIII, 387 ff.

out everything that has taken place and reducing the action of the play to incidents of no consequence whatever. Molière, by the use of this type of ending, somehow creates a feeling of disproportion, a sense of discrepancy between cause and effect. By this device, the comedy as a whole tends to reflect the absurd causality which marks many of the individual scenes.

Scapin reminds us of a gambler who cannot lose: everything seems to lend itself to his genius for intrigue. Right after our hero has extorted a sum of money from Argante, who quickly leaves the scene, Géronte conveniently makes an appearance: "Je n'ai qu'à chercher l'autre. Ah, ma foi! le voici. Il semble que le Ciel, l'un après l'autre, les amène dans mes filets" (II, 6). Scapin appears to have signed a pact with Heaven, or with destiny, or with the author of the plot. And each of his tricks fits easily into its expected place. His intrigue works like a well-oiled machine except in one instance: a misunderstanding between Scapin and Léandre not only leads to a beating but to the confession of three typical *fourberies* with which he had fooled his master.

The lack of a real obstacle, the alliance with destiny do not reduce Scapin to the traditional role of "valet intriguant," or of *deus ex machina*. In Mascarille we could discern the avatar of a Cornelian hero; in Scapin we find the very soul of the plot —a sort of inspired being who seems to create the plot as he goes along. The hero of *Les Fourberies* not only appears to improvise the action, like a character from the *commedia dell'arte,* but he seems to contain within himself every ounce of intelligence available, a commodity in which his fellow-characters are sadly lacking. Silvestre, Léandre, Octave, the two girls, and the two old men lack initiative and must rely on Scapin for their every move. This unequal distribution, whereby Scapin appropriates all the skills and the other people must willy-nilly act as his pawns, inevitably puts the hero in a peculiar position, for he becomes almost indistinguishable from the author himself! Moreover, Molière, strange as this may seem, has centered the entire play around the idea of literature, of literary creation, of appreciation.

SCAPIN AS STAGE DIRECTOR

Molière must have taught his Scapin all he knew about the
theater. In many scenes, he shows consummate skill as an actor.
He impersonates Octave's father, Argante, so successfully that
Octave himself remains tongue-tied, because, as he admits,
"... je m'imagine que c'est mon père que j'entends" (I, 3). It
is through his acting that he lends an air of plausibility to his
many lies, particularly the one about Léandre's kidnapping.
At the end of the play, he makes Géronte and Argante believe
that a stonecutter's hammer has fractured his skull and "dé-
couvert toute la cervelle"—the seat or headquarters of his wits.
And he can disguise himself almost at will: with Géronte in
the bag, he easily impersonates, merely by changing his voice,
a Basque soldier and then a Swiss mercenary. Moreover, he confesses that, in order to frighten Léandre, he had masqueraded
as a werewolf.

In this forced confession to his master, Scapin reveals his mastery in the techniques of the theater. In addition to his werewolf
act, he had made Léandre believe, by bloodying his face and
putting mud on his clothes, that thieves had stolen the watch
intended as a present for Zerbinette. He shows even greater skill
in directing the other characters. If he consented to play the
part of Argante for the edification of Octave, it was only to give
the young man a chance to prepare for the inevitable quarrel
with his father: "Répétons un peu votre rôle, et voyons si vous
ferez bien" (I, 3). He achieves his greatest success as a director
when the uninspired Silvestre arrives on cue to play the part
of Hyacinthe's imaginary, swashbuckling brother. And Silvestre
performs his part to perfection, for Scapin had coached him
well: "Tiens-toi un peu. Enfonce ton bonnet en méchant garçon.
Campe-toi sur un pied. Mets la main au côté. Fais les yeux
furibonds. Marche un peu en roi de théâtre. Voilà qui est bien.
Suis-moi. J'ai des secrets pour déguiser ton visage et ta voix"
(I, 5). Obviously, Scapin leaves nothing whatever to chance.

SCAPIN AS A CONSCIOUS ARTIST

The mock-heroic Mascarille had frequently boasted of his artistic talents: "Vivat Mascarillus fourbum imperator." His successor, Scapin, sees himself, from the beginning of *Les Fourberies,* as a creative artist of the first rank:

> A vous dire la vérité, il y a peu de choses qui me soient impossibles, quand je veux m'en mêler. J'ai sans doute reçu du Ciel un génie assez beau pour toutes les fabriques de ces gentillesses d'esprit, de ces galanteries ingénieuses à qui le vulgaire ignorant donne le nom de fourberies; et je puis dire, sans vanité, qu'on n'a guère vu d'homme qui fût plus habile ouvrier de ressorts et d'intrigues, qui ait acquis plus de gloire que moi dans ce noble métier: mais, ma foi! le mérite est trop maltraité aujourd'hui (I, 2).

In the checkered field of intrigue, Scapin has received a divine gift. By calling his *fourberies* "gentillesses d'esprit" he transforms them into intellectual skills. Society, with its stress on morality and convention, with its opposition to trickery, shows a complete lack of artistic appreciation. Only the "happy few" have the knowledge and the insight to understand the finer points of his art. He regards his more-or-less criminal pranks as a profession, as a "noble métier." The ironical complaint that merit goes unrewarded—the typical cliché of the frustrated artist—brings to a climax the more-or-less hidden comparison between Scapin's artful dodges and Molière's own profession. In discussing with Silvestre his difficulties with the law, he further develops his veiled comparison: "... je me dépitai de telle sorte contre l'ingratitude du siècle, que je résolus de ne plus rien faire." He sounds indeed like a disappointed writer, discouraged by the indifference of the public or, perhaps, like a dramatist, who has run into difficulties with the rigors of censorship. Can we claim that Molière is ironically referring to his own predicament as actor-director-dramatist, excommunicated by the Church, and all but reduced to silence by the suppression of two such outspoken masterpieces as *Tartuffe* and *Dom Juan?*

Scapin takes care to stress the esthetic aspects of his practices and his precociousness: "... je n'étois pas plus grand que
cela, que je me signalois déjà par cent tours d'adresse jolis" (I, 2).
Like most writers, he is exceedingly vain and proud. He insists,
for that reason, on getting even with Géronte, who had unwittingly led to his confession of three *fourberies* that otherwise
would have gone undetected. Throughout the comedy, he appears to share the esthetic attitudes of a professional writer. He
rails against peaceful love, exclaiming: "... Il faut du haut et
du bas dans la vie; et les difficultés qui se mêlent aux choses
réveillent les ardeurs, augmentent les plaisirs" (III, 1). At the
end of this scene, he proclaims his own philosophy of life:
"... je hais ces cœurs pusillanismes qui, pour trop prévoir les suites
des choses, n'osent rien entreprendre." His parting words suggest that very same attitude. When Argante says: "Allons
souper ensemble, pour mieux goûter notre plaisir," Scapin adds:
"Et moi, qu'on me porte au bout de la table, en attendant que
je meure," which means, more or less, "Eat, drink, and be merry,
for tomorrow you may die."

LITERATURE

Scapin not only shows mastery in all the arts of the theater,
but he knows how to tell a story persuasively. Indeed, the term
récit, together with such expressions as *conte* and *histoire,* reappear frequently. Scapin's imaginative account of Léandre's
shotgun marriage easily convinces Argante, and his strange story
about Léandre's abduction by pirates sounds just as convincing
to Géronte. Naturally, Scapin accompanies each narrative with
a wealth of dramatic gestures. In short, this valet not only
has a fertile imagination, but he knows all the tricks of rhetoric.
And when eloquence fails to convince, he can rely on his mastery
of theatrical techniques.

Scapin's hoodwinking of the stupid Géronte becomes itself
a narrative, a *récit,* capable of amusing the other characters.
Zerbinette asks the valet to tell her about his latest prowess:
"Tu sais qu'on ne perd point sa peine lorsqu'on me fait un conte,

et que je le paye bien par la joie qu'on m'y voit prendre" (III, 1).
Zerbinette thus sees herself as the perfect audience, the type
of audience so devoutly wished for by the dancing master in
Le Bourgeois gentilhomme. By transforming the dramatic scene
of the abduction into a narrative, into a story, she tends to transform Scapin's theatrical trick into a literary creation, having
no other function than to please an audience. The impressive
material results achieved by Scapin, namely the extortion of
five-hundred ducats for the purchase of this same Zerbinette
from the gypsies who owned her, recede into the background.
Scapin's feat, reduced to its esthetic essence, almost becomes a
gratuitous act.

This metamorphosis of action into narrative leads to the scene
where the hilarious Zerbinette chokingly gives Géronte a de-
tailed account of his own undoing. She thus transforms into a
story an event which the audience has already witnessed and
through which the now suspicious Géronte has lived. The old
man sees himself in the most ridiculous light possible and, like
Arnolphe before him, must play the passive part of audience
in order to discover the entire truth. In this scene, Molière has
forced together two mutually exclusive types of "audience reaction." Molière had already used a similar device in his *Impromptu de Versailles* as well as in *La Critique de l'Ecole des
femmes,* plays in which he had put the "audience" on stage.
But its effect in *Les Fourberies* is much greater, for the real
public finds Zerbinette's irrepressible laughter contagious and
enjoys the suffering of Géronte, who no doubt deserves this type
of punishment. The reward for all this laughter belongs to
Scapin, alias Molière: even before telling Géronte about the
incident of the *galère,* she had referred to the entire adventure
as *notre conte,* describing the valet as "un homme incomparable"
who deserves "toutes les louanges qu'on peut donner." After
her victim's departure, she tells Silvestre about her mistake:
"... je me suis adressée à lui-même sans y penser, pour lui conter
son histoire" (III, 4). It would seem that the author cannot
insist too strongly on the transformation of a purely theatrical
event into story-telling.

There is a general tendency throughout the farce to tell stories, so much so that _Les Fourberies_ appears to contain a greater number of narratives than any other play of Molière. The author goes so far as to include a _récit_ in a _récit,_ when Octave discusses Léandre's love for Zerbinette: "Il ne m'entretenoit que d'elle chaque jour; m'exagéroit à tous moments sa beauté et sa grâce; me louoit son esprit, et me parloit avec transport des charmes de son entretien ..." (I, 2). But in Octave, Léandre by no means found a suitable audience: "Il me querelloit quelquefois de n'être pas assez sensible aux choses qu'il me venoit dire, et me blâmoit sans cesse de l'indifférence où j'étois pour les feux de l'amour." But can we blame Octave for being bored with his friend's rather wordy love affair with the garrulous Zerbinette? When Scapin shows impatience at Octave's story: "Je ne vois pas encore où ceci veut aller," the young man eloquently recounts his own infatuation. The scene that he then describes would tempt a Greuze. It all starts with "quelques plaintes mêlées de beaucoup de sanglots" which he overhears. Molière definitely wanted to prepare Octave and the audience for the ensuing spectacle: "Une femme nous dit, en soupirant, que nous pouvions voir là quelque chose de pitoyable en des personnes étrangères, et qu'à moins que d'être insensibles, nous en serions touchés." His acquaintance with Hyacinthe will thus begin as a touching spectacle. After the insensible Scapin's interruption—the valet definitely does not play the part of receptive audience in this scene— Octave continues his narrative: "... nous voyons une vieille femme mourante, assistée d'une servante qui faisoit des regrets, et d'une jeune fille toute fondante en larmes, la plus belle et la plus touchante qu'on puisse jamais voir." Octave's ensuing description of Hyacinthe definitely has a theatrical quality: "Ses larmes n'étoient point de ces larmes desagréables qui défigurent un visage; elle avoit à pleurer une grâce touchante, et sa douleur étoit la plus belle du monde." An actress could not have done any better. And this sad spectacle, which Scapin's sophisticated comment—"Je vois tout cela"—transforms into just another absurd incident, has found in Octave a most receptive audience. The star of the show "faisoit fondre chacun en larmes"—everyone except Léandre who, quite unmoved by all this melodrama, "la trouvoit assez jolie."

Silvestre, who has heard this before, impatiently interrupts him: "Si vous n'abrégez tout ce récit, nous en voilà pour jusqu'à demain." He then continues this pathetic story, but at such speed that the whole love affair becomes ludicrous. Silvestre actually increases the tempo of the narrative as he goes along: "Voilà son amour augmenté par les difficultés. Il consulte dans sa tête, agite, raisonne, balance, prend sa résolution: le voilà marié avec elle depuis trois jours." It almost seems as if Silvestre had overshot his mark. He moves at so great a pace towards the crucial event, that he somehow relegates it to the past at the very moment he reaches it: "depuis trois jours." The sudden *dénouement* of this story makes the audience move, mentally, three steps backward. Thus the author, in recounting a single event, succeeds in expressing a variety of "audience reactions": curiosity, impatience, boredom, sentimentality immediately degraded by irony, before coming to a conclusion, which takes the spectators by surprise. The narrative concerning the tearful Hyacinthe appears quite early in the play, whereas the story told by Zerbinette occurs almost at the end. In all likelihood, Molière wanted to establish the same sort of contrast between these two girls as between Octave's appreciation of witty remarks and Léandre's enjoyment of pathos. And we find the same sort of contrast in the two narratives just discussed. The play seems to move from one extreme to another, mechanically.

The *dénouement*, like Octave's narrative, contains just about all the ingredients of "bad" literature. We can put the story of the rich young man who marries a poor orphan in precisely the same literary class as that of the fathers who finally discover their long lost daughters. By combining the two, one might obtain a sickly sentimental tale that would make an intelligent eight-year-old blush with disbelief. Molière does not fail to underline the absurdity of the ending. Silvestre exclaims: "Voilà une aventure qui est tout à fait surprenante!" (III, 7); and even Hyacinthe says: "O Ciel! que d'aventures extraordinaires!" (III, 11). Literature has come to the help of literature in order to ensure a happy ending. Or perhaps heaven has put itself on the side of the inspired Scapin, that creative demiurge. This ending actually resembles the incredible *dénouement* of *L'Avare;* but instead of bringing a feeling of relief, the happy pairing off of sons and daughters makes the whole thing collapse, for Scapin, throughout the play, had shown much more inventiveness than chance or the *deus ex machina*. He had managed, by his skill, to put himself above destiny and to treat existence as a sort of mechanical contrivance.

20

Food for
Thought

*A*FTER *Les Fourberies de Scapin,* Molière
wrote a slight but effective ballet-comedy entitled *La Comtesse
d'Escarbagnas,* which contains a series of performances within
a performance. Moreover, the author develops one of the major
themes of the previous play: literary appreciation. This pleasant
divertissement was followed by one of Molière's most savage
plays, *Les Femmes savantes.* Critics have often pondered the
cruel treatment of the abbé Cotin, named Tricotin and then
Trissotin in the comedy. Previously, the author had seldom
satirized specific individuals; but here he rivals Aristophanes
by the directness of his attack. And it would be difficult to determine whether his main purpose consisted in exposing a certain
type of intellectual preciosity, or in destroying an enemy.

In Trissotin, Molière has created a character almost as repulsive as Tartuffe, but somewhat more clever. According to A.
Adam, who finds this comedy disappointing, the real Cotin
was a vitriolic hypocrite. This alone would justify Molière's
venom in caricaturing him. Actually, the idea of attacking Cotin
may have occured to Molière as an afterthought, for the metaphorical structure of the play suggests that Molière's prime aim
in writing this work was, at least from an intellectual standpoint,
to renew his attacks against verbalism and, at the same time, to
expose a particularly virulent type of tyranny. In Trissotin,
Molière has stigmatized the most dangerous type of user of
words; and in his female admirers, he has portrayed the usual
gullible victims of this kind of fraud. The author goes even
further than in *Le Misanthrope* or *Dom Juan,* which, among
other things, exposed the futility of verbalism, or even *Tartuffe,*
where he had revealed the equivocation of gesture. In *Les
Femmes savantes,* words and concepts serve mainly as a means

241

to achieve unavowed material ends, such as the power to dominate; and they become the most effective instruments for deception and even self-deception.

VERBALISM

A key scene in the play is the summary dismissal of Martine
for infractions against the rules of grammar. Chrysale, the submissive husband, upon hearing that Philaminte has dismissed
his favorite servant for some heinous sin, enumerates three
different crimes, one more serious than the other. At each of
these guesses, his wife asserts that Martine has committed a
felony incomparably worse. Chrysale then taxes his imagination
in order to discover her atrocious crime, but Philaminte cuts him
short:

> Elle a, d'une insolence à nulle autre pareille,
> Après trente leçons, insulté mon oreille
> Par l'impropriété d'un mot sauvage et bas,
> Qu'en termes décisifs condamne Vaugelas (459–62).

Philaminte's aberration makes us laugh; and it would seem
that it was only for the sake of a good joke that Molière invented so preposterous a reason for firing an otherwise exemplary
domestic—the only one who performs her duties efficiently instead of writing books! Actually, the attitude of Philaminte
towards Martine brings out one of the major themes of the
comedy: these blue-stockings consider words sacred. For this
reason, any infraction against correct speech will necessarily
appear more serious and more dangerous to them than, for instance, theft.

Philaminte, Armande and Bélise differ from Cathos and
Magdelon in that they wilfully attempt to substitute a universe
of words and concepts for the "real" world. The *précieuses ridicules* had merely wished to live in the literary paradise of Madeleine de Scudéry's novels and, vicariously, indulge their budding
vanity. The ambitions of both Philaminte and Armande go
way beyond that, for they wish to found an academy that will

dominate the cultural life of the country. Thus, they assert their will to power by means of words:

> Pour la langue, on verra dans peu nos règlements,
> Et nous y prétendons faire des remuements.
> Par une antipathie ou juste, ou naturelle,
> Nous avons pris chacune une haine mortelle
> Pour un nombre de mots, soit ou verbes ou noms,
> Que mutuellement nous nous abandonnons;
> Contre eux nous préparons de mortelles sentences,
> Et nous devons ouvrir nos doctes conférences
> Par les proscriptions de tous ces mots divers
> Dont nous voulons purger et la prose et les vers (899–908).

Although these pitiless proscriptions involve only the bloodless world of the dictionary and will spill nothing more gory than ink, Armande sounds like the youthful Cæsar Octavius addressing his associates Marcus Antonius and Lepidus. In this massacre of syllables, antipathy and hatred play a dominant part, with tyranny as the goal. Armande's ambition resembles that of Arnolphe, who tried to make himself absolute in marriage. From the standpoint of style, this speech provides another example of the mock-heroic mode, for Armande expresses her will to dominate a verbal universe as though she intended to take over the state. Although their ambition may strike the reader as ludicrous, it is by no means innocuous. Philaminte and her elder daughter want above all to tyrannize the world around them. And Philaminte's browbeating of her husband, as well as the sway Armande used to hold over Clitandre, merely corroborate this same drive to power. In short, these predatory females do not really care about ideas or even about the purity of the French language; they merely use philosophy as a means of asserting something much more basic. Deprived for obvious reasons of military or political dominance, they find in these learned academies some form of compensation.

In substituting words for reality, Armande and her mother tend to materialize, to concretize concepts. It is this tendency that made Martine's crime so heinous: she had not only committed a crime against Vaugelas, but she had unwittingly ques-

tioned their authority, and endangered the only world they
regard as real. The materialization of concepts appears most
clearly in the "femmes savantes'" admiration for Trissotin's
poetry. These women who, previously, had dismissed the cook
for spoiling French grammar, equate his verse with food: "Servez-
nous promptement votre aimable repas" (746). Trissotin blithely
adds new variations on this metaphor: [1]

> Pour cette grande faim qu'à mes yeux on expose,
> Un plat seul de huit vers me semble peu de chose,
> Et je pense qu'ici je ne ferai pas mal
> De joindre à l'épigramme, ou bien au madrigal,
> Le ragoût d'un sonnet, qui chez une princesse
> A passé pour avoir quelque délicatesse.
> Il est de sel attique assaisonné partout,
> Et vous le trouverez, je crois, d'assez bon goût (747–54).

Our three *précieuses* prefer a wordy diet to more sustaining fare.
They almost live on words and concepts, which take the place,
among other things, of money. Philaminte cannot help but
regard Trissotin, an impoverished poet, as a man of great worth.
For this reason, she has arranged a match between him and her
younger daughter Henriette. The poet will compensate for the
girl's lack of intellectuality, in the same manner that a wealthy
but no longer youthful husband might provide a young, well-
born, but dowerless bride with the finer things in life. And
Philaminte considers this match between Trissotin and Henriette a *mariage de raison* in every sense of the term.

KNOWLEDGE AND FEELING

Molière makes fun of his three *précieuses* by punctuating with
typically feminine expressions of enthusiasm their pursuit of
knowledge, e.g. Armande's "Epicure me plaît," or Philaminte's
"Pour les abstractions, j'aime le platonisme," or Bélise's "Je
m'accomode assez pour moi des petits corps" (III, 2). All three
women sound as though they were selecting a new dress or com-

[1] Cf. *Grands Ecrivains, Ed.,* IX, 122.

paring the latest craze in lace. When they learn that Vadius speaks Greek, their enthusiasm knows no bounds. Armande squeals: "Du grec! quelle douceur!" and Philaminte even hugs the pedant: "Quoi? Monsieur sait du grec? Ah! permettez, de grâce, / Que pour l'amour du grec, Monsieur, on vous embrasse (III, 3). Vadius appeals to them not only as a master of words, but of words in their most sacred and select form: Greek words. Hence, their ridiculous display of emotion. Base words, as we have already seen, elicit hostile emotions.

If feelings tend to distort their knowledge, we can expect that knowledge will, in return, give a strange twist to their feelings, even to the point of distorting their femininity. Philosophy definitely affects Philaminte's conception of feminine beauty and charm. She tells Henriette:

> La beauté du visage est un frêle ornement,
> Une fleur passagère, un éclat d'un moment,
> Et qui n'est attaché qu'à la simple épiderme;
> Mais celle de l'esprit est inhérente et ferme (1063–66).

Philaminte, a self-styled idealist, despises the body and its skin-deep attractions. Her daughter Armande, a confirmed Platonist, regards love as a meeting of disembodied spirits: "Ce n'est qu'à l'esprit seul que vont tous les transports, / Et l'on ne s'aperçoit jamais qu'on ait un corps" (1211–12). Armande, in spite of these theories, will finally accept baser forms of love, such as "nœuds de chair" and "chaînes corporelles" (1238), in a futile attempt to wrest the no longer faithful Clitandre from her sister Henriette. In short, our "femmes savantes" cannot avoid foisting their feminine feelings into the domain of knowledge where they do not belong and, conversely, introducing idealistic metaphysics into the world of sex where it is out of place. Molière has created a preposterous exchange, whereby the body is denied its material existence and baseless ideas emerge into concreteness.

This paradoxical exchange or transformation appears in the quarrel between Armande and Henriette which opens the comedy:

> Quoi? le beau nom de fille est un titre, ma sœur,
> Dont vous voulez quitter la charmante douceur,
> Et de vous marier vous osez faire fête? (1–3).

Marriage, unlike "fille," is a dirty word which suggests dirty thoughts:

> Ah, fi! vous dis-je.
> Ne concevez-vous point ce que, dès qu'on l'entend,
> Un tel mot à l'esprit offre de dégoûtant?
> De quelle étrange image on est par lui blessée?
> Sur quelle sale vue il traîne la pensée?
> N'en frissonnez-vous point? et pouvez-vous, ma sœur,
> Aux suites de ce mot résoudre votre cœur? (8–14).

Throughout the scene, Armande's passionate Platonism combines with her jealousy to give her speech an absurd kind of eloquence:

> Laissez aux gens grossiers, aux personnes vulgaires,
> Les bas amusements de ces sortes d'affaires;
> A de plus hauts objets élevez vos désirs,
> Songez à prendre un goût des plus nobles plaisirs,
> Et traitant de mépris les sens et la matière,
> A l'esprit comme nous donnez-vous toute entière (31–36).

Desires, pleasures, and the unstinted gift of one's self somehow lose their substance, and even feelings are metamorphosed into an ethereal form of knowledge. Armande's argument reaches some sort of climax when she says: "Loin d'être aux lois d'un homme en esclave asservie, / Mariez-vous, ma sœur, à la philosophie, / Qui nous monte au-dessus de tout le genre humain" (43–45). According to this reasoning, the pursuit of knowledge will inevitably lead Henriette to a kind of abstract and disembodied marriage. As to Armande herself, she intends to keep Clitandre enchained, if not as a possible husband, at least as an admirer, because, after all, "... l'on peut pour époux refuser un mérite / Que pour adorateur on veut bien à sa suite" (103–04). This at least is the answer she gives to Henriette, who had ironically echoed her own bizarre proposal: "Votre esprit à l'hymen renonce pour toujours, / Et la philosophie a toutes vos amours" (97–98). Armande unfortunately makes the mistake of arbitrarily trying to substitute emotions for ideas and, at the same time, ideas for emotions to the detriment of both. In poor Bélise, a similar substitution brings about a state of utter confusion, for she believes that every man she happens to meet must fall madly in love with her though in the chastest manner possible. She indulges in a sort of Platonic promiscuity and indiscriminately accepts every male's hommage as a tribute to her irresistible charms. Differing in this respect from her counterpart in Desmarets' *Visionnaires,* she expresses her misguided Platonism in pseudo-Cartesian terms: [2]

> ... nous établissons une espèce d'amour
> Qui doit être épuré comme l'astre du jour:
> La substance qui pense y peut être reçue,
> Mais nous en bannissons la substance étendue (1683–86).

As for Philaminte, she shows greater consistency in her philosophical views than Armande who has deceived herself all along in her attempt to rise above her instincts. Upon hearing the news of her total financial ruin, she reacts as a true stoic should. She definitely shows her superiority over her husband, who is crushed by the disaster: "Ah! quel honteux transport! Fi! tout cela n'est rien. / Il n'est pour le vrai sage aucun revers funeste, / Et perdant toute chose, à soi-même il se reste (1706–09). Her stoicism takes the form of self-assertion, worthy of Corneille's Médée. Clitandre, however, behaves just as nobly as Philaminte, for he offers to take Henriette without a dowry. And Henriette surpasses the other two, for she refuses to burden the man she loves by adding her own poverty to his. Thus, love proves to be more than a match for Philaminte's stoicism. As for the self-seeking Trissotin, he naturally behaves like a cad.

OBEDIENCE

On the level of the plot, everything depends on whether Chrysale or his wife will be obeyed. Between the two, there

[2] Hespérie merely believes that every man loves her.

rages a ludicrous and rather one-sided struggle for power—
a struggle which produces an impression of futility, because the
husband, in spite of his common sense, has abdicated his rights,
and the wife, who holds all the power, has lost touch with reality.

The earthy Chrysale, however, tends to substitute words for
action. He always shows courage when people happen to agree
with him:

> Et moi, je lui commande avec pleine puissance
> De préparer sa main à cette autre alliance.
> Ah! je leur ferai voir si, pour donner la loi,
> Il est dans ma maison d'autre maître que moi.
> Nous allons revenir, songez à nous attendre.
> Allons, suivez mes pas, mon frère, et vous, mon gendre
> (1441–46).

At the critical moment he will of course give in once more. His
brother who, all along, has expected the worst, must at the
last moment invent the stratagem of the lost lawsuit and the
false bankruptcy. Chrysale, in spite of the fact that he always
submits to his wife, frequently expresses his feelings in her presence. After having given his reluctant consent to the dismissal of
Martine, he bitterly criticizes the conduct of the "femmes
savantes," prudently addressing his admonitions to the innocuous Bélise. He uses strong language in accusing them of madness
and his entire household (with the exception of Martine) of
inefficiency. His brave words do not lead him to reverse his decision: in this respect at least, he resembles Armande and Philaminte, who use words as a form of compensation. By substituting
speech for action, Chrysale gives himself if no one else the illusion of being master in his own house. Like Armande, he tends
to materialize words. The best example of this tendency appears
at the end of the play in the orders he gives to the notary:
"Allons, Monsieur, suivez l'ordre que j'ai prescrit, / Et faites
le contrat ainsi que je l'ai dit."

The idea of obedience goes much deeper than the simple
struggle for power between Chrysale and Philaminte. It often
takes the form of a hierarchy of values, going from the basest

or most material to the highest and most ethereal. Obviously, mankind must give full allegiance to these immaterial and spiritual values. Because Henriette wants a husband, Armande accuses her of baseness: "Mon Dieu, que votre esprit est d'un étage bas! / Que vous jouez au monde un petit personnage" (26–27). Moreover, she constantly opposes the lowly pleasures of marriage to higher objects where a woman worthy of the name should perpetually elevate her desires. Throughout the play, there are reiterations of the antithesis between high and low, between terrestrial and celestial, between material and spiritual, as well as a consistent striving, usually quite inauthentic, to put oneself above the contingencies of everyday existence. Philosophy will put Trissotin above the shame of being a cuckold (cf. 1545–46). Against the alleged betrayal of Clitandre, who has switched his affection to the less learned Henriette, Armande asserts: "Contre de pareils coups l'âme se fortifie / Du solide secours de la philosophie, /Et par elle on se peut mettre au-dessus de tout" (1145–47). Molière, by constant repetition of this spatial metaphor, makes the idea of hierarchy appear ridiculous, especially when we remember that the three bluestockings intend to place Trissotin's poetry and Vadius' Greek higher than almost anything else. Clitandre, in his speech to Philaminte, stresses the absurdity of this hierarchy: "Et ce qui m'a vingt fois fait tomber de mon haut, / C'est de vous voir au ciel élever des sornettes / Que vous désavoueriez si vous les aviez faites" (1260–62). The surprising antithesis between the familiar *tomber de mon haut* and the expression *au ciel* emphasizes the absurdity of Philaminte's insistence on levels of being.

The idea of hierarchy carries with it a whole concatenation of laws and obligations. As Philaminte despises the so-called lower aspects of existence, she feels that she has the right and perhaps even the duty to dominate her husband, who prefers good cooking and a well-managed home to the values that really count. Philaminte, who wants to identify herself with everything spiritual, would like to occupy in her milieu the same lofty position that philosophy occupies in the realm of knowledge: philosophy gives sovereignty to reason and submits our

animal nature to its laws. In their opening quarrel, Henriette
had reminded Armande that their mother, after all, had not
been above marriage; and she therefore suggests the following
line of conduct:

> ... dans nos desseins l'une à l'autre contraire,
> Nous saurons toutes deux imiter notre mère:
> Vous, du côté de l'âme et des nobles désirs,
> Moi, du côté des sens et des grossiers plaisirs;
> Vous, aux productions d'esprit et de lumière,
> Moi, dans celles, ma sœur, qui sont de la matière (67–72).

Previously, she had indicated that Armande could occupy "Les
hautes régions de la philosophie" whereas she would confine
herself to the nether regions of "terrestres appas." Thus, the
usual antithesis between high and low appears in her speech,
colored of course with a generous tinge of irony. Henriette, in
addition, suggests the existence of a dual order, each one based
on instinct, each one exemplified in the noble life of Philaminte,
taken, though perhaps not too seriously, as a model. And Henriette affirms the validity of both of these orders: "Ne troublons
point du Ciel les justes règlements" (61), for Heaven always
will take the side of diversity. Armande, mainly for selfish reasons, proclaims the absolute superiority of the "high road":
"Quand sur une personne on prétend se régler, / C'est par les
beaux côtés qu'il lui faut ressembler" (73–74). This statement
shows quite clearly that Armande wishes to introduce at all costs
a hierarchy of so-called spiritual values or, as it will soon appear,
a tyranny of empty idealism over nature, leading inevitably to an
utter confusion of values.

  In this quarrel Henriette speaks rather ironically, as we have
already noticed, of the idea of hierarchy. Moreover, she never
fails to point out the contradictions in her sister's attitude.
Armande, upon discovering Clitandre's preference for Henriette, had shown her anger. Henriette cruelly refers her sister to
the moral laws which she had so stoutly proclaimed: "Eh! doucement ma sœur. Où donc est la morale / Qui sait si bien régir la
partie animale, / Et retenir la bride aux efforts du courroux?"

(159–61). Armande, for lack of a better answer, refers to a quite different kind of law, that of parental authority (cf. 162–68). She thus appeals to the principle of authority rather than to the lofty idealism which, up to that moment, she had always preached. Philaminte, in discussing with Armande her younger daughter's rebellion, will complete this confusion between the two antithetical types of moral law:

> Je lui montrerai bien aux lois de qui des deux
> Les droits de la raison soumettent tous ses vœux,
> Et qui doit gouverner, ou sa mère ou son père,
> Ou l'esprit ou le corps, la forme ou la matière (1127–30).

These lines are among the most subtly ludicrous in the entire theater of Molière, because of the identification between metaphysics and family authority. By adding to this confusion her dislike of Clitandre, who shows no interest in her writings, her choice of a poetaster who dabbles in philosophy as a husband for Henriette, and the constantly repeated antitheses between high and low, between spiritual and material, we reach a state bordering on intellectual and moral chaos. Philaminte's statement may strike us as absurd; actually, it is only more extreme, but hardly any worse, than most of our reasoning, even today, on the subject.

Molière introduces the notion of hierarchy into the relationships between Chrysale and his wife: "Il a reçu du Ciel certaine bonté d'âme, / Qui le soumet d'abord à ce que veut sa femme" (207–08). His brother advises him to assert his authority against his wife's assumption of sovereignty:

> Votre femme, entre nous,
> Est par vos lâchetés souveraine sur vous.
> Son pouvoir n'est fondé que sur votre foiblesse,
> C'est de vous qu'elle prend le titre de maîtresse;
> Vous-même à ses hauteurs vous vous abandonnez ... (677–82).

Molière uses throughout such lofty terms as *souveraine, pouvoir, empire, loi,* to express Philaminte's henpecking of the weak and foolish Chrysale, which shows how frequently the author relies

on the mock-heroic style for his comic effects. Chrysale himself
sees a moral issue in his struggle with the redoubtable Philaminte:
"C'est une chose infâme / Que d'être si soumis au pouvoir d'une
femme" (699–700). He sometimes sounds like a conspirator,
willing and ready to risk his neck in order to overthrow a cruel
tyrant.

The principle of authority and the idea of law characterize
most of the human relationships in the comedy, for instance the
now vanished love of Clitandre for Armande:

> J'ai souffert sous leur joug cent mépris différents,
> Ils régnoient sur mon âme en superbes tyrans,
> Et je me suis cherché, lassé de tant de peines,
> Des vainqueurs plus humains et de moins rudes chaînes
> (141–44).

In this manner, the conventional vocabulary of preciosity enters
the picture and fits perfectly into the metaphorical scheme of the
play. Armande will take this fashion of speaking seriously and
transform Clitandre's trite metaphors into so many moral obligations: "Au changement de vœux nulle horreur ne s'égale, / Et
tout cœur infidèle est un monstre en morale" (1173–74).
Clitandre does not hesitate to return the compliment:

> Appelez-vous, Madame, une infidélité
> Ce que m'a de votre âme ordonné la fierté?
> Je ne fais qu'obéir aux lois qu'elle m'impose;
> Et si je vous offense, elle seule en est cause (1175–78).

Clitandre refers to a tyrannical law imposed on him by arrogance
—a law quite different from the obligation of fidelity. Armande,
in her confusion, attempts to justify her arrogance and her con-
trariness in Platonic terms. Like her mother, she automatically
identifies her pride and her will to power, even in the realm of
love, with the loftiest idealism. And because of this inauthentic
idealism, she will necessarily lose Clitandre to the clear-sighted
Henriette.

Now, hierarchy, laws, rules, and other absolutes can dominate
completely only in the realm of words. This explains why our

bluestockings attach so much importance to vocabulary and syntax. Grammar must reign supreme: "La grammaire, qui sait régenter jusqu'aux rois, / Et les fait la main haute obéir à ses lois" (465–66). Thanks to grammar and to philosophy, Philaminte and Armande hope to fulfill their dream of absolute authority. And they assert this authority, as already mentioned, by firing the cook whose errors in vocabulary and syntax endanger one of the hierarchies with which they identify their very essence. Their admiration for Trissotin and Vadius actually helps to bolster their authority, and by founding an academy they would really become absolute. Unfortunately, the quarrel between Vadius and Trissotin makes Philaminte's reliance on hierarchy appear ridiculous, even before the latter's betrayal of his principles.

From an intellectual standpoint, it would seem that Molière wrote *Les Femmes savantes* in order to satirize those people who wilfully try to confuse one hierarchy with another, especially if they derive their prestige and their status from a false identification with a scheme of values which they hardly understand, such as Platonic philosophy or Cartesian metaphysics, or else with purely linguistic categories such as the rules of grammar. By false identification, Philaminte puts herself above other people and therefore regards her every whim as an infallible law of nature. And to this false identification, Molière opposes another, no less false, but so silly that it brings out the complete absurdity of Philaminte's vision of the world. Martine tempestuously takes the side of Chrysale against his wife:

> Les savants ne sont bons que pour prêcher en chaise;
> Et pour mon mari, moi, mille fois je l'ai dit,
> Je ne voudrois jamais prendre un homme d'esprit.
>
> . . . .
>
> Et je veux, si jamais on engage ma foi,
> Un mari qui n'ait point d'autre livre que moi,
> Qui ne sache A ne B, n'en déplaise à Madame,
> Et ne soit en un mot docteur que pour sa femme (1662–70).

Martine has confused the issues as badly as Armande or Philaminte in spite of the fact that she moves in the opposite direction. Instead of witnessing the invasion of the realm of sex and marriage by some misguided form of spirituality, we see an illiterate husband becoming a "docteur pour sa femme." This unexpected invasion from the bottom actually seems to be a caricature of Philaminte's confused reasoning and therefore can serve as a fitting revenge for her lack of pertinence in intellectual and moral matters.

Molière has also made fun of Cartesianism, referred to in such terms as *tourbillons* and *petits corps,* as well as in the opposition between "substance qui pense" and "substance étendue" (V, 3). Descartes, because of his reliance upon clear and distinct ideas, upon thought rather than experience or experimentation, sought, according to a Gassendist point of view, to impose new hierarchies where they do not belong. And one can hardly deny that Descartes' metaphysics, or at least his ontological proof of God, is based on hierarchy and on the superiority of thought over extended matter.

21

The Doctor's Curse

Le Malade imaginaire readily lends itself to conflicting interpretations. Several scenes do not quite make sense if the spectator or reader regards Molière's satire as directed only at physicians. Does Purgon behave like a doctor of medicine when he curses Argan with all the diseases ending in -*ie,* as though he had the power of life and death over a disobedient patient? The author criticizes the *Faculté* for stressing the importance of ancient languages and of dogma instead of the exigencies of the present. But it so happens that these same strictures can apply as easily to the Church as to medicine. The play actually gains in coherence whenever a metaphor, an attitude, a gesture suggests an analogy between medical doctors and theologians—the type of analogy which had already made an ominous appearance in Monsieur Filerin's long speech to his colleagues in *L'Amour médecin.*

WORDS AND CANT

Molière once again satirizes the willful confusion between words and objects, but more violently and more explicitly than ever before. In a futile attempt to cure Argan of his madness, his brother, Béralde, insists upon the distinction between fact and word, between effective knowledge and pure nomenclature. Physicians have achieved mastery only in the realm of words: "Ils savent la plupart de fort belles humanités, savent parler en beau latin, savent nommer en grec toutes les maladies, les définir et les diviser; mais, pour ce qui est de les guérir, c'est ce qu'ils ne savent point du tout" (III, 3). Their knowledge of disease is limited to discourse—to those verbal classifications dear to the hearts of grammarians. Unfortunately, language cannot cure—

or at least it lacked this power in the seventeenth century. Later in this scene, Béralde emphasizes even more strongly the wordy nature of medical "science": "... Toute l'excellence de leur art consiste en un pompeux galimatias, en un spécieux babil, qui vous donne des mots pour des raisons, et des promesses pour des effets." Finally, Argan's wise brother opposes facts to discourse: "Dans les discours et dans les choses, ce sont deux sortes de personnes que vos grands médecins. Entendez-les parler: les plus habiles gens du monde; voyez-les faire: les plus ignorants de tous les hommes." After Purgon curses Argan, Béralde will reiterate this same distinction in an even simpler and more succinct form: "Et ce qu'il dit, que fait-il à la chose?" (III, 6).

Throughout the comedy—from Argan's comments on Monsieur Fleurant's bill to the concluding masquerade—physicians and apothecaries achieve a measure of success only in their use of language. Argan is reading out loud the pharmacist Fleurant's bill for the month: "Plus, du vingt-quatrième, un petit clystère insinuatif, préparatif, et rémollient, pour amollir, humecter, et rafraîchir les entrailles de Monsieur." And Argan observes: "Ce qui me plaît de Monsieur Fleurant, mon apothicaire, c'est que ses parties sont toujours fort civiles" (I, 1). Monsieur Fleurant's art consists in making even an enema sound attractive and graceful by the deft use of appropriate terms. This language, however, strikes Argan as inflationary, but in quite a different manner: "... vingt sols, en langage d'apothicaire, c'est-à-dire dix sols." One may wonder how many creative writers have derived as many solid benefits from their verbal mastery as Molière's soft-spoken pharmacist.

The fledgling doctor, Thomas Diafoirus, is described even by his father as deficient in imagination and wit. Nevertheless, he is extremely verbose in his compliments to Argan, Béline and Angélique. As he had learned his lengthy compliments by heart, he can no longer pursue his speech after Béline has stopped him in his tracks. He affects a style, fashionable perhaps in the day of Puget de La Serre: this old fashioned rhetoric, coming from a young man, must have struck Molière's contemporaries as even more ridiculous than it seems to us today, now that it has become merely archaic. Toinette, upon hearing his ornate oratory, exclaims sarcastically: "Ce sera quelque chose d'admirable s'il fait d'aussi belles cures qu'il fait de beaux discours" (II, 5). Granted the antithesis between talking and curing, young Diafoirus' patients may not fare too well.

As physicians are proficient only in their use of language, we can expect them to invest medical terms with an almost sacred power: hence, Monsieur Purgon's curse of Argan and his patient's terror. As Argan's illness remains purely imaginary, he is bound to attribute to the names of diseases a frightening quality. Like Milton's Satan, our hero, abandoned by his doctor, will fall from one morbid state to the next—*bradypepsie, dyspepsie, apepsie, lienterie, dyssenterie, hydropisie* until deprivation of life. This horrible sequence will result from Purgon's malediction: "Et je veux qu'avant qu'il soit quatre jours, vous deveniez en un état incurable" (III, 5). To Argan, the rhyming names of these diseases sound like so many devils, endowed with occult and malignant powers, which Purgon has called forth to punish him for his disobedience. Indeed, medicine itself strikes him as an occult force or a vengeful deity having a will of its own: "Je n'en puis plus. Je sens déjà que la médecine se venge" (III, 6). Purgon's language contrasts sharply with the insinuating tones of Monsieur Fleurant and also of the notary. In the irate doctor, Molière has portrayed the true believer, who never doubts the value of his doctrines—the disinterested dogmatist, who subordinates life itself to the rules of his profession: "... il ne fera, en vous tuant, que ce qu'il a fait à sa femme et à ses enfants, et ce qu'en un besoin il feroit à lui-même" (III, 3). Béralde describes Purgon's faith in medicine as a "roideur de confiance." Because of his rigidity, through thick and thin, the good doctor persists in applying systematically the principles of his art; and he need never refer to observed facts and experience.

THE THEME OF OBEDIENCE

In *Le Malade,* Molière gives a new twist to a theme which had played a dominant part in *Les Femmes savantes:* that of command and obedience. In Argan's specialized universe, only the hierarchy of medicine and disease really matters. Physicians have discretionary powers, and the patient must obey them without murmur. For that reason, Purgon feels entitled to curse the apparently rebellious Argan and anathematize him by abandoning him to the weakness of his constitution in the same manner that the Church might abandon heretics to the corruption of human nature.

Within the hierarchy of medicine, Monsieur Fleurant takes orders from Purgon. When Argan attempts to put off for a while his enema because of Béralde's intervention, Monsieur Fleurant protests: "De quoi vous mêlez-vous de vous opposer aux ordonnances de la médecine, et d'empêcher Monsieur de prendre mon clystère? Vous êtes bien plaisant d'avoir cette hardiesse-là!" (III, 4). The term *ordonnances,* which generally signifies a medical prescription, subtly takes on its original meaning, that of a government or a church decree, for the apothecary does not refer to the "ordonnances de Monsieur Purgon" or "du médecin," but to those of a more august power: "de la médecine." He may, for that reason, accuse Béralde of *hardiesse.*

Béralde's answer is masterful: "Allez, Monsieur, on voit bien que vous n'avez pas accoutumé de parler à des visages." Fleurant must then appeal to higher authority—to Monsieur Purgon. The latter, sensing the danger of rebellion, rushes over and repeatedly accuses his patient of disobedience before uttering his final curse: "Voilà une hardiesse bien grande, une étrange rébellion d'un malade contre son médecin. ... Un attentat énorme contre la médecine. ... Un crime de lèse-Faculté, qui ne se peut assez punir. ... Puisque vous vous êtes soustrait de l'obeissance que l'on doit à son médecin ... . Puisque vous vous êtes déclaré rebelle aux remèdes que je vous ordonnois" (III, 5). Purgon's attitude shows that Molière meant by *ordonnance* much more than a medical prescription, for the mad physician really believes that Argan's disobedience deserves the direst punishment, as though his patient had committed a crime against the king or against religion.

Argan apparently believes that the mortal sin of disobedience has put his life in jeopardy. Béralde implies as much when he tells him: "Il semble, à vous entendre, que Monsieur Purgon tienne dans ses mains le filet de vos jours, et que, d'autorité suprême, il vous l'allonge et vous le raccourcisse comme il lui plaît. Songez que les principes de votre vie sont en vous-même ..." (III, 6). But our hypochondriac cannot help believing everything that his doctor has told him: "Il dit que je deviendrai incurable avant qu'il soit quatre jours." Argan does indeed attribute to Purgon absolute power over life and death as though he actually held sway over destiny itself which, like Fleurant and like his patients, must obey his least command. Béralde's surprising statement: "Songez que les principes de votre vie sont en vous-même" appears to transcend the realm of medicine and to deny all externalized occult powers that men, including priests as well as physicians, invoke for bodily and spiritual salvation. And taken out of context, it could serve as an epigraph to almost any work of Jean-Paul Sartre! Béralde's wisdom has hardly any effect on his brother: "Voyez-vous? j'ai sur le cœur toutes ces maladies-là que je ne connois point, ces ..." (III, 7). In other words, Argan fears the unknown, fears those mysterious forces that his disobedience has unleashed.

The hierarchical aspects of medicine reappear in the burlesque masquerade which ends the comedy:

Totus mundus, currens ad nostros remedios,
Nos regardat sicut Deos;
Et nostris ordonnanciis
Principes et reges soumissos videtis.

Although physicians may impress a minority of their patients by their power, although rulers submit to their prescriptions, they tend throughout the play to behave in a most obedient manner. Purgon, as we have seen, slavishly follows the rules of his profession; and Thomas Diafoirus, like his father, does not dare depart from the teachings of the ancients. Moreover, young Thomas requires his father's permission for everything he does, even outside the realm of medicine. After having recited his lengthy compliment to Argan, he asks Diafoirus senior, as though he were speaking to a schoolmaster: "Cela a-t-il bien été, mon père?" (II, 5). And when he meets Angélique, he asks his father whether or not he should kiss her hand. Finally, when he gets mixed up in his compliment to Béline, Monsieur Diafoirus orders him: "Thomas, réservez cela pour une autre fois" (II, 6). May we then say that physicians, because of their submissive attitude to dogma, their complete lack of skepticism, their authoritarianism, tend to suggest the behavior of priests and monks?

As a foil to this type of subservience, Molière has introduced the filial obedience of Angélique to Argan. Angélique, who somehow believes that her father intends to marry her to her beloved Cléante, carefully emphasizes her submissiveness: "Je dois faire, mon père, tout ce qu'il vous plaira de m'ordonner" (I, 5), and "C'est à moi, mon père, de suivre aveuglément toutes vos volontés." But when it transpires that Thomas Diafoirus, and not Cléante, is the intended bridegroom, Toinette questions Argan's authority in the matter and, despite her low rank in the household, speaks as though she had as much power as Argan. She tells the father that this ludicrous marriage will never happen because Angélique will never give her consent. The scene reaches a climax in the following exchange: ARGAN: "Je lui commande absolument de se préparer à prendre le mari que je dis." TOINETTE: "Et moi, je lui défends absolument d'en rien faire." Their quarrel ends with the hypochondriac running after the servant and ordering his daughter to help him catch her: "Si tu ne me l'arrêtes, je te donnerai ma malédiction." Toinette, in her retort, usurps the role of father: "Et moi, je la déshériterai, si elle vous obéit." Her behavior differs from that of Dorine in *Tartuffe*, for instead of rebelling against her master, she simply assumes his authority and his prerogatives. Whereas Dorine had been content to play the part of Mariane, who did not dare oppose her father's will, Toinette reduces the whole idea of authority to absurdity. Moreover, this usurpation of power makes Argan behave like an enraged but perfectly healthy and vigorous human being. It may, for this reason, correspond dramatically to the usurpation of authority which characterizes the *corps des médecins*. This correspondence or parallelism is much more obvious later in the play when Toinette actually "creates" the part of a famous physician, so drastic in his prescriptions that even Argan voices some timid objections: "Me couper un bras, et me crever un œil, afin que l'autre se porte mieux? J'aime bien mieux qu'il ne se porte pas si bien. La belle opération, de me rendre borgne et manchot!" (III, 10). By their very absurdity, Toinette's drastic remedies emphasize the perils of contemporary medicine. She actually reasons about disease in much the same manner as Monsieur Purgon or Diafoirus, father and son. Her prescription may contain, however, an allusion to religion: "Si ta main est pour toi une occasion de chute, coupe-la: mieux vaut pour toi entrer manchot dans la vie, que de t'en aller, ayant deux mains, dans la géhenne, dans le feu inextinguible ... Et si ton œil est pour toi une occasion de chute, arrache-le: mieux vaut pour toi entrer borgne dans le royaume de Dieu" (Marc, IX, 43–47). Could Molière be alluding to the symbolic denial and amputa-tion of the human spirit, which appears so scandalous to a *libertin,* and even to a humanist? Perhaps Toinette's gruesome joke coin-cides fortuitously with a passage in the New Testament; but there are so many suggestive retorts in the play that we cannot entirely ignore the irreligious implications of Toinette's drastic cure. After all, the Christian denial of the body and of nature may, from a certain point of view, render man, as Argan says, "borgne et manchot."

The idea of hierarchy leads, in the course of the comedy, to several ludicrous situations based on Argan's belief in a close connection between his physician's *ordonnance* and his eventual cure. This aspect of the play particularly impressed Madame de Sévigné, who even quotes passages which Molière or at least his editor did not retain. She does, however, refer directly to a well-known passage concerning the exercises which Purgon has prescribed for his patient: "Monsieur Purgon m'a dit de me pro-mener le matin dans ma chambre, douze allées et douze venues; mais j'ai oublié à lui demander si c'est en long, ou en large" (II, 2). Argan's attitude strikes us by its absurd rigidity—by the idea that the organism closely depends upon the exact num-ber of steps that Argan will take in his daily constitutional. Earlier in the play, the same Argan had established a numerical relationship between the amount of treatment he had undergone and the state of his unhealth: "Si bien donc que de ce mois j'ai pris une, deux, trois, quatre, cinq, six, sept et huit médecines; et un, deux, trois, quatre, cinq, six, sept, huit, neuf, dix, onze et douze lavements; et l'autre mois il y avoit douze médecines, et vingt lavements. Je ne m'étonne pas si je ne me porte pas si bien ce mois-ci que l'autre. Je le dirai à Monsieur Purgon, afin qu'il mette ordre à cela" (I, 1). The use of figures throughout this scene is rich in comic effects, for it brings out the idea of rigidity, all the more so because it attaches to these exact quantities of medication a very precise price tag. The main result of all this medication is the depletion of Argan's purse, a fact which makes the other type of causal relation—the supposed rapport between medication and health—all the more preposterous. Monsieur Diafoirus, no less than Argan, insists on the numerical aspect of remedies. When the hypochondriac asks him: "Monsieur, combien est-ce qu'il faut mettre de grains de sel dans un œuf?" he receives this strange answer: "Six, huit, dix, par les nombres pairs; comme dans les médicaments, par les nombres impairs" (II, 6). This reply shows that Argan derives his superstitious reliance on exact figures from the doctors themselves, and that he has merely exaggerated a normal tendency of the profession.

We may wonder why Molière has attached so much importance to these numbers. Was he concerned only with the hilarious reaction of his public or did he have another axe to grind? Moreover, the author insists also on Argan's ritualistic punctuality in taking his various medicines and in relieving himself. By combining this ludicrous punctuality with the idea of quantitative precision we obtain a bizarre type of causality, tantamount to the complete denial of nature. Medicine has finally transformed Argan into a strange, biological mechanism, quite devoid of human qualities, as Béline's outspoken funeral oration over his supposed dead body shows. Argan, with his pharmaceutical mathematics, has metamorphosed himself into a gut: "Un homme incommode à tout le monde, malpropre, dégoûtant, sans cesse un lavement ou une médecine dans le ventre ..." (III, 12). It would seem that Molière has satirized the tendency of physicians to introduce a rigid, mathematical type of reasoning into natural processes; but he may also be poking fun at certain religious practices and beliefs. Mathematics plays a not unessential part in the system of indulgences: such and such a prayer, such and such a pious gesture will pay for a specific number of days, months, or years in purgatory, either for oneself or for other sufferers.[1]

PLEASURE AND THE IMAGINATION

The term *plaisir* provides one of the metaphorical keys to the comedy. The idea of pleasure or diversion provides, for instance, a transition between the play itself and the second *intermède,* of which Argan is a spectator. He apparently does not have anything to do with the first, and he of course plays the main part in the third and last. And this transition does more than serve as a connecting link between two disparate parts of the play, leading from the actual comedy to the diversion and then back again: "Ce sont des Egyptiens, vêtus en Mores, qui font des danses mêlées de chansons, où je suis sûr que vous prendrez plaisir; et cela vaudra bien une ordonnance de Monsieur Purgon. Allons" (II, 9). At the beginning of the third act, Béralde continues his comparison between medicine and entertainment: "Eh bien! mon frère, qu'en dites vous? cela ne vaut-il pas bien une prise de casse?" Toinette adds, sarcastically: "Hon, de bonne casse est bonne" (III, 1). But why should Molière compare entertainment to a mild form of purgation? Actually, the dramatist had all along injected into the medical aspects of the play the idea of pleasure, and the double transition between the second and third acts serves to make the blending of medicine and pleasure more explicit. This strange analogy appears for the first time in Monsieur Fleurant's bill, couched in insinuating language, which Argan is reading out loud when the curtain rises. The latter is pleased by the style but revolted by the prices: "Ah! Mon-

---

[1] James Joyce, in his *A Portrait of the Artist as a Young Man,* dwells on the spiritual mathematics of indulgences, and with as much humor as Molière. Cf. pp. 170 ff. in Modern Library Edition.

sieur Fleurant, tout doux s'il vous plaît; si vous en usez comme cela, on ne voudra plus être malade." This excellent joke implies that Argan regards disease as a sort of hobby, as though he could take it or leave it!

The theme of pleasure reappears in the very next scene in the course of Argan's quarrel with Toinette. The latter exclaims: "Si vous avez le plaisir de quereller, il faut bien, que de mon côté, j'aye le plaisir de pleurer: chacun le sien, ce n'est pas trop. Ha!" Most people would consider quarrelling as scarcely more pleasurable than sickness. And later in the same scene, Toinette actually connects pleasure with medicine: "Ce Monsieur Fleurant-là et ce Monsieur Purgon s'égayent bien sur votre corps." Admittedly, the word *s'égayer* means, according to Littré, *se donner carrière*—to display activity; nonetheless, it definitely evokes its primary meaning of having fun or even of making fun, which implies that the doctor and his soft-spoken apothecary derive enjoyment as well as money from their tender treatment of Argan's complacent body.

Still later in the play, Cléante, after having listened to Thomas Diafoirus' second display of eloquence, establishes a clearer and more ironical connection between disease and enjoyment: "Que Monsieur fait merveilles, et que s'il est aussi bon médecin qu'il est bon orateur, il y aura plaisir à être de ses malades" (II, 5). It remains, however, for our fledgling physician to bring out the inherent absurdity of this connection: "Avec la permission aussi de Monsieur, je vous invite à venir voir l'un de ces jours, pour vous divertir, la dissection d'une femme, sur quoi je dois raisonner." And Toinette takes advantage of this remark to cross all the t's and dot all the i's: "Le divertissement sera agréable. Il y en a qui donnent la comédie à leurs maîtresses; mais donner une dissection est quelque chose de plus galand." It is then Cléante's turn to entertain the company. He produces a pastoral scene in music in which he explains his love and his intentions to Angélique. Argan, who appears to have seen through Cléante's little stratagem, is not amused: "Les sottises ne divertissent point." More than anything else, he enjoys his illness: "Ah! que d'affaires! je n'ai pas seulement le loisir de songer à ma maladie" (II, 8). He sees his imaginary disease as a sort of pastime, which lesser activities tend to interrupt. It will take the final entertainment, where Argan becomes a doctor, to conciliate these antithetical types of pleasure.

It is of course outlandish to combine disease, even imaginary disease, with songs and dances. Molière may have enjoyed the absurdity of this combination. Nonetheless, the pleasure involved has, to say the least, a dubious quality, because Molière, who chose to play the part of Argan, states within the comedy that he is seriously ill: "... il n'a justement de la force que pour porter son mal" (III, 3). Molière has put these words concerning his illness in the mouth of the wise Béralde, entrusting, on the contrary, Argan with the cruelest remarks about himself: "... quand il sera malade, je le laisserois mourir sans secours," and: "Crève, crève! cela t'apprendra une autre fois à te jouer à la Faculté" (III, 3). The author has made the scene highly paradoxical from a dramatic point of view; and Béralde, in defending Molière against Molière himself (Argan), puts the audience in a piquant situation, partly pleasurable and partly disturbing. Argan is both Molière and not Molière; both a malingerer and a sick man; both a madman who enjoys his imaginary illness and a sufferer who, with barely enough strength to support his disease, has done his utmost to entertain the audience. Molière had used a similar trick, though in a less unnerving manner, in his *Misanthrope,* where Philinte meanly compares Alceste (played by Molière) to the Sganarelle of *L'Ecole des maris.* In *Le Malade imaginaire,* however, it is more than a clever device, not only because of the constant equivocation between pleasure and medicine, but because the idea of impersonation plays a fairly important part in the comedy. Toinette, as we have seen, had impersonated a famous physician who happens to look just like her—just as Argan happens to look exactly like Molière. But then, why should Molière want to make fun of theatrical illusion by destroying it at the very moment when he seems to be creating it?

Strange as this statement may appear, we can find something *wrong* with almost every action, situation, and character in the play. Argan is both terribly ill and perfectly healthy; disease brings both suffering and pleasure; the notary, instead of limiting his activities to legal matters, mentions lawyers who fail to understand what he calls *détours de la conscience* (I, 7) or, in other words, casuistry: Monsieur Purgon speaks more like a theologian than a doctor; Cléante and Angélique discuss their love in terms of entertainment. . . . A willful distortion of one kind or another marks practically every event in the play.

There is something rather puzzling, comic in a breathtaking sort of way, in the scene where the hypochondriac feigns death. His little daughter, Louison, had put on a similar performance earlier in the play in order to avoid a whipping. She had even succeeded in frightening her not too intelligent father. Argan's mimicry of death allows him to discover the truth, not about himself, but about his mercenary wife. Illusion will also play an important part in the burlesque travesty that ends the comedy: it will arrange everything, particularly the marriage between Cléante and Angélique. But in every illusion, whether or not it acts as a catalyst of truth, reality must enter the picture. The separation between the real and the illusory, at least on the stage, should never become too sharp. Molière, for this reason, makes his hypochondriac say: "N'y a-t-il pas quelque danger à contrefaire le mort?" (III, 11). After all, his imaginary death might suddenly become as real as his imaginary disease! And we should not forget in this particular instance that Molière, then a dying man, took it upon himself to impersonate a corpse. Contemporaries of the author dwelled at length on this morbid paradox.[2] Death thus emerges as a spectacle and, temporarily, steals the

---

[2] See the many epitaphs concerning Molière's death, published in various *recueils,* for instance in the *Mélange de pièces fugitives tirées du cabinet de Monsieur de Saint-Evremont* (Utrecht: François Galma 1697), which accompanied an edition of the *Voyage de Messieurs de Bachaumont et de La Chapelle.* Here is a fairly typical one:

> Cy gît un qu'on dit être mort,
> Je ne sçays s'il l'est, ou s'il dort,
> Sa Maladie Imaginaire,
> Ne peut pas l'avoir fait mourir,
> C'est un tour qu'il jouë à plaisir,
> Car il aimoit à contrefaire,
> Quoy qu'il en soit, cy gît Molière;
> Comme il étoit grand Comedien
>   Pour un mort imaginaire,
> S'il le fait, il le fait bien (p. 134).

show from Argan's imaginary disease. Toinette, dressed in a doctor's habit, had introduced herself to Argan as an admirer, as a fan: "Vous ne trouverez pas mauvais, s'il vous plaît, la curiosité que j'ai eue de voir un illustre malade comme vous êtes; et votre réputation, qui s'étend partout, peut excuser la liberté que j'ai prise" (III, 10). Toinette addresses herself to Argan as though he were a celebrity, a fascinating spectacle worthy of a long trip. In this joke, the author attempts to combine illness with spectacle, suffering with entertainment. Toinette's admiration suggests that Argan has actually transformed himself into an "illustre malade"—illustrious in the sense that an actor can make himself famous. Her words take on an additional meaning if we consider that she addresses them to Molière—to Elomire Hypocondre—rather than to a character in the play.

Theater as metaphor appears almost everywhere. Cléante's courting of Angélique takes the form of a performance, or at least of a rehearsal. Moreover, Angélique had met Cléante at a play, where one of the spectators had persecuted her with his insults. Béralde puts on a show for the benefit of his brother who, in turn, performs a part in order to discover Béline's and Angélique's true feelings. And the whole thing ends with a burlesque ceremony put on by a troupe of actors. Dissection itself becomes a spectacle performed no doubt in an *amphithéâtre*. Everywhere we turn, we witness a triumph of the theater, particularly over sickness and death. Living and dying become gigantic systems of make-believe in a world that has become meaningless. As Béralde claims, the veils are too thick, and only the present requires our attention. Only entertainment really counts, for, as Béralde puts it, "... chacun à ses périls et fortune, peut croire tout ce qu'il lui plaît" (III, 3).

22   *Conclusion—*
The Choice of Comedy

$\mathcal{M}$OLIÈRE stands out as by far the greatest creator of dramatic forms in the entire history of French literature, comparable in this respect to Shakespeare in England. He never actually repeats himself, even though certain comic devices may recur in nearly every one of his works. Even the various scenes of "dépit amoureux" which, superficially at least, appear so similar to one another, take on different meanings and, more important still, have divergent functions in different plays. And, as we have just seen, Molière, far from stereotyping his doctors, makes them behave sometimes like lawyers, and sometimes like priests. Finally, he knew how to take advantage of every kind of *genre* within the general framework of comedy, from sustained five-act plays in verse to elemental farces, from coarse and brutal humor to poetic ballets, from exuberant gaiety to bitter satire. And the reason for his success in such diverse types of writing—so diverse that Pierre Louys and M. Henri Poulaille were led to imagine, in the so-called "great" comedies, a collaboration between the actor Poquelin and that creative genius Pierre Corneille—is that, in all probability, he viewed each work as an organic whole, requiring its own peculiar comic and poetic rhythm, a rhythm that had to be maintained from the first to the last line. Indeed, from the standpoint of the creative imagination, the lyrically poetic differs only in degree and not at all in nature from the basely ludicrous; and the so-called tragic spirit is closely related to the comic spirit, however we may define it. Both *Le Médecin malgré lui* and *L'Amour peintre* are comic poems, even though the qualities of the poetry involved would appear to exclude one another, even though Molière's most brutal and boisterous farce may have very little in common with his most delicately suggestive composition. As for tragedy, Arnolphe has as

268

much hubris in his make-up as Œdipus or any other suffering protagonist. Take away his kingly rank and his imminent peril, and Œdipus, who displays a willful ignorance second to none, whereas every one else concerned shows a fair degree of lucidity, might become the hero of a farce. Moreover, modern criticism has shown that a pun, moderately funny in most contexts, can become mysteriously evocative when suitably disguised. That magic tenseness which characterizes tragedy and, sometimes, lyric poetry, does not at first sight have much in common with the incongruities and interruptions so characteristic of many forms of laughter. However, these apparently contradictory reactions, which occur at opposite ends of the literary spectrum, function, at least in one respect, in the same manner: they break with the even tenor of everyday experience and ordinary perception. Indeed, laughter can arise with the sudden awareness that we have lost touch with reality; and we are moved when we have the strange sensation of transcending the real, for instance when we identify our destiny with that of a hero, victimized by a supernatural force. Lyric poetry, tragedy, and comedy resemble one another in their willful distortion of experience. In fact, art by no means confines itself to an imitation of reality, of human action, as Aristotle and his innumerable disciples maintain: the artist uses reality as a spring-board to an imaginary and therefore unreal realm, quite unlike anything we might witness in our everyday experience. The creative writer uses this so-called reality as a sort of sacrificial victim which he sets up in order to destroy it. Of course, the stronger he makes his intended victims appear, the more powerful will become the ritual of immolation. Many moralists, including Baudelaire, have commented on the cruelty and evil involved in most types of laughter; and Freud has convincingly shown that aggression decuples the intensity of laughter. In short, comedy, tragedy, and lyric poetry seem to base their strategies on one form or another of destruction, a destruction which corresponds, paradoxically, to the affirmation of creativity—of an inner consistency and illusory permanence. Tragedy and comedy are closely related not only because of this reliance on destruction, but also because dramatic techniques remain rather similar whatever the genre. That omnipotent but man-made Fate which can dominate the entire existence of a king differs mainly in intensity from the skilful contraptions which drive puppets to clash against each other, or the contrived coincidences which foil the plans of systematic clowns. The author finds it as easy to pull the wires himself as to let the audience believe that some deity or inner Nemesis has accomplished the dire deed. To the creative artist, *Deus, deus ex machina,* or simply *machina* pose the same sort of problems.

Why then did Molière, with his exceptional poetic gifts and his penetration of human motives, choose to write only comedies, some of them quite inacceptable to the intellectual elite of his day because of their vulgar slapstick? And why, after he achieved success, did he continue to waste his creative talents by acting in them? Why, when he no longer had to, did he insist on entertaining the crowd, and that till the article of death? After all, he might have acceded to an easier and more rewarding career by limiting his activities to writing or to entertaining the court as did Benserade. Racine, whose tragedies eventually brought him a brilliant career as a courtier, had started as low on the social scale as Molière. Any answer to these questions must obviously remain conjectural and speculative. But we feel that Molière must have chosen once and for all the artificial world of the theater in preference to any other. Unlike Racine, he could not use the theater as a stepping stone to social success, for such an action would have been the worst kind of betrayal. He thus chose the theater, chose entertainment, as others choose the priesthood or a contemplative life. He became a militant entertainer—one who considered his own make-believe universe as no less valid than the hierarchical jungle where he quarried his audience. In order to write a tragedy, he would have had to transcend that very society whose values he challenged and from which he had alienated himself, and, at the same time, he would have had to go beyond that spirit of *divertissement* which made up his entire existence. Comedy, which requires interruptions, separations, and discontinuity rather than a desperate reconciliation between man and the incomprehensible forces which surround him, provides the dramatist with a perhaps illusory mastery over his own fate. As a result, the usual predicaments of mankind can be shorn of their imagined mystical dimensions. Only in that entertaining world which Molière created and in which he chose to live could seventeenth-century man be entirely himself.

INDEX

(Numbers in italics refer to subjects discussed at length; authors are indexed even when only their works are mentioned in the text.)